The Lord God of Truth Within

The Lord God of Truth Within

A POSTHUMOUS SEQUEL

TO

THE DAYSPRING OF YOUTH

by

M

The Lord God of Truth Within
A Glorian Book / 2020

Originally published in 1941.

Print ISBN 978-1-943358-10-6
EBook ISBN 978-1-943358-11-3

Glorian Publishing is a non-profit organization. All proceeds
further the distribution of these books. For more information,
visit gnosticteachings.org

DEDICATION

This book is reverently dedicated to
all the children of Manu.

*"Adore, oh my child, adore the very good
and the very great god of the sages, and never
all yourself to become puffed up with pride,
because he sends one of the children of wisdom
to initiate you into their order, and to make you
a sharer in the wonders of his omnipotence."*

With this salutation, we greet you.

INTRODUCTION

*"To him, who in the love of Nature holds communion with her
visible forms, she speaks a various language."* —Bryant

Before entering the portal of his great initiation, our brother was preparing this supplement to *The Dayspring of Youth*. His
notes form the text. Scan well this quartz, for mystic gold may
nugget in a flash. Such is the cryptic elemental code.

May the Lord God of Truth within make his face to shine
upon you, and bring you peace. So mote it be!

CONTENTS

PUBLISHER'S INTRODUCTION

This book was written in 1941 before the true heart of the teachings that lead to liberation from suffering was revealed to the public in 1950 by Samael Aun Weor. One can say then that this book was opening the door to that knowledge, and that is precisely what it still accomplishes. Yet, now that those teachings are available to everyone, this book is even more powerful; when you know that the source of liberation is within you, and you are using it daily for that purpose, the knowledge in this book is made truly practical, effective, and invaluable. Without that practical, daily transformation, this book remains veiled, impenetrable.

There are several words in this book that are used in a way that is different from modern use.

The author called his teachings Yoga, in the true sense of the word. The word Yoga does not mean the Hatha Yoga people are fascinated with today, but the true yoga, which is the science of awakening consciousness. He wrote here:

"The end of all true Yoga is to bring God realization to humanity which is union of the lower self with the Lord God of Truth within... Nature awaits man's discovery of his power to reclaim his own lost birthright, the gift of the spirit. This lost birthright, when man seeks union with his Innermost, brings a greatly expanded consciousness to his mind."

M uses the words "man" and "his" in the classical English way to indicate any person, whether male or female. Thus, "when man seeks union with his Innermost," means when **anyone** seeks union. Therefore, do not be distressed by his use of the word "man," and wrongly interpret it as sexist or somehow discriminating against women. Nothing could be further from the truth. In esotericism, men and women are viewed as equals in every respect.

Another word to be aware of here is mind (or mental), as in "brings a greatly expanded consciousness to his mind." In this word "mind" M in synthesizing a variety of psychological arenas within us. For instance, he wrote:

"When the student is taken out of his body for the first time and accompanies his teacher upon a mental flight..."

This "mental" flight could refer to an astral projection, or a trip in any number of sephiroth on the Tree of Life, not merely Netzach, the mental plane.

Additionally:

"Initiation is the conscious attainment of illumination, of knowledge, and of power. It is an expansion of consciousness on the mental plane."

Initiation is related to many sephiroth on the Tree of Life, not merely Netzach, the mental plane. The way to understand this use of the word is given here, by Samael Aun Weor:

"The entire universe is condensed mind. Universal mind waves saturate the infinite space... Even the astral body itself is nothing but the crystallization of the mental matter and the physical world is also condensed mind. Therefore, the mind is matter and it is very gross, whether it exists in a physical state or in that state called astral or manasic..."

So, M uses the words mind or mental to indicate the non-physical, psychological aspect, which as you know, has many levels. He synthesized many sophisticated concepts into simple words.

On that note, we encourage you to read this book carefully. There is very profound knowledge here, but it is not given explicitly or obviously.

Most of the footnotes were written by the original editor of the book in 1941. We added a few more for additional clarity.

CHAPTER ONE

SEEKING THE PRESENCE

IN YOGA teaching the causes of evil must be sought in the self-created universe where dwells the "I am." Long has humanity sought to explain the why of evil by objective analysis. But the cause of a thing is not within the thing, and the cause of the underworld is to be found neither in the crime, nor in the underworld. Until man, the son of Manu, the Thinker, by contact with the Lord God of Truth within, has come to understand the cause of his affliction and sufferings, he can neither avoid, nor profit by them. He who seeks to know Truth and the cause of things, must avoid ceremonial and experimental magic as he aspires upward through the world of mind, the realm of memory, and the plane of conscious nature.

Starting upon this path man awakens to a consciousness of confusion within his own mind world. Sprightly and alert his thoughts refuse to concentrate, decline to contemplate, but wildly leap from bough to branch, until exhaustion welcomes sleep. As he presses on the seeker finds the agitation less, his wanton thoughts yield sequence to his will until, the borderland of memory reached, he knows and knows that he knows. The lower mind no longer blinks the lights, but now it grasps the thought like moving pictures cast upon a screen, and then man knows that *Truth* is what he sees. Tis thus he gains the plane of conscious nature and there perceives the cause of all those things he knows, yet not by the process of objective thinking, as in the outer world. In this realm within one sees himself an "It" in the apricot-colored atmosphere of conscious nature, teeming with other "Its," all pinhead size, but devoid of body separation. This is a tremendous moment, for this is the presence of the Great Reality to which we aspire. Doubts fade, from the left surges the vibration of infinite love and from the right, a vibration of beauty indescribable. Suddenly he is in the Presence, and an intense and subtle joy surges through him. Henceforth nothing matters, but the attainment of this consciousness. Here he analyzes the vibration of Love, and discovers that it is the Law in all its majesty. He attunes himself to Beauty and, in its constant rhythm, he finds it is the mask of strength and gentleness. 'Tis here he learns the cause of Law is love and wisdom; the cause of Beauty, strength and gentleness.

All Yoga training has the attainment of this consciousness for its aim and many books have thrown light upon this subject, yet the true secrets come to the pupil only from the lips of his teacher.

Once man has found, and been touched by the Presence, an atomic link always connects him in his everyday life. Within his self-created universe the quality has changed, and Law and Beauty stand as heavenly twins, expressing love and strength.

This is the thought expressed by a great soul, when asked regarding the reward of a true seeker, "To him who will seek, comes the knowledge of Truth and Beauty."

It is on this plane of conscious nature that the student sees the cause of evil hid within the law, exemplifying love and wisdom. The three main causes of evil in this world are:

Gratification of our animal passions and desires.

The evil of the intermediate worlds (which the average person knows little about).

Lack of devotion to Truth (the perfect attribute of God).

Only when man has gained experience in the underworld and, by aspiring, risen above it, can he find the plane of conscious nature. This may take many incarnations, perhaps not always in the body of a human. To the initiate the meaning or equivalent for reincarnation or rebirth is metempsychosis, or transmigration of souls. It signifies a passing of the conscious entity to higher, or to lower states of being. It is here that we find a clue to the cause of much of the evil of everyday existence. Born a man, one who has led an evil life, worked contrary to the law of his own environment, and given way to his animal nature, may reincarnate in a sub-human form with the animal nature. Thus karma states the debt, and the conscious entity gains experience in the world beneath our feet. An old saying of the East is, "The miser seeks to guard his hoard." Therefore, when the natives see a cobra entering his hole they

try to find his hiding place, in hope to find the miser's treasure of a former life. The miser's love carried over, although
the treasure did not last. Thus, the underworld consists of the
debris cast off from civilization. The underworld is the plane
of consciousness where evil souls are reborn, where the law
of the beast rules. Thus the human debris, while working out
its karma in this submerged world, yet serves to stimulate the
beast to higher living purpose. In this world dwells Pan and
all his satyrs. They are principles of nature upon the lower, or
underworld plane—and herein lies the danger of experimental
and ceremonial magic by amateurs. A sincere aspiration for
truth both ascends and descends. It rises into a higher and
inner sphere of consciousness, and sinks into the depths of
the submerged world beneath us. Thus is the magic evoked
on the earth plane brought to the attention of the denizens
of both spheres. Toward it they turn and if the student be
unprepared the horrors of the lower plane so shock the senses
that often several lives must pass before he can overcome
the shock. The world little realizes the countless number of
magicians who practice the darker side of magic. Neither does
it realize the number of white magicians who spread their
protection about those who seek union with the Lord God of
Truth within, and urge them to aspire.

In every large city throughout the world some great soul
dwells, whose mission is to stimulate youthful minds to
search for Truth. Many people nowadays are becoming sensitive, and apprehend the thought atmosphere of others, be it
good or evil. It is through this thought atmosphere that the
occult students of the darker side, when extending their range
of consciousness, seek to form groups. Thus, they gain power
and substance to carry on their work, and easily gain their
bread and butter. But no student of white magic will set a
price on the things of the spirit.

It is through such extension of consciousness and sensitivity to thought atmosphere that certain undying immortals
living in this world today seek to further its evolution.

This natural system of thought transference, among those
sufficiently developed to respond to thought vibration, is

one of the surprises of Yoga practice. America has a number of holy men living in seclusion, remote from the world, sometimes in etheric bodies, who watch over her destiny, and when an earnest student sincerely seeks truth, he is protected by these Elder Brothers. When the student is duly and truly prepared, and has been found to be worthy and well qualified, he is given his instruction. One student was watched over during seven years of preparation, by one of these Elder Brothers, before the instruction came which set his feet upon the upward path, which will lead him through conscious nature to the plane of heavenly peace—the presence of the Lord God of Truth within.

While the ordinary man's vision can detect a living intelligence expressing through the flame, only the Yogi has come to realize that the elements of fire, air, water, and earth are inhabited by elemental intelligences of different degrees of development. In Persia the intelligence of fire is fervently and sacredly worshipped as the giver of all life. This intelligence, symbolized by the flame, is revered and there are altars in that land where the sacred flame has burned continuously for thousands of years.

The intelligences of air, water, and earth can likewise be seen. It is with these intelligences that the Yogi communicates, when in his practice he enters nature's consciousness. In his search for the Presence, the Yogi links himself with nature's will, which is in the plane of intuition. When this is reached man no longer "thinks," he "knows." He has tapped the *knower consciousness* and, as it works in nature, so will it function through him. Even in his present condition man has flashes of intuition where he knows, without thought. When he receives this guidance he should act upon it at once, for "He who hesitates is lost." In a higher sense this intuition is a manipulation of nature's will. The genius of Edison often so manifested that through him nature gave many wonderful gifts to man. But the average man has never learned to recognize an intelligence separate from the human body. Take the element of fire; it is a symbol of our sovereign sun. As an intelligence is found in fire, so from the sun flow those forces which have so much to do with the development of our earth. These forces which affect our earth, are manipulated by a great positive intelligence residing in the sun. There is also a great solar intelligence which manipulates the forces that activate the sun. Those solar beings, who work under the positive or right-hand intelligence of the sun, periodically make their presence known and they regularly appear in certain Zen temples. The representatives of the reigning houses of China and Japan are supposed to be descendants of these beings. The sun is an emblem for each of these countries, as it was also a symbol on the first American flag.

While China regularly worships the solar intelligence it also, at certain seasons of the year, worships the intelligences of fire, air, water, and earth. The Chinese recognized, and we must not forget, that our bodies are made up of these elements.

Through Yoga practice the student develops the higher vision, and man's body resembles a gaseous figure with variously colored radiations quivering about his nerve centers. Thus, man's limited physical vision is extended through Yoga by developing centers in his body seemingly atrophied by disuse, until his range of consciousness is greatly extended, and he sees with the *knower consciousness*.

The student comes to realize that there is a division in nature where the noble minds of the hierarchal devas dwell, and that these devas watch over different parts of the earth. This is a plane of vibration where the brooding of the spirit can be sensed. Beneath is a plane of action where nature acts as the Lords of the Law demand. Wind storms, torrents, and lightning are not whims, they are the instruments by which man is scourged into a recognition of his true place in conscious nature. When man, through selfish greed, destroys forests and vegetation, nature causes rain and floods to manifest, bringing death and destruction to many. When he destroys wheat and other food products, nature responds with wind and drought. Someday science will discover, as the Yogi has done, that nature is teeming with intelligences. This will come about, and is even now coming about, through the development of two types of clairvoyance, which extend the range of perception.

Behind the five senses there exists the higher counterpart, which can be seen by eyes that have come to harmonize themselves with vibrations which exist in the seven planes of consciousness, but the ordinary man can apprehend only the three lower ranges.

At the beginning the student is conscious of his physical body, which he has been accustomed to refer to as "I." When, in his study, he thinks intensively, he shuts down upon the body's activities and enters the world of mind. As he aspires and meditates more deeply he becomes conscious of the world of the spirit. After that, if he has one-pointedness of mind, and earnestly seeks the Lord God of Truth within, he slowly, and in this world and life, can enter the kingdom of heaven and there he finds peace and happiness. He has become an atom in a great unit and realizes that "I Am That." But few people are interested to search for and find the Lord God of Truth within. The concern of most is with pleasure, sex, and their problems of living. They read only what interests them in the newspapers. Since they avoid all mental exertion, they think little, belong to the herd, and follow the dictates of those in power and position. As their physical forces decline some people will, perhaps, begin to question their future and review their experiences in life. Such are preparing to profit by their experiences. Someday science will test and measure people, not by their ability to memorize, but by their ability to learn by experience. It is what one learns from experience that really counts in his progress towards Truth.

It is by experience in this mundane world that man learns that the Kingdom of Heaven is within. So the student in Yoga learns of things which are happening in his own real universe within himself, by experience. When this stage is reached progress is rapid and active, for the student has found a vantage point from which to view things which are happening both within his self-creative universe, and in the objective world about him.

In the objective world man is a prisoner and is seldom able to see what is happening in his environment. When the student consciously enters the universe within, a broad expanse of energy confronts him, and he passes through many different divisions of activity in his quest for Truth.

On this earth, and in the objective plane locomotion is slow, but in the higher mental plane the student can travel with the speed and quickness of thought. He begins to realize that Time and Space are terms which man has created, and in this higher consciousness, time and space do not exist. Everything in the presence of the Truth, of the Reality, *is* and, from this different viewpoint, the student learns that he is of no race, creed, or epoch, but that his atoms are of all races and periods. Race and creed distinction disappear, for he is composed of all strata of all races through which he has migrated and, by research within, he finds there is no such thing as racial distinction, and thus he becomes a brother to all men—a brother of the White School.

CHAPTER TWO

THE FALL OF ATLANTIS

In the Atlantean records are to be found the happenings which have been preserved to us in the book of Genesis. There were adepts in those days so closely in tune with nature's consciousness that they created forms and images which they were able to endow with mortal significance. If they desired a plant or flower to assume a certain shape, this was impressed through the medium of their thoughts upon, and executed by the parental stem of activity with which the plant was endowed. This power was one of the causes of nature's upheaval, which brought about the destruction of that great civilization. By the exercise of this endowment of nature the Atlanteans were abundantly furnished with supplies for nourishment. But they went beyond this permitted and legitimate use and used this secret power, which was referred to as "Nature's permitted instinct," to engender all living things with an increased activity. They ruthlessly destroyed nourishing supplies, while they were also increasing yields, and forcing development. By the self-determination of their minds, endowed with nature's will, they would hasten the growth of a plant so that in a single day it would mature, blossom, and wither.

But the law that would permit them to tap the forces of nature for the welfare of the people, when those forces were used illegitimately, brought about monstrosities both in nature and in mankind. That law would not permit the Atlanteans, by their own determination and for the purpose of creating want and suffering, to enlarge, or to confine nature by the control of her art. Thus this race, able to create forms of speech and learning out of mind stuff matter, and to endow nature's products with an activity similar to personal will, was destroyed. The great secrets were drawn back into nature, but the mental debris which was cast off was a dynamic power which controlled malformations, want and suffering both in nature and in mankind.

This debris became the natural environment in which these monstrosities lived and on which they fed. Hence these robots of the later Atlantean period still live within themselves and subsist in this mental debris, which enslaves and molds their minds, and in reacting to this mental debris, they believe they are exercising what they call today "intellect."

Following the destruction of Atlantis this mental debris has been disseminated and man to-day, entranced in pursuit of learning, feeds his mind on these forces through the reading of books on what others have experienced, rather than by searching within himself for the records of his own experiences.

Some few professors, using books as a stimulus, delve deep into the past in their research work, in order to discover something which may have escaped the observation of other clever minds. They are like miners following a vein of gold, seeking for a greater deposit of wealth. While the ordinary man seeks happiness and finds distress in the gratification of his passions and desires, the intellectual student gains the greater happiness through the pursuit of intellectual gold. But it is only the intellectual giant that dares reveal his treasure to a world where the consensus of opinion is adverse.

However surprising, intellect is not experience. From experience man gains intelligence, but not intellect. From intelligence he attains to the greater wisdom. But he does not gain the greater wisdom from the perusal of other people's experiences, disseminated through this Atlantean mental debris.

The later Atlanteans made use of the forces of malformed mind stuff, to give their robots and monstrosities the power of governing.

The Atlanteans conveyed their thoughts through syllables of speech far different from our own. They used the sound vowels of nature, and could thus converse with her creatures and inhabitants. Thus did they converse with the intelligences of earth, air, fire, and water, and with the devic creations which assist nature in her design and framework.

The work of these devic beings is to instill into humanity the intelligence of the fixed principle in nature, so that man may become qualified to understand her purpose.

This fixed principle in nature is her governing force, and is similar to human, personal will, by which we seek to determine our actions. Long ago man lost this understanding, but it can be reattained in some degree through Yoga practice.

When man seeks to harmonize himself with the nature of his own Lord God of Truth, within his own self-constituted world, the gift of intelligence is then bestowed upon him.

In allying ourselves with this great principle of nature, we ally ourselves with the Lord God of Truth within, for when we assume responsibility to nature and her works, we slowly begin to assume her character of expression. This is governed by this determinative principle—the will of conscious nature—God.

Down the long ages man has sought union with God, but man images God as outside of himself. Until man learns to align himself with the "God within" he is but a blind wanderer upon the perilous sea. In order to energize the spirit of truth within, he must ally himself with this fixed principle of nature, a principle which commands, but never heedlessly destroys.

In other words, the will to power, the will to knowledge, and to truth, and the understanding of truth comes not from man's self-created personal will, but from the power given by nature's will and understanding. It is a return in thought and desire to union with the truth within.

In its terrific passage through space our earth picks up much cast-off Atlantean debris and, in certain places, it stimulates the earth to mental activity, and to the gratification of intellectual desire.

Sometimes intellects so stimulated argue that murder, rapine, lust, and unnatural vice must be experienced in order to know the Good (God). The student recognizes, however, that out of the body men are easily known by the light they radiate about them. In the dark twilight sphere the true character of a man expresses itself. On the earth plane only a sensitive can see this light, which reveals man's true character. When I was living with a tribe of red Indians in America I discovered that they had nine-tenths vision. I have been told that the average man has only four-tenths vision, but before long people will be born who will be able to determine a person's character by the atmospheric color, which betokens his true nature of being. Jesus has said that by a man's light is he known, and the deva creations say that when a man advances to that period where he can discriminate between the true and the false, he has received his first degree in the acquirement of knowledge of the truth.

When nature calls on us for service the devas expect us to obey. It is just before nightfall, and at certain other times of the day, when nature calls upon us to assist the Elder Brothers in our tribal community. This is a time when self-interest should be laid aside, and we should assist in some way the aged and infirm brothers of our community, for nature's laws are manifested in order that the strong may assist the weak. It is only through self-sacrifice and clean living that the weaker brothers can be brought to the higher levels of well-being, which are enjoyed by the others of the community.

Binding ourselves to the consciousness of well-being determines the speed at which well-being will approach our human minds, since the activities of a thing determine its place in nature's manifestation. For instance, if we look at a globe of crystal and notice its florescence, we determine its speed of activity by its atomic radiations which encircle our minds. When we tap a thing with our knuckles, we bring about a relation between the thing we touch, and the sensation which we receive with our fingers—therefore, unconsciously our mind brings about a union with the thing we tap.

A mantel surmounting a fireplace is a favorable absorbing station for the minds gathered about it, and a seer can easily discover their type of mentality, for the people living in the house have thrown their mentality into the mantel, and by this means the history of the past is easily read.

The moment the student aspires inwardly for truth, he unconsciously taps nature's will, and from that moment he

slowly begins to build up an alliance with nature's understanding. Nature's will, as the Yogi understands it, is totally
different from that outer framework with which we have built
up our personality. The miracle worker, in all the sciences,
arts, and professions, is he who goes to nature for her truth
and understanding.

CHAPTER THREE

THE SEALED BOOK OF THE UNIVERSE

When we enter into the consciousness of nature, we discover that the Great Sealed Book of the Universe is intermittently open to those who are inwardly seeking Truth.

The Great Law has something to give to humanity which will regenerate the race, so that we may gain consciousness of the law of justice, for nature desires to unfold to the student the understanding of the law of cause and effect (karma). In Yoga practice, as the student goes inwardly and studies the many lives and incarnations through which he has passed, he is instructed in the knowledge of this law regarding the different states of his evolution. He is, as it were, resurrected in these lives, and learns that he has brought upon himself untold suffering through injuring others, and has gained knowledge for himself through the Path of Experience. He is then taken over into another division of nature's consciousness, where he studies the beginning, rise, and fall of nations, and analyzes the causes and effects which have brought about their destruction. Great empires have been destroyed, yet history does not tell us much about the cause of their decline. The student discovers, however, that the nation which does not build itself up in the security of the greater powers of nature and God, eventually passes into oblivion. Thus Egyptian civilization quickly passed away when it no longer attuned to nature's determinative energy.

The lawgivers of Egypt were at first guided and directed by the Great Architect of the Universe and had recourse to the laws of nature, but when that nation no longer responded to the direction of truth and the rulers secured personal gain by building up laws for the government of the many, then their knowledge of truth was withdrawn. Later, the priesthood of Amun Ra (no longer fulfilling the Law's original purpose) became very powerful, and built up laws of their own. They became so powerful that the occasional God-enlightened ruler, who sought to administer justly the greater Law, was unable to break their power. So we see that "a house which is divided against itself cannot stand."

There exists today in nature the plan of a great temple to be erected near the Great Pyramid and the Sphinx. The Great Architect planned the pyramid, and its builders are again being brought out of time to manifest as nature's law demands, in an edifice plan which will give security and instruction to the efforts of races who seek union with the law of nature. This temple will be a "plan form" symbolizing man's achievement throughout eternity. We all recognize this "edifice plan" in the inner spheres, which symbolizes nature's fixed principles for the attunement of our mind world.

A great domed building will be erected in homage to our foster parent, the sun, for truth travels like a ray of light, and sometimes its beams are reflected into the secret chambers of the Pyramid. [1] Already the Sphinx (the moon symbol), constantly looking towards the East, awaits the time when the sovereign purpose of this moon god may be known, and its book of revelation opened.

The Great Pyramid was constructed according to the law of nature, and symbolizes periods of destructive, as well as constructive activity. It is the map of both the constructive and destructive forces of nature and man, and it acquaints us with the fact that Truth can only be attained by humanity in an ascending spiral scale, and that the apex of our pyramid can only be reached through the secret chambers of our hearts, by entering our interior states of being, where the Lord of Wisdom is seated upon his throne, the administrator of the law of justice—Truth.

The great temple of the Sphinx is within the finer essences of nature, and the student can see the great mundane elemental being who guards its entrance. Information regarding the wisdom books, relating to the present, past, and future, is to be found within this temple, and there is a machine which measures the direct and retrograde movements of learning.

---

1   (The great pyramid was so constructed that each year, when the parent sun is in line with the Dog Star, the light falls upon the square Stone of God at the upper end of the great gallery, and thence descends upon the head of the high priest.) See *Comte de Gabalis*, page 88.

The theory of evolution, as conceived by our scientists, does not in the least conform to the accuracy of these instruments, for they measure the movements of nature, and the understanding of these things is given to the advanced souls, the wisdom seekers of humanity.

A great discovery regarding nature's consciousness will shortly be made, which will shake the minds of humanity. Those who have knowledge of nature's mysteries, and who have consciously attuned themselves to her truth, will be able to bring down this primordial consciousness of nature into people's minds. Thus will nature's presentment of truth come to the human understanding. This primordial consciousness reflects the truth and falsity of each to others, and the evil man cannot stand in it. It lights the torch which every true seeker after knowledge possesses, and will prove dangerous to any sham or falsity which the student may possess.

This great shining orb of nature's truth gives us the power to pursue our own voyage of discovery, and a positive, one-pointedness of mind for union with Truth. This manifestation is nature's justice sword, and an understanding of the law which governs it will give the knowledge of truth to its possessor.

Few people have any knowledge of our sun, or its higher counterpart, the Sun behind the sun, nor have they knowledge of the other suns which are creating another great globe, called by the Mohammedans, "The Globe of Akhama."

Truth is like a flaming sword, and all the darkness hovering about our world cannot extinguish the book of wisdom records guarded by the Sphinx, for the Great Architect has so recorded. When man can stand in the presence of the torch of truth, then this wisdom knowledge of the Sphinx will become common property, for the secrets of the Law are guarded only until the wisdom religion is again known to the teachers of Truth.

The scientists of our world think that evolution is gradual, but this is not so, for there are *forced* movements in nature, both backwards and forwards, similar to the tides of the sea. The movements which built up Greece, and the knowledge given to Egypt of the forces of nature, were all measured. The Renaissance, and the retrograde movements which came after, were measured, and even now we can see the path of a new civilization, and measure its dark age of destruction and turmoil, and also its emergence into peace and security in the future.

The student often goes into the elemental world in his practice of Yoga and, in a temple there, he can see the revolving globe of our world, the surface of which he is told to watch. Where it appears most bright, is where its people register an appeal to know God. This brightness appeared over the Mohammedan countries during the time of the Great War, while some of the European countries became very dark, and heavily clouded with shadow. To the minds of the Mohammedan followers of God at that time, Christianity seemed to be only on the surface.

As the student enters into nature's consciousness he begins to realize the differences which exist in its various elemental properties, just as he would notice the difference between the waters of a clear stream and those of a murky, muddy pond. In order to enter this clearer vision, he harmonizes himself with the different organs and nerve centers within his body. Thus he establishes a correspondence between nature's seven grades of consciousness. If the student wishes to harmonize himself with the devas and chains of initiates, which belong to that division of nature's understanding, he determines the best method of approach by tuning in to their vibration through the pitch of his voice, or by mantras, or else by his Silver Shield, [2] the node points of which attune themselves to any particular intelligence or consciousness of the devic creation.

There are minute membranes on our mental body, and on the Silver Shield, which receive the communications which nature can deliver to us, and these communications, through our body's organism, are transferred to our human brain. We aspire for purity, in order to reach the higher of these devic

---

2   See *The Dayspring of Youth*.

types and ask for instruction. If worthy, we may be instructed in their magic and understanding of nature's laws.

We give to these devas our trust and, as we give to them, so they return their trust to us, for that is the law. The devas communicate with us by means of a projected thought form, or thought energy, and also through small impulses towards organization and regeneration. They do this in order that our thoughts may be embodied with purity, and that we may have the desire to express ourselves as truthfully as possible.

The devas will say to us: "Do not tell us what you think, tell us what you *know*," for we always speak from the *knower* consciousness of Truth. They approach us from the consciousness of the world of intuition, where truth underlies all expression. The deva will ask, "How can you change this expression of Truth, as you are ever in its presence." This presence of Truth flows through us, and according to the degree in which we have made it our own, we shadow forth its force to the world.

Humanity has built up a false creation of its own, which it conceives to be truth. *Real* thinking is not like our ordinary process of thinking. The Yoga student should know a thing by its development, according to its "plan image," and its state of action, and it is our duty to assist in its efforts to complete its circle or plan.

Why does mankind hesitate? Because it is their way of preparation towards what they call thinking. The student should *know*, without any preparation. Love, tolerance, joy, intelligence: we should know all these things without going through a process of building up their form or state of activity. To build a bridge takes time, experience, and care, in order to conform to all the architect's plans, but, when we build a thing in nature, using nature's materials, it is done immediately, conforming to the law of its existence. Everything is completely planned and keeps its original species, its atoms cluster about its central "node" point, and its builders conform to the direction of its principal parental stem.

If, for some reason, it evolves an adverse characteristic, its atoms instantly adjust themselves again around its parental nucleus. This is done instantly, without thought, as we know it. So it should be with us, for all men possess that higher mind, which we use to gain the light of truth and justice, although few acquire its use. In order to acquire its use the student must pass from the mind of this illusion world into that inner world where justice and truth abide in the sanctuary of our mind bodies—the presence of the Lord God of Truth within.

This requires a cleavage from the government of our lower mind body, and the establishment of a union with our higher selves. There are simple laws of nature's unfoldment, which the student must learn, and he should try to attain the consciousness of nature's higher counterpart in everything, for this is to know God. Unfortunately there are few men eager and persistent enough to seek this knowledge, which would give them peace and happiness, even while in this dense and corporeal body.

The devas are the recognized "bringers" to the Yogi. They teach him when to expect movements of a new type of understanding which will be given to man. It is they who open and close the book which measures to man the duration of a religion. Great religions spring up, blossom, and disappear, like the flowers of the field, leaving but few memorials of the real work of the avatar. We see this in the evolution and development of a religion such as was given to Egypt, Greece, and Rome. At one time these religions were just as vital and resplendent as the teachings of our great advocates of justice and truth in later days. But the devic knowledge is given only to those who seek the services of the devas.

We measure space and time here on our earth, but as we go inwardly into the finer essences of nature, space and time disappear and we find ourselves in the presence of love and beauty. We desire union with the consciousness of the knower, for in its presence there is bliss and knowledge.

CHAPTER FOUR

MESSAGE OF THE DEVAS TO AMERICA

There are many destructive elements at work in the American Commonwealth, which cause nature to change her original plan and purpose. In recent years man has destroyed her forests, has diverted her rivers from their natural and original courses, and has abused her bounty by willfully destroying her products to produce shortage, and now the law of nature is beginning to take effect upon the country, and the consciousness of humanity in these localities is fast becoming impressed by the barren state of nature.

The soil, no longer husbanded according to nature's plan, is not producing its accustomed yield, and this is causing havoc and suffering to humanity on account of man's interference with nature's system of development.

Since we, the devas of nature, are no longer respected, it is most difficult to find anyone who can serve our purpose. We wish you to warn the American people that filth and evil cast upon the surface of springs, lakes, and rivers has befouled humanity's mind and that we, the guardians of nature, can retaliate and use weapons of destruction as well as of propagation. Nature is never idle. She seeks to supply man with those gifts which the real soul of humanity needs; but man has disregarded our affection for him and for all living things, and has interfered with the elements in order to make so-called improvement, and profit.

We will keep to our resolves and work for the good of mankind, but we will not see our work ruthlessly destroyed. Therefore, we wish you to write down the seven commandments of nature:

Do not heedlessly destroy that which we build up, unless it is for the good of mankind.

Do not cut down or destroy that which nature provides as a manifestation of her plans of organization.

Do not build habitations and buildings (factories, etc.) the emanations from which are destructive to our being, except in the waste tracts of lands where the soil is infertile.

We seek to fertilize the soil with nature's own nourishment, to make it healthy for the production of crops. In the season when this fertilization is proceeded with, do not destroy nature's craftsmanship in her moulding. The soil should lie fallow for a year before the workman disturbs it, and he should plant only what is indigenous to the soil. Nature is endangered by cross-fertilization, the crossing of one plant with another, and foreign growths should not be planted in alien soil. The tiger and the bear should not be mated, nor should native plants be fertilized with foreign pollen. The soil is endangered by grafting foreign shoots upon a native tree, for these shoots need different soil nourishment from the parental stem, and this brings a destructive element into the soil. There is a movement backwards and forwards, like the tide of the sea, between the soil and the tree. The tree derives nourishment from the soil, but it returns atomic elements of its own back to the soil—hence the confusion.

Do not replace nature's beauty by ugliness which breeds disorder, and is repugnant to us (the devas.) We can be destructive as well as constructive and we can introduce into the soil and its products elements which are destructive to body and mind. Fear is the chief element, and fear can be more deep-seated than people imagine, for it passes into the deeper channels of man's being and reacts upon the functioning of his mind, bringing periods of great distress and anxiety. We can also bring about drought and famine through our power to withhold water from the land.

The lack of reverence for nature and her powers causes sorrow to us, the devas of nature. Man no longer places the handful of grain, or the fruit of his harvest upon his family altar, in thanksgiving to the giver of all good. Do not neglect this.

We consider the greatest crime is man's heedless waste of nature's products, and his inhumanity to nature. The idleness of the husbandman who neglects to reap the grain that he has sown is criminal, as is likewise the activity of any man who causes the products of the field to perish, causing scarcity, suffering, and want. Do not sanction waste.

The interesting thing about the deva creation is their power to portray to the student the condition of his higher self in nature's consciousness. We may describe this power in their own words by saying, "He becomes the barometer of his soul, and of the conditions about him."

Through this power the devas may project into your mind the vision of a beautiful brook, a placid lake, or a quiet sea. The water may be clear and moving gently, and perhaps you can see the stones and the trout at the bottom. When you have this kind of vision, the conditions about you are good; but when you see rapids and foam, the devas say that in your struggle for light the conditions are bad. When your barometer shows a placid, quiet, and beautiful stream, then it is a good time for aspiration towards light. It is not wise to meditate or aspire when you are in the midst of turbulence and discord, just as on the psychic plane it is not wise to bring one's clairvoyance into play during a violent storm, when the lower intelligences of the wind are at work (for they are destructive), nor on a dark, foggy night, for earthbound spirits find it easy to materialize in a damp atmosphere, since it gives them a place of residence, and the power of propulsion and pressure.

A man suspended in air cannot jump, for he has no density or resistance from which to spring. This is also true of a discarnate entity. The Yogi must learn of the other worlds that are about him from experience, and he soon learns that he has other planes beside this physical world in which to make discoveries. In time there will come the period when he will gain his schoolroom experience in nature's consciousness. The planned economy of nature will then put to shame the selfish arguments of the world's pseudo-planned economists.

Since men began to destroy wheat in America, hurricane and drought have destroyed the farming communities, but before long men will begin to realize that nature is the law-giver and that man, at his peril, runs counter to her will. We have only to look at China and Spain to realize what havoc nature can bring about, when her forests are destroyed and her bounty wasted.

According to the law of nature, those who have enriched themselves unlawfully, and have caused privation and suffering are placed, after death, in a world where the habitants recognize the sham in each other. Here, when man meets man, the true character of each is revealed and they find themselves in a hell of their own making. In these purgatorial states they must remain until they follow the gleam of the far distant star of Truth.

The world never realizes what becomes of the fortunes these destructive agents hope to secure for their posterity. Occasionally they are used for good, but more often like pirate gold they find their way back into the underworld of crime, ever impregnated with the curse of suffering.

Nature wars against everything which breaks down her natural productions for humanity. Civilizations have passed away in a single week, and the jungle and the desert sand now cover vast cities where nature was dethroned from her mercy seat.

There are three divisions in nature:

Creative

Destructive

Protective

—and until man seeks union with his own Lord God of Truth within, he is but the cat's paw of nature's movements. Whilst man seeks happiness through his passions and desires, and through his five senses, he is living only in the objective world and spiritually he will be unsuccessful. When he turns within to find his own Kingdom of Heaven then his day of happiness will begin to dawn. This is the aim of all Yoga practice. When man withdraws within, he finds that the present world in which he lives is similar to a dream and an illusion and, by seeking union with the Lord God of Truth within, he enters nature's consciousness and perceives the reality which lies around him.

Few have stopped to consider what a man who tends a machine all his days gets out of life. How much nearer does he attain to the Truth? He may live a clean and honorable life of toil, yet, in his old age he comes to ask, "What has it

all amounted to?" Suddenly, there will come the desire to
know Truth and he begins to wonder about the world within,
which he has not had leisure previously to know and enjoy.
He discovers that the wall which separates him from nature is
the wall of "ignorance of his own Self," and he awakens to the
significance hidden in the lines,

"This above all: to thine own self be true,
And it must follow, as the night the day,
Thou canst not then be false to any man."

Hamlet.

CHAPTER FIVE

FOOD ADULTERATION

Nature's purpose is to give freely of her surplus to provide nourishment and food for the toilers of the earth. It is not the purpose of nature to fill the pockets of the minority through buying and selling. Nature bountifully supplies the needs of mankind, but her purpose is often frustrated by capitalism and through adulteration of the essential characteristics of natural food. Nature resents this and penalizes man by bringing about sickness, famine, and disorder, for she supplies only the just demands of the people.

Many of our native foods today are so adulterated that they are highly destructive to man, and nature's vitality, purveyed through food, no longer finds entrance to the human body. Food laws, which good men have placed before our legislative bodies, have been rejected, owing to the influence of advertisers and adulterators, who claim that they would be ruined if these bills became law. Very little is openly spoken about this condition in the underworld of crime, so nature often assumes the place of the lawgiver and destroys the areas of supply.

Professions depending for their livelihood on sickness caused by food adulteration, resent any legislation which would tend to reduce their incomes. Today most professional men are in the "racket," and it will be difficult to combat human nature until the State gives the doctor and the surgeon an assured income, so that he can look after the people's health and have time for research, without worry over money matters. In the medical and surgical professions at present we find men sacrificing themselves for the good of the community, but usually they are very poorly compensated.

Always there are many who carry on their operations contrary to the laws, seeking to enrich themselves by extortion from those in trouble, or by blackmail of the unfortunate. In this class we find many patent medicines well advertised, being sold for exorbitant prices, when the cost of such is little, and the curative value less. Alas, people do not interest themselves deeply in things which do not touch them, and are callous to the welfare of their unfortunate fellow man.

CHAPTER SIX

NATURE THE BROADCASTER

As the student aspires for Truth, he discovers that he has definitely penetrated other spheres of consciousness than those with which he is familiar in the daily expression of his ordinary life.

He slowly becomes acquainted with many different divisions of nature, of which formerly he had been ignorant, and he begins to realize that his body has become a sounding board upon which the different vibrations of nature's movements play intermittently. New worlds appear before his vision and, if he is earnestly seeking the light, he discovers the inhabitants of several of the divisions of nature and gradually learns to associate himself with their different degrees of intelligence and attunes himself with their vibrations.

His body becomes the instrument which puts him *en rapport* with the intelligences who are the governing powers in nature's kingdom. The "engineer" atom within his body signals to him when he is in tune with a being of the deva creation, and he "listens in" to the communications which immediately come to him, while aspiring for truth at the same time, and thus with a higher clairvoyance he sees and tests each source of information. In other words, the student should see the being he is in communication with, and by the radiation of its light test its degree of knowledge.

When the student goes inwardly and draws himself away from the objective world, he instantly recognizes the forces which wish to communicate with him. Purifying his mind, he "listens in" to the communications coming through. Nature has become his instructor and he has no need to go into his ordinary world of experience for knowledge. He earnestly aspires for the greater wisdom which these instructors in nature may reveal to him.

The reader may wish to know what type of instruction is supplied by these angelic devas of nature. They instruct him in the purposes of nature. For instance, the student may ask himself, "What is the meaning of an oak tree, what part it plays in the manifestation of nature, and what relationship it has to the human kingdom?" As he analyzes its form and its purpose he asks himself other questions, "What does it symbolize?" "What is the purpose of its creation?" "What use is it to humanity?" "What are the characteristics which differentiate it from other species?" "What relationship it has to the animal world?" "To air, fire, and water?" "What relationship it has to other species, such as the tall sycamore, and the drooping willow?" "How does its purpose and manifestation become known to the human consciousness?"

The asking of such questions sets in motion that process which will in time attune him to the deva intelligence.

It is the deva instructors who give us this information and they will approach us when, by right thinking and right action, we have purified the elemental nature within us. The body is a constantly evolving structure, either becoming more refined and pure, or degenerating in density and sluggishness.

In this process of refinement the student first becomes conscious of the intelligence which is symbolized in the "water" of his nature. Although previously he may have been slightly "aware," he now becomes conscious of nature's instruction. In his youth the writer was greatly impressed with a tribe of American Indians with whom he lived during a whole summer. Whilst walking with some of the "wise men" of the tribe he noticed that one would suddenly stop, cross his arms upon his breast, and with great veneration "listen in" to something which had escaped the writer's notice. It took the writer a year and nine months living close to nature, before he began to apprehend nature's movements and instruction.

Gradually he learned that nature, through her broadcasting station, often heralds forth to man glad tidings of the presence of a great teacher, whom the Indians call the "Child of God." The great teachers of humanity, whether in the body or out of the body, often herald their approach by the coming of a devic form.

When the deva wishes to attract the attention of the student, he projects into the consciousness of the student some form, as of a seagull, bird, swan, deer, or a beaver. A red

Indian initiate will often say, "The king of the beavers is about to speak," and it is from this source that the Indian gets his knowledge of the laws of the beavers. These laws show how men should live. They are a canon of human conduct and, among the Indians, the different degrees of intelligence are symbolically summed up by saying, "He belongs to the 'beaver' lodge, or to the 'blue bird' lodge."

Many sensitives have been conscious of that movement in nature which announces the approach of the dawn, called by the Greeks, Aurora, the herald of the dawn. As God gives of his bounty to the human body, in the fruits of the earth, so do the heralds of the dawn give a mental stimulation of splendor and brightness to those who attune themselves by "going inwardly" to receive their message of the day.

In time humanity will await eagerly the announcement of God's messengers for the day's instruction in music and in beauty. Our greatest composers have touched only the fringe of nature's symphony, and eventually the radio and the other toys which God has given to man through science, will become refuse heaps of twisted wire and discarded mechanism, for in time man is to know and enjoy God.

The ascetic in his cave is often pitied by civilization's bright wits. They think he must be very lonely; whereas, in the deeper states of Yoga practice nature unfolds herself and the ascetic listens to symphonies greater than the ear of man has ever heard. It is well to seek union with the Lord God of Truth within, so that nature may reveal herself and man become an artist, conscious of his own creator—the Lord God of Truth within. When he so becomes conscious, he quickly realizes that his objective world is but a sphere of illusion, like a dream. It is in the illusion world that magic is encountered.

A great deal has been written about magic. People who cannot produce any tangible proof talk about it with authority. The true magician is a seeker after Truth, and as he perfects himself he begins to discern in nature her wonderful unfoldment. In proportion as he merits Truth, nature rewards him with a knowledge of her secrets and gives him dominion over some small division of her consciousness. This is in

order to enable him to perfect himself in the government
and knowledge of her constructive principles. In recognition
of his worth and one-pointedness of mind in seeking the
Truth within, there is a guardian appointed to instruct him
in nature's phenomena. He is rewarded by attaining to a
greater or less degree of knowledge of nature's law, and the
deva becomes his guardian spirit, allowing him to use nature's
materials within a certain range of authority. It is only when
Truth appears to the mind—when primordial light, through
devotion to Truth, descends—that man is given his first real
lesson regarding the cause of things—the knowledge of the
laws of cause and effect. But the student must constantly
aspire for truth and purity of thought, before the Lords of the
mind and of the deva creation will enter into a close relationship with him for, as the devas say, "The mind must be bound
through merit, which is at the disposal of the Gods."

The student must enter into the consciousness of the real
"mind body" of nature. This means passing over the void
from the material world into the mind just back of nature,
as well as detachment from all things which would agitate or
keep back ascertainment of the truth of a thing.

CHAPTER SEVEN

OBSERVE OTHERS

When the physical man is sick and diseased, his mind becomes weakened and is more easily preyed upon by the evil of the intermediate worlds, but a healthy body and mind invariably bring healthy thoughts.

It is a revelation to an ordinary man to enter a group of men engaged or interested in physical culture, for a fit body is dynamic. It radiates health and attracts people who have been unable to lead natural lives.

A healthy man whose liver is normal invariably radiates good nature in the morning. When the minute brain at the tip of the liver is out of order, man becomes suspicious of his fellow men. He is restless and sluggish, and his mind does not seem to function normally. On arriving at the office one quickly notices if the boss is "liverish" and if so, he expects a "spot of trouble." Likewise, when the upper third of the lungs is not normal, man is subject to mental depression and a high state of nerves. Again the so-called spiritual "man of the cloth" sometimes finds that his organs of generation are out of order. A healthy body is needed to combat the evil of the world. The body that constantly preys upon the mind causes its owner to talk about "ill health," not health.

The student will also observe a vampire class, who have generally led indolent and selfish lives. I know of a lady, provided for by other people, who is supposedly engaged in good works. When she entered a room in which there were eighteen people, she came in pale and worn. Five minutes afterward she left, glowing with health, but those remaining all felt like rags, and simultaneously gave sighs of relief at her departure. I have never noticed this vampirism, except among people who were selfish and self-centered. Old people often seek the society of youth for the stimulation which youth and health bring, and a list of crimes some day may be placed under the category of "old age." Yet I have never seen this vampirism in old people who had the "light," for they radiated the "spirit which is

within," as the healthy athlete radiates physical vitality and
magnetism.

In Yoga we begin to perceive distinct differences in types of
humanity, and we grade people according to these canons of
observation, although this sometimes causes us much torture
of the mind.

In beginning the study of Yoga one should start with a
long period of physical culture; the second step is the observation and analysis of others, not calling upon the use of the
"third eye," which is developed later. The way in which a man
stands gives you an index to his character, just as the place-
ment of the ear gives the sign of the criminal. One is taught
self-protection through observing these higher and lower
types in society.

As a man thinks in his heart, so is his body actuated, and
the man who is telling you a falsehood gives himself away. At
the end of this second period the teacher says, "Go and get
knowledge from all sources, for that reason you came to this
world; hence gather experience. Seek and pray for knowledge,
and the light of Truth will enter the mind."

It will be many centuries before man realizes that the
wisdom teaching of Jesus, "Agree with thine adversary quickly,
whilst thou art in the way with him," and "A soft answer tur-
neth away wrath," are fundamental truths. Witness the jujitsu
expert, who easily overcomes his adversary by softness in his
physical attack. It is far better after a fight to shake hands,
seek to forget all differences of opinion, and start friendship
anew, for the law of opposition is the law of attraction, and it
links two persons together in the case of quarrels.

CHAPTER EIGHT
THE TIGER MAN

In Yoga practice, on returning to our bodies, we often find
the covering of our mental sheath befouled by particles of
matter foreign to its natural state. We do not normally realize
the foulness of the atmosphere in which we live. The average
man who has not built up his Silver Shield of protection, can
not protect the node points of his mental sheath from being
soiled by the debris and mire of ignorance. In Yoga the mental
body protected by the Silver Shield becomes vibrant, strong,
and responsive to all the finer vibrations in nature.

It has been written that we "see through a glass darkly."
When we energize our mental body and see the primordial
light within us, we are taken out of our darkness and use this
screen which nature gives us. We then see face to face. Man's
range of observation is limited, and his sensitivity registers
only a certain limited range of vibration.

When we descend into the underworld, the beings there
often implore us to tell what happiness is in our world of
being. To them, our world, of which they sometimes gain faint
glimpses, is a world of light, although when we progress into
the higher planes we find it a world of twilight. Our world
becomes brighter, however, when we can remove the debris
from our mental sheath, so that the primordial light can
illuminate our own dark mental world.

After the Yoga student has met his teacher, for the teachers
who possess real knowledge hand it down only by word of
mouth, there comes a great moment when he is taken out
of his body in full consciousness, and shown the evil of the
world. One such pupil was taken out of his body by night
for a period of a year and seven months, and was shown all
the evil of the world, the degree to which the beast in man
can sink. Think not that this is a fairy story. Not only is the
student shown the evil of the world, but he is taught how to
impress the mind of the wrongdoer with the sense of punishment. He is often shown how the innocent may be protected

by the "fear of God" impressed upon degenerate minds, and
how many souls may be ministered to in their distress.

The horror of the lust and brutality of men and women
is a subject the world knows little about. When first seen the
student cries out in anguish: "Is there no such thing as goodness, kindness, charity, or love?" It is then the teacher switches
him over among the unknown helpers of humanity, both in
and out of the body, and he will meet living men who in deep
sleep pass out of their bodies, and are then instructed to be
helpers of humanity.

There are many men and women who are looked upon as
failures in this world, who are doing great works out of the
body. Some of these great souls, known to the initiates for
their work, realize only in their dreams what they have been
doing, but it is to those great workers that the teachers bring
initiation and God realization.

As I have said before, man's so-called senses limit him in
the knowledge of his own activities. Could he trace the power
behind his personal will, he would realize the havoc caused
both to others and to himself by misdirected thought. He
would realize that his own thought atmosphere can bring
good or evil instincts to birth in the minds of those about
him, and that a thought is a *thing,* and is like a bullet from a
rifle which, if illegitimately used, can cause great havoc.

The business man especially is fond of the game of life. He
realizes his power and likes to play the game of impressing
his personality upon others, thus evolving his own ego. It is
this dynamic force in business which brings the knowledge of
power and releases into the business atmosphere the dynam-
ics of the underworld. As he plays this game, the business man
becomes greedy for money, position, and power, and he learns
how to prey upon the weakness of others. He attracts corrupt
minds which exist in the worlds of evil, and through this
added mental pressure he links himself with the destructive
forces of man and nature.

The forces of nature are either constructive, destructive,
or distributive. The distributive forces segregate a group of
humanity from their state of unity, and weaken them by

such separation. The big corporations say to the little manu-
facturer, "Come in with us, or we will ruin you," but when
they get what they want, they care very little what happens
to the "small man." It is the law of the jungle—diamond cut
diamond, steel cut steel.

President Lincoln, in his time, foresaw and warned people
of the ferocity of the tiger man. Today, crime has developed
as the trusts and large corporations have developed, and their
combinations have very little trouble in getting the aid of
bankers and others, holding so-called responsible positions in
society. It is a network of cooperation among men of criminal
instincts, but if these evil-doers could only realize the punishment which is coming to them, they would seek a way out
of it all before it is too late, for his own higher self will judge
each of them.

Discarnate, earthbound spirits, who are made witnesses
of the suffering they are causing and have caused others,
often ask in their misery for men to pray for their souls. The
purgatory in which they pass their discarnate existence can be
realized only by one sensitive enough to take on their mental
conditions, when their atmosphere touches him. It is very difficult to get these beings to aspire to the Lord God of Truth
within. In this purgatory there is one class of beings whom
the lords of justice clothe in sage green apparel—a single piece
costume, with a hood similar to that worn in Italy in Dante's
time. This costume is to them a symbol of hope.

The reader must realize that the laws made by men are not
always God's laws. Viewed from the inner planes of being,
God's laws are often contrary to man's. The great avatars and
teachers, who have brought spiritual truth to this world, all
agree that, "As you do to others, so will you be done by." All
of them have taught, "Love thy neighbor as thyself," "That
no man is altogether evil; that within all things is the divine
spirit of God; and that the ultimate end of all being is God
realization." When men have learned these truths ignorance
will be banished from the mind and the Lord God of Truth
within will come into his own. Some students desire this more
than do others, and it is they who hasten on the path. Some

play with their passions and desires, and see not the light that is above them. Many do not realize the goal which sooner or later all men must reach.

We think of murder as the worst crime that man can commit, but man's thoughts are often far more destructive than the weapon of the murderer. People injure each other by the use of envy, hatred, malice, and uncontrolled desire; then comes a day when man is brought face to face with true justice. His actions of good and evil are summed up within him, and he sees the balance struck.

Man does not take much interest in the sufferings or happiness of his fellows, as long as the actions of others do not annoy him. But, when he has cast up his balance of good and evil, he begins to analyze the happiness and sufferings of his environment. Then he realizes the immensity of the karmic debt that the tiger man must cancel before he can start on the path that will lead him to the Lord God of Truth within.

CHAPTER NINE

NATIONS - THEIR RISE AND FALL

This world is designed with many divisions by the Architect. There is a partition separating each division, and hovering over each there is a deva whose mission it is to instil into the minds of those devoted to Truth the consciousness of the spirit, that clarifying nectar which brings the properties of matter within the mind vehicle. This results in a composite unity of expression. Its manifestation is similar to brushing away ashes from the fire in order to allow the flame to spring up and blaze.

The earth is dear to these devic overlords of nature. They radiate their love to all living beings and growing things—to the flower as well as to the beast of the field. They desire that men shall know happiness, and that the lion and lamb shall become friends. It is these great beings, the "watchmen on the hills," who inform the Yogis when one of the intermittent manifestations of God's bounty is to be expected within their territory.

Nations are born, spring up, and die. Greece took two hundred and fifty years to attain to her supreme moment of culture—culture such as has not appeared since on this earth. Then the tide turned and the height of the next wave was not until the time of Constantine the Great.

When a nation seeks right direction from God, nature unfolds her bounty and man becomes great in thought and deed, for then beauty and truth are worshipped, and the devas smile.

When man assumes a one-pointed direction of mind, he separates himself from the debris and larva of discordant thinking and assumes the final essence of his true nature. It is, then, the part of the deva to vibrate these properties of mind stuff matter, so that the real finer and truer properties of mind are ensouled by the spirit which broods over the lower world. To the Yogi this one-pointedness is the emergence from darkness (ignorance) into a preparation to bring in the light and intelligence of the spirit. A hierarchal being

of a devic nature watches over those minds which seek union
with the spirit, and manifests in man's higher self, but seldom
penetrates into his objective lower nature.

There are devas who act as guardians of countries, nations,
and peoples, and watch over their aspirations for right government. When crime and corruption creep in they attract
elemental nature's scourge: then famine, flood, and pestilence
appear, and continue until man tries to think for himself and
find out the truth. When man seeks to know the cause of
crime and its punishment, he asks why "the rich man gains in
a day what the steadfast poor man toils for over a long period
of time," and he learns why the "strong man's arm becomes
weak in battle."

The criminal classes are similar to a pack of wolves entering a forbidden country, carrying destruction in their wake.
These are souls incarnated from the animal world into ours
through magic and misunderstanding of the laws of nature,
and they prey upon all who oppose their activities. They
are after loot and the gratification of their lower desires, at
the expense of the labor and toil of honest men, who seek
to provide better conditions for their children than those
which their early environment had given them. These men are
known to the initiated as the "freemen of the earth." These
freemen are seemingly in chains today. They are chained to
the machine, to the pay check, and to the taskmasters above
them. They are economic slaves, when all men should be free,
and know God.

A great many professions are filled with these predatory
animal souls. Among doctors and lawyers we find some who
say that if disease and crime were prevented, they would
starve. Oh, that Galen and Solon might reincarnate, in order
to purify these two great professions! Our lawyers and our
doctors should be in a position where their livelihood would
be guaranteed by the State, so that their labor would be for
the good of the community. For the sake of justice, and the
health of the nations, doctors and lawyers should be paid
according to their merit. So also with artists. Whistler once
said: "Poor artists! In the strength of my youth, I was too poor

to hire models and to pay for my materials! What wonderful things I could have painted then! Now I have plenty of this world's goods, but I am too weak to work!" The ignorant knows not the powerful concentration that the great artists put in their work. Sargent, the painter, once said, turning to the thirty-two pictures in an exhibition: "Every brush stroke has cost me a drop of blood. I do not wish to paint any more pictures now, for I want to rest."

Both Sargent and Orpen died of overwork and exhaustion, yet the mysterious energy of some criminals has equalled in destructiveness all that these great painters have done for the ennoblement of the human mind. I once asked a criminal why he carried on his profession and he said that he did not want to do it, but that something within him forced him to do so.

Often those engaged in international espionage enter it more for the sake of adventure than from a sense of loyalty and devotion to their country. They will tell you, "We like the game of diamond cut diamond, and steel cut steel."

Like attracts like, and if man has hatred and malice in his heart towards his fellow men he attracts souls of the under-world, and ushers them out of that dark world into his own world of being. He thus gives them the opportunity to incarnate through his vehicle into his sphere of consciousness. This type of incarnation can also be brought about by the ignorant use of magic, and the result is always a destroyer. One never finds creative artists, craftsmen, or geniuses among them.

Observe that the followers of Mohammed pillaged Persia, they destroyed the beautiful works of the creative artists. Later they tried to perfect their own art by imitating the creative Persians, but imitation is not creation. This was again demonstrated when the attempt of Lord Leighton and Alma Tadema to imitate Greek art in England, with English models, failed.

When diseased atoms of these submerged souls permeate our earth, a militant force is engendered by their ideal that "might is right," but when warlords are born, who seek to oppose civilization's ideals of security, the closing chapters of a nation are being written. Such dictators are dethroned when Truth (intelligence) prevails. In China great warlords have sought to exterminate the castes of intelligence, but in the end intelligence always survived. A Chinese adept once told me that the warlords have often swept over his country, but that the caste of intelligence always won. Among Chinese adepts the military castes are looked upon with so much disdain that when a son enlists, his family hold a council and declare him dead to them forever.

We must not forget that man has two natures within him, the 'white' atom in the heart, and the 'black' atom at the base of the spine,[3] and it depends upon the man's aspirations as to which atom rules, the higher, or the lower self. By giving away to lust and the desires of the flesh the 'black' atom becomes powerful and seeks to overthrow the higher law within. In Yoga practice the student tries to balance the good and evil natures within him. This being done, he opens a path within himself to God Realization, and is able to distinguish between the true and the false—the good and the evil in man. He sees the 'caste mark' which every man wears upon his brow, and learns an occult law of which many possess the secret; that softness is greater than strength. This is taught by those initiated in the mysteries of life and death.

To seek knowledge is to illuminate the intelligence and to perfect the heart; it is to interest by the true, to move by the beautiful, and to persuade by the good. By his great devotion to nature, the Yogi perceives the light of Truth, and once having touched this divine flame, his whole being undergoes a change towards perfection. He becomes conscious of the essence of the world about him, so that his eyes perceive in all things the activity of the spirit. Henceforth he ennobles whatever he touches, for he sees in nature the perfection of the spirit—the handiwork of God. Illusion, which formerly surrounded him, disappears as he stands in the presence of "The Infinite—The Great Reality." This is the goal of the freeman, for in truth and beauty is everything that he needs to know. Truth is like a flaming sword. If you oppose it, it cuts you. If you accept it, it is placed within your hand, and then begins the lesson of its use. While a nation makes use of the flaming

---

3   Sometimes called the Secret Enemy.

sword of truth, it blazes forth as a meteor, and naught can stand against it. But when it sinks into a greedy despotism, balancing sordid benefit against universal rights, it shatters its pillars of protection and the end is delayed only until the universal law of karma is fulfilled.

CHAPTER TEN

BEAUTY AND ITS FUNCTION

The primordial light of Truth exists in the upper strata of mind stuff matter. When we plunge deeply into the mind's lower densities, we enter a realm of darkness and misery.

Often the fear of poverty beclouds human vision, and we cannot perceive the light which really is shining in our mind. This absence of the light of Truth within us plunges us into the realm of misery and despair lying beneath our feet, and we open ourselves to the pressure of minds which are imprisoned in these submerged strata. Often, when a man is idle, and suffering from cold and hunger, he unknowingly contacts these submerged strata and their inhabitants put pressure upon him to increase his misery.

Evil is able to affect the ignorant in three ways:

The bombardment of our uncontrolled passions and desires, and the activity of animalism in our mental atmosphere.

The influence on our minds of discarnate spirits who have imprisoned themselves in the lower spheres of the animal world.

The lack of devotion to Truth (God).

It may seem strange to the reader that when a man does not give time for devotion to God, he is open to contact with evil, but one learns early in Yoga practice that the presence of God within oneself is the greatest protection. This world is the school room of experience, and children learn by experience that if they play with fire they get burned. As soon as a man sincerely aspires to know the Lord God of Truth within, a shield of protection of an elemental and angelic nature is placed about him.

Children have this protection until they reach the age of maturity. Thence onwards they have to endure the conditions of their environment until they seek union with the Lord God of Truth within. In other words, the soul must henceforward fight its own battles. Devotion to Truth is one of the greatest revealed mysteries of this age. Man must seek the light

and truth within the strata of his higher mind, for there are
the places where the light dwells. Devotion to God (Truth)
gradually purifies and perfects the mind, until at last the light
enters its lower dense strata.

Since the body is the instrument of the mind, we must
purify our bodies. The body is constantly evolving in response
to the finer vibrations which refine its gross nature.

Thus, when man becomes harmless in word and deed,
the higher law manifests, and Truth descends into the lower
strata of the mind. This brings the student the power to discriminate between the true and false, and, when the authority
of the lower mind no longer controls him, he is given freedom
(happiness). When the authority of the lower mind loosens,
man experiences a complete change. It is a moment of illumination, when fear, anger, and hatred no longer exist for him,
and things are seen from a cosmic wave of thought. The student witnesses humanity's endeavor to escape from its prison-
house, from the mental darkness of the illusion world and he
seeks through sacrifice to bring to humanity the knowledge
of Truth. The mind is a veil which, if controlled, allows the
primordial light to show us our path. When we no longer have
devotion to God the light which should illuminate the mind
is scarcely perceived. By devotion we protect ourselves from
the thoughts of envy, hatred, and malice, for in the world
"like attracts like" and devotion to Truth protects us from the
onslaught of forces of a demoniacal nature.

When spiritually we realize the presence of the Lord God
of Truth within, those earth-bound spirits cannot enter our
atmosphere unless we will it. There is danger in all seances
held in the dark, for God's messengers make themselves
known in the light. Giving away to our passions and desires
make this world unhappy, as the great Persian mystic said,
"The world is an old hag, with a thousand wooers."

When the light of the spirit enters our mind body, it enters
our presence and nature unveils herself. No man can be
really evil when beauty enters his mind, and the perception
of beauty depends upon the evolution of one's own soul into
Truth. No two people can agree when discussing art, because

to some people Truth manifests to a greater extent than to others. Michael Angelo, in his old age, when his sight became dim, asked to be led to the Greek torso of the Hercules in the Vatican, and spent hours lovingly running his fingers over its chiselled surface. A great sculptor, after looking at himself in a mirror, was heard to remark, "I, who am so ugly, love beauty so much!" The evil man who loves beauty finds a way of escape to a nobler purpose. Canfield, the gambler, loved beautiful things, and he will be remembered for his love of beauty. In this way the victims of circumstances often find a means to a higher and nobler expression. When humanity at last realizes the value of art, artists will no longer starve, or degrade their art into a lower commercialism.

When a man seeks to be and to become, he begins to advance into his own time and has a perception of everything that goes on around him, but the average intelligent man is living many years behind the present. For instance, he is only beginning to perceive slightly the cause of the recent Great War. Let him fall not again into the trap led by a minority of the greedy, ambitious, and dishonest people.

Habit causes man to revert constantly to the past. The student must seek to project his mind into the present and future, as man measures time. Thus he is horrified by the crime of the present time and he thinks seriously of the future. He observes a man accumulating a great fortune to provide for the future. In ninety-nine cases out of one hundred the fortune goes with the first generation. Were man only to reestablish nature, where her bounty has been destroyed, he would provide security for those who follow after, for nature is grateful to those who nourish her purpose. In China it is the grandfather's custom to plant trees for the pleasure of those who are to come after. Those who wantonly destroy the products which nature provides for humanity, become detached from their fellows and, through the transmigration of souls, reincarnate in the underworld beneath our feet. Nature, though loving, is a severe mother. She enforces the law of her domain, seeking thus to bring her children out of ignorance into knowledge. The red Indian has often received devic instruction through some animal, and the laws governing its species. The actions of beavers have often enlightened the wise men of the tribe in the laws of nature, and in the mystery of nature's animal world. The devas are beings who watch over the development of different divisions of nature's elements, and they taught the red Indian the Law.

A great red Indian soul demonstrated his power over animals, called rabbits out of their holes, and stroked the wild deer in the forest. He sent the "love note" out to my cat, which responded immediately; and he afterwards sent her a danger signal, which caused her to run out of the room in panic, with her hair standing on end. He did this by means of the unspoken word. He told me that if only the white man had the graciousness of heart to approach the red Indian properly, he could receive much knowledge of great benefit to him.

The great avatar who appeared to the Indians in the eastern part of the United States, taught the initiated the written language, and they still have two books in their possession which, in some future period, as the devas wish, will be made known to humanity. The law of karma (cause and effect) will some day return justice to the Indians, and to the yellow race as well, for the armed superiority of a warring and greedy race will disappear in time, and the pendulum will swing in the opposite direction—for justice tempered with mercy will prevail.

Strength is followed by weakness, and out of weakness comes strength. This is the rhythm behind beauty's shield. The prophet Merlin has said that war will become so terrible that nations will cry out to each other for love. Then will the emulation of nations express itself in beauty, not in war and trade.

CHAPTER ELEVEN

THE LORD OF THE MIND

Man does not realize that although his mental self has jurisdiction over his mind body, a force outside of his ordinary concept of thought has power to build, or destroy it, to increase its range of activity into the consciousness of Truth, or to retard its activity. Unknowingly man possesses within him a lord of the mind who acts according to the will of nature.

The student recognizes a consciousness of the power of direction which precedes each manifestation of nature. This lord of the mind, if we accept its truth, can change our entire outlook and bring us release from the turmoil and tribulation which normally agitates our mind bodies.

When we have a real intelligence in the temple of our mind, the spirit (light) enters the lower regions of our mind body, and brings about a change of attitude in ourselves. When we view things on the mental plane, we perceive new qualities in them, which we have not discovered previously. On the physical plane we perceive light or spirit in its activity. On the mental plane we observe its quality, and nature's expression undergoes a complete change, for we have advanced in our perception of Truth. This attainment brings us into a closer study of the law of cause and effect. For instance, we have been studying society as a whole, seeing only the surface, but now we begin to understand and study the laws *underlying* society. We have been seeing the effects, but now we begin to study the causes of the different states of society which we observe about us, and when we seek to understand the framework of society and its cause, we at last begin to understand the relationship which exists between nature and man.

We see man's law, and we perceive what nature's law is doing for man. This comes to the student when the light (Truth) of the spirit has entered his consciousness. He then observes the disorganization of society and sees how nature shakes up the framework of our organizations and gives them a new impulse for better organization. Thus the student discovers that Mother Nature is the lawgiver and in time all men must serve her purpose.

The student comes to realize that crime leads man to recognize the Truth which is apparent in all things. Crime is the misdirected result of the nature which man has within him and knows nothing about. When man realizes the errors he is accountable for, he seeks redemption and tries to attain a knowledge of nature's law. In his ignorance man little realizes the power which he possesses. Crime is the ignorant use of what is good, and until man seeks union with his own higher self he will remain in ignorance of the dynamic powers which nature's instruction will reveal to him when he is worthy of her confidence.

An unworthy man is not allowed the knowledge of the "forbidden fruit."[4] That is secret information which this lord of the mind may reveal to him when he becomes worthy. This knowledge of nature's laws has been preserved intact by the lords of wisdom in nature, and is given only to those who will use it as the Law allows. Many people in their present incarnation have shown themselves worthy of nature's instruction. Yoga practice is a means of linking man consciously to his wisdom records of the past.

Those who attained to God Realization in the past find it easier, by aspiration, to attain to the wisdom periods of their own time. I speak of these things, for they may be helpful to the student. Often a sincere student attains easily to a change of mind, to the great surprise of his fellow students, and he sometimes suddenly becomes a leader in wisdom.

When man no longer seeks direction from the Lord God of Truth within, the lord of the mind snuffs out his light and man plunges deep into the mire of illusion. He becomes submerged in an environment in which incest, murder, hypocrisy, envy, malice, and crime abound. Submerged in this environment man ceases to act with regard to his well-being and good.

But the seekers for Truth, who are slowly emerging again into this New Age—the beginning of a Golden Age foretold by

---

4   Editor: as of this writing (before World War Two), this was true. Things changed in 1950. Read *The Perfect Matrimony* by Samael Aun Weor.

the prophets of old—recognize that the density of the shadow of today results from the brightness of the light of Truth, which is beginning to shine. In the ancient records it was written, "For man was created to know and to enjoy God."

CHAPTER TWELVE

THE PAN CONSCIOUSNESS

There are some activities of the Pan consciousness, which may prove instructive to the student. In considering them the reader should realize that our thought creations are ensouled by elemental nature and hence all of us are pursued by our own ensouled chimeras.

An officer residing in India caused a Yogi to be hanged for an offense. Later it was discovered that this Yogi was innocent. From that time on the officer's young wife could not stand sunlight and lived in rooms with drawn blinds. When her child was born it likewise could not stand the sunlight and was happy only in a darkened room. Other symptoms developed and the lady was in a London nursing home, when I was asked, if possible, to diagnose the trouble. The doctor and I were at dinner, when the nurse told the doctor of the recurrence of an attack. We went upstairs and found two attendants holding the girl down on a mattress on the bare floor. I cautioned the attendant about using too much pressure of his knee upon her arm. The girl was snapping and snarling like an enraged dog.

At such times the student, seeking to make himself impersonal and pouring forth all his love, is permitted to call upon his teacher for help. The girl suddenly ceased her attempts to bite the attendants and, in a beautiful voice cried out: "Jesus, hold me in your arms." I then asked the attendants to leave the room, only the doctor and the matron remaining with me. In my arms she began to sing a little religious song, taught to her when a child by her nurse. The doctor began looking around, trying to trace the origin of a queer noise, a whisking movement which had become noticeable in the room. There in a corner, sitting on its haunches, was a being from the world of Pan, half-human, half-dog, with terror-stricken eyes. The arms and body were covered with long hair and the pedal extremities more human than paw-like.

I told the matron, "This is the best paying guest that you have here, but if you will live up to the highest principles within you regarding this girl, we can cure her. It will mean pecuniary sacrifice on your part. You must give her freely of your love and make no charge for your services, and you are to place her out of doors in the sun at ten o'clock tomorrow morning." The matron did as she was told, and this was the first time since her attack that the girl was able to bear the sun's rays on her face.

Another slight seizure came over the girl shortly afterwards and she complained that a black mummified hand passed over her face. It was an Egyptian entity. (Before the execution of the Yogi in India, he had warned the officer that he was innocent, and that a curse would come upon him.)[5]

Another visit was made to deal with the Egyptian condition, which was a very strong one, and two weeks afterwards the matron brought the young girl to my house. The young lady was most enthusiastic, like a happy child, for that week she had been to see the Benson Players in *Much Ado About Nothing*. This was the first time in her life she had been to a theater, although she had been well educated in Shakespearian literature.

The Pan entity had also to be succored and I did not get into bed until three o'clock one night, for I had to take the poor Pan creature back to his own element. Imagine this stray entity crouching in his corner, or being chased by people actuated by fear and hate. However, it immediately responded to love, just as a starving dog responds to kindness.

The Egyptian, earthbound and personal, was more difficult to deal with, but in time he also responded to love and

---

5   [Original] Editor's Note: Two questions present themselves:

1. Why would the innocent Yogi permit himself to be hanged?
The Ancient Wisdom teaches that spiritual powers may not be used for personal ends. Of the Christ it was said, "He saved others, Himself He cannot save." To have saved himself would have been black magic, because used for personal ends.

2. How can the Yogi justify the curse?
The blundering officer had raised a karmic debt, which he must pay. The fullness of love required that the folly be reprehended with justice. So far it could not be forgiven, but eternal damnation was no part of the Ancient Wisdom.

aid. Elemental nature, when it is recognized, will respond to love, and the fear which elemental nature casts over a person coming through a deep wooded ravine at night, will turn to welcome, if the person will send love, untinged with personality, into that ravine.

Again, there is a beautiful strip of shore in the Highlands of Scotland which, until recently, little children avoided if possible. Living in the district, I had been awakened a number of times by a cool hand placed upon my forehead and, when I looked up, I would see a habited monk saying, "Pray for my soul, I am in hell." I would often meet him in the evening and he would come up to me gibbering and grimacing like an infuriated ape. I knew then that he was controlled by a master adept in ceremonial black magic. The cause of his earth-bound condition was that his master had made him procure a child for sacrifice. Living in the submerged spheres beneath our feet, this master intermittently possessed a power similar to hypnotism, and when so influenced the earth-bound monk would threaten me with all kinds of disagreeable things. He is now no longer earth-bound.

So we see that the creatures of this lower animal world are ushered into our world through magic and the breaking of the Law. The presence of such entities is often felt, although unseen by the normal eye. The development of one's clairvoyance is a purely scientific thing, but it is more quickly developed when we aspire to the Lord God of Truth within. We must not forget that our bodies are made up of the elements of air, earth, fire, and water, and that we attract from the elements what we are, thus bringing to our atmosphere our true elemental nature, be it good or evil. Therefore, we must purify our lower elemental nature by right conduct and aspiration towards Truth.

Whatever our mind is placed upon, that we attract, be it the dwellers of heaven or of hell. If we harbor anger, hatred, or malice in our hearts, we attract these elementals of destruction into ourselves. If we concentrate on fear, we are pursued by our own specters. Henri Martin, the painter, once pictured a procession of people crossing a desert, each carrying upon his back his own chimeras, the financier his moneybags, the artist his model, the roue his courtesan, and the others their appropriate burdens. Each creates his own burden, and he must carry it until he finds the path of wisdom and the place of understanding. Such is the Law.

CHAPTER THIRTEEN
THE COMING AGE

In the teachings of the past, instruction was conveyed by parables, or symbolic word pictures. A new system of expression is being engendered in the race, and youthful minds will speak what they think, regardless of the older minds about them.

This will mark the beginning of the emancipation of those living under normal conditions in the Northern and Southern Hemispheres. Even now youthful minds, though ignorant, often speak with authority, and this is bringing about an entire change in civilization's output. For when a man speaks with authority he links himself with the greater essence of Truth within his own interior world. A man conscious of the Truth manifesting within himself speaks with a corresponding authority, for he is then under the shekinah[6] of nature's consciousness.

In the Golden Age of the remote past, before man developed a personal will, he was guided by intuition and spoke with authority and truth. Much later, in the Age of Copper, and this present Age of Iron, man developed a personal will. Therefore, we must be patient with the youth of today, for the urge of nature, calling for cyclic change, is driving him to a pronouncement of his true character. As the age progresses, the youth will be less outspoken and will conserve his thought, so that when he does speak, he will be able to assert himself and make people listen.

So will begin an Age of Emancipation, when men will think for themselves and openly express their authoritative character. They will no longer be ruled and governed by a minority of the so-called "master minds" of the politicians, [7] and by those in authority who rule the masses. The Doctrine of Emancipation is the unfoldment of the law of becoming. Within every man lies that atom of the infinite and great reality which to the Yogi is the Lord God of Truth within. The great avatars

---

6   In Kabbalah, shekinah is the feminine aspect of God (the Divine Mother) that inhabits the temple when Israel is in harmony with God.
7   Sometimes called "The Brain Trust."

have all said, "The Kingdom of Heaven is within," and to attain
to the consciousness of the Lord God of Truth within is the
ambition of every true seeker (Yogi). Criminal souls, which have
been rejected by their own level of consciousness, group themselves together in the spheres beneath our feet. In the animal
world souls are not individualized as in the ordinary person on
the physical plane. Hence we find some individual semi-human
souls mingling with the animal group souls. The animals reject
and fear the presence of these semi-human individualized souls
and hence they flock together for protection. These beings
always ask us what is going on in our sphere and earnestly desire
to enter it. They are similar to the earth-bound spirits which
inhabit our world, and often their magic gives them the power
to incarnate here. This state is like the close association of a
human being with his dog, which causes the animal, through
love, to take upon itself the thought atmosphere of its master.
The master also in some degree enters into the consciousness
of the animal world, by projecting his atmosphere into the dog.
When the people of a nation can find sympathy and love only
through the devotion of a dog, or other animal, it is a sign of a
nation's decadence.

In early days people lived together in community groups,
sharing with each other the fruits of the field which they had
cultivated, and binding themselves together for the protection
of the tribe. They slowly became individualized and powerful,
making slaves by conquest, each man taking land under his own
jurisdiction, the products of which he no longer shared with
his tribe. In time, being separated from his neighbors he built
walls around his property and became distrustful of his fellow
creatures. He built himself a castle, for he lived in fear, and he
trained dogs to protect him and guard his domain. He placed
his affection upon his dog, because he trusted no human; hence,
no one trusted him. But the picture of the past is changing, and
the present merely awaits the next great human cataclysm to
shift the tide of destiny into the channel through which it is to
gain experience in the coming age.

CHAPTER FOURTEEN
ENSOULED ELEMENTALS

In order to get behind the screen of nature and discover what is back of the flower and back of the plant, the Yogi taps the higher kingdoms of the devas and in their vibration and consciousness he learns the cause of things. As he enters the realm of intuition, he gains the realization of truth and beauty and knows his place and plan in nature's manifestation.

These devas, or higher elemental beings, show the student the crucible of nature. They show him the creation of man from the beginning, and what takes place in elemental nature up to the time it is ushered into the physical world. It is from these higher beings that the Yogi obtains the knowledge of phenomena and is taught to obey the law of these planes of being.

Man little realizes how much of the elements are within himself; how his thoughts are seized upon by the elemental nature within him, and seemingly ensouled. Thus man acquires the character of his own mentality. He has both a physical and an elemental mind, with which he must familiarize himself and, when he becomes acquainted with the powers of his own elemental nature, he becomes a magician and miracle worker. Ignorant of his own creations, man tries by illegal methods to stop nature's process of creation. An expectant mother considering a miscarriage or abortion, should realize that she carries around in her atmosphere a human intelligence, a half-human, half-elemental child, who derives nourishment from the life stream which flows through her. If she is a sensitive, she often becomes entranced by these half-human children, who remain beside her sometimes as long as twelve years.

Such children can intermittently see our world through the eyes of a sensitive, and the education of these spirit children is three times as rapid as of those born in the ordinary way. Such entities often control and entrance their mothers. For instance, a friend who is often entranced by her guide (so-called) will sometimes go into a shop. She buys some article, and when it arrives at her house, she will always find a red thread, which she is unconscious of ever having perceived. I have spent hours with her family, and whenever I appeared I was greeted by the voice of a small child, who did not leave her mother's body until just before my departure. If you have the vision, you can communicate with these children. You learn to love them, for they will come to you whenever the mother is near you, and will ask for help. They like parties of children and often bring with them their little friends who are often as mischievous and troublesome as those in actual life.

The Yogi is often asked by his teacher to minister to a soul in its mother's womb, in order to give it courage, strength, and love; this to prostitutes, as well as to more fortunate mothers. In *The Dayspring of Youth*—(Yoga Practice Adapted for Western Minds), we have spoken of the "white atom" of the heart, and also the "Secret Enemy," or black atom at the base of the spine, the seats of the two natures in man. Each man is a magnet and attracts into his own atmosphere those conditions which are of the nature of his being. Man attracts that which he seeks, and that on which he places his mind unknowingly forms the nature of his own elemental being.

If we read the criminal records and the confessions of many murderers, we find that two or more intelligences dominated the man. One of these plunged his mind into its own consciousness of hatred and anger toward the world. It thus caused the poor sensitive to commit some crime, often leaving him with a blank consciousness, but with the fear of the law in his heart.

In the sub-human world the criminal classes are a division set apart, for generally they are rejected by the group souls in the animal world as being unsuitable in their present environment. They therefore seek by every means possible to reincarnate into the human kingdom, but generally their lower nature prevails and they war against society, in an effort to find an easy way to gratify their passions and desires.

The advanced souls leave beautiful things behind them in our world, which ennoble our minds and hearts. If we look at a beautiful piece of Chinese porcelain, we do much to discourage the onslaughts of discordant minds, for the alliance of beauty and truth is a protective force. This also applies to literature. It is always a good thing to have in our vicinity something which our hearts can recognize as beauty, for it will intensify in our minds the search for beauty in everyone we meet. It will start our imagination to work, which is the instrument the soul uses to make us aspire for higher things.

There is a secret mystery understood among the Asiatics and Yogis concerning the existence of a plane of consciousness which gives one control over the human mind. On this plane of consciousness the mind functions from a central fixed point of attraction and this gives a man the power to hold the lower mind in abeyance.

This realm is the sphere of the unformed consciousness in which the higher types of the devas reside, and here man is assisted to concentrate with fixed purpose upon one thing. It is as though an arrow which, when shot, had its limits of projection, was seized upon and carried forward into a consciousness of Truth.

Thus there comes a time during meditation and concentration when our fixity of purpose is increased and taken into another dimensional side of nature. The sensation is similar to stepping into another world of creation in which the mind is held true to the point upon which we meditate or aspire. This quality can be best summed up as fixity of purpose. Here the deva creations make their appearance and assume shapes often familiar to us in Chinese and Buddhistic paintings. We are also connected with a living chain of ancient teachers, who had gained realization of this sphere of the deva creation.

In Yoga we pass through the different dimensions, as we know them, and approach the subject from the background; namely, from that which is behind the thing we meditate upon. For instance, if we think of love or of war, and try to analyze our thoughts, we must approach and enter the consciousness *behind*. For example, the consciousness of the mother is behind the child and we approach the child consciousness by becoming immersed in the mother activities, which caused its creation.

The first teaching that comes from nature is to stand alone. Do not depend upon the assistance of others for your well-being, and do not depart from the original plan and purpose for which you came into an earthly body. Before a man incarnates, his higher self, the Lord God of Truth within, gives him the plan of his mission, and he is generally given choice of three ways of carrying out the plan. He is shown that it is possible to carry out the entire plan in a single life, but if he wishes to incarnate in the lap of riches his progress will be slow, and it will take him more lives than one. He discovers that his plan is to gain a certain range of experience, and that from this range of experience he will gain a greater wisdom knowledge. It might even be called Wisdom Teaching, because it is the result of his own personal experience before his plunge into matter. He must decide the course which he will take. The more advanced soul desires to gain his wisdom as quickly as possible. This plunges him through a range of experience which usually brings with it suffering and exertion. The wise man, whom we meet on earth today, has passed through a greater range of experience than his fellows; he is learned in the ways of mankind through *actual experience,* and he learns to see and feel as his fellows see and feel.

Man is happy only when he is carrying out the plan for which he incarnated and the gaining of this experience gives him a "round consciousness," which brings him no sense of separateness from his fellows. The unhappy man is he who cannot carry out his desire to do this or that. I once met an old gentleman, eighty-two years of age, who impressed me as being exceedingly happy, and radiant with good will towards his fellows. He was attending a class for piano tuning and I asked him why, at his age, he was engaged in that work. He replied, "All my life I have had one desire, to learn to tune instruments, but I have had to work for others, and have been a slave. Now, at last I am free to carry out my early desires, and I am learning much from the vibration of these chords. All my life I have been out of tune. Now I am getting into it, not only with myself, but with others, and I am just beginning to feel alive. I am also beginning to be truthful to myself for the first time, and I understand now what Plato said regarding music."

The second principle of nature is that of honesty, honesty of purpose and honesty of mind. To be really honest is to acquire right direction and truth through nature's instruction.

The Yoga student, in first becoming acquainted with the elements, is taught by a sylph and, before he is taken into their consciousness he is asked not to break their laws, or interfere with their state of government. He is also taught the care of his physical body, for the human odor and general atmosphere is most obnoxious to the higher elemental beings of the air. His mind is also subjected to their system of analysis to determine his honesty of purpose. The gnomes, like the human beings of earth, dislike ridicule of any kind, and measure your attitude toward them by a quick glance in your direction.

The student is first given instruction regarding his form and nature before he came on earth. He witnesses the powers of creation and sees how a human being is built up and instructed in the womb of its mother, long before it takes earthly form. The plan and purpose of his present incarnation is also shown, and then the part which he did not fulfill in his former incarnation. As he contemplates these omissions he may perhaps ask the sylph teacher what Shakespeare left out of his works, and he will be instructed in subjects of Shakespeare's past experience which he never dwelt upon. This brings a new fact to the student's consciousness and a new vision of man's achievement. He comes to realize the plan, and the part nature plays in man's incarnation and in his evolution.

In the finer worlds the student is at one with nature's intelligence, according to his degree of development. Here he discovers that nature grades him according to his devotion to Truth. She demands, "Honesty above all things."

It is falsity in our natures which constantly endangers us. Like school children we must work through the different grades of nature's teaching. By our mundane education we are supposed to be fitting ourselves to earn a living and take up our position in society. Also, we must aspire for the instruction of nature, in order that her cloak of protection may encircle us, and that we may gain the wisdom of our Lord God of Truth within.

This is a process of retiring inwardly to bring us into the higher realms of consciousness, and it is only by aspiration that we can approach the knowledge and wisdom of the laws of nature. We have within us our wisdom records of nature's experiences, besides the records of our human experiences in former incarnations, but it is only when we seek to unite ourselves with Truth that we begin to regain our place in nature.

The third principle of nature—to be of service—has a double meaning. In order to be of service we must seek to become an instrument of the Lord God of Truth within. In serving humanity we serve the presence whose "spark" is in the mind of all things. Thoughts which are beneficent and helpful to our fellow beings link us with them through all eternity, but the result of this linking brings us sadness. We experience compassion, or a desire to serve our weaker brothers. People often wonder what is the difference between a holy man and a saint, but if we think deeply we find that a saint is a miracle worker, who has the power to answer the prayers of humanity. Some consider that saints belong only to the remote past, yet in our day and time there are many saints, who have the divine note of nature within them and who, having gained God Realization (understanding the laws underlying nature's consciousness), no longer use "personal will," but the will of nature—God. By this means they have unified themselves with nature and man, and have become one with the spirit that governeth all things. After he has developed his finer forces, the Yoga student often meets these miracle workers, these men and women of God, for they stand in all time. Some remain behind, after the death of the body, to help the seekers after Truth in the world of darkness, and miracles are being performed under our very eyes today by these servants of the God of all creeds and races.

Out of the body, the aspiring student is brought en rapport with these unseen helpers. He may meet Mohammedan, Christian or Buddhist saints who passed away recently, or centuries ago. It is his services for humanity that bring to the student the help of the higher beings, and he is often given aid when he least expects it. Also, a time will come when the ancient spiritual teachers, who have attained to the greater Realization through many incarnations, will appear to him and give him their instruction.

Untruthfulness and falsity to self erects a barrier within the student and dims his perception. He thus blocks his path to knowledge. We have all *read* about the consciousness of peace and compassion but, when we meet a saint we learn for the first time the *meaning* of love, peace, and compassion. When I registered the compassion which was the chief characteristic of a Mohammedan saint, he switched my thoughts to the great compassion that Jesus had for humanity, as if the virtue which I registered in him was negligible to that of Jesus.

The three principles of Nature which the student must acquire are:

Ability to stand alone.

Honesty of purpose.

Devotion to God and to humanity.

CHAPTER FIFTEEN
MIND STUFF MATTER

We must never forget that we are living in mind stuff matter, and that what we attract, we become. This is because we absorb into our minds and bodies those atoms which are similar to our own nature of being. We must also realize that nature has her seven classified degrees of atmosphere, and that this seemingly solid earth has its own lungs, and breathes in and out as humanity does.

The degree of man's density follows the law of his development. We perceive the son of Manu in mankind and observe in man the different degrees of mental density. There are minds which are sluggish and slow in perception, and there are mercurial minds which work with great rapidity and accuracy.

Where we place our thoughts reveals to us, through Yoga practice, that division or density in which we are classified. For instance, we can place our minds in the air, fire, earth, or water densities of nature's elemental substance. The Lords of Creation watch our aspiration for Truth, and when we work through these different densities and, by aspiration for purity, place our minds in the element of fire then, if we are worthy, the Lords of Creation light the torch of our intelligence.

Yoga teaches us to aspire and to seek union with the Lord God of Truth within. Symbols of these divisions of elemental nature are placed before us and, by the proper use of these symbols, we attract into our mental atmosphere the atomic chain which links us with the intelligence of these elemental spheres and we listen in on this intelligence for instruction.

When we seek union with the Lord God of Truth within, the "engineer atom" within the body signals us when it has put us in communication with the intelligence within some division of nature's consciousness. Through Yoga practice we are given instruction as to how to develop the nerve centers within our bodies, so that they will respond to the seven divisions of nature, for these nerve centers are receiving sets through which we attune ourselves to nature's consciousness.

When the student communicates with nature, awareness of space and time does not enter his consciousness; rather, a realization of the "eternal now" impresses him with a consciousness of unity with all nature, a consciousness that he is a part of her: Above all, he feels the Presence, and that he is not separated from nature. He has the sensation of coming into a something in which to rest, which heals him and gives him strength. In his own daily work he is conscious of something in nature which gives him a strong urge to know and to become. He has only to shut his eyes for a moment and he can rest in this peace and love, in this realm of intelligence and instruction.

What you have given to nature in thought and deed, she will return to you threefold, and when you are able to break through into nature's consciousness, the intelligence there will inform you that there is "joy in heaven."

We speak of these things in order to stimulate the student to aspire for nature's Truth, for when the mind is linked to nature's consciousness, if trouble comes and you pause a moment to go inwardly to nature, on your return you will bring into your atmosphere peace and confidence.

When the student prepares himself for this voyage of discovery into nature's consciousness, he must ascertain the basic principles concealed in answer to the following questions:

Are you ready to bear your responsibility towards man and nature?

Are you ready to stand alone, and to serve unselfishly your fellow beings?

Are you ready to serve nature according to her laws?

What is nature's position and purpose regarding humanity?

What is your responsibility and underlying purpose in serving according to nature's law?

Other questions to be answered are:

Where are you standing?

Are you marking time, going forward, or retreating in time?

What self-knowledge have you acquired?

Are you one of the herd, or do you dare speak your thoughts?

With calm consideration ask yourself, "For what purpose did I come here?"

After some consideration you will discover that you lack self-control. If you imagine that you do not, try to stop thinking, or to think on one subject and hold the thought. A great initiate once said, "He who can control his mind for three-tenths of a second can become a master of this world."

Only by going inwardly and seeking union with the Lord God of Truth within can you come to know yourself and be yourself, and it is by the process of aspiration that you may enter the realms of conscious nature, and receive her instruction. Man gains little by the outer, objective knowledge of this world. The great avatars have all pointed out the *one* path— that "the Kingdom of Heaven is within."

Nature's higher counterpart commands the student to be truthful, for only then can you fit into your place in society, find *your own* level, and the level of other men.

To be true to nature, as in the earlier Greek and Egyptian days, means to serve the gods, and to serve all Truth that exists in nature and man.

To be of service to your fellow men means to serve those who are truthful, to seek and serve the honesty in men. Here nature begins to give the student one of her greatest gifts, discrimination of purpose. This is a power to discern the type of life a man is living, to perceive whether he is a builder towards God, or a distributor of ignorance; whether he is seeking to bring intelligence into his circle, or to put pressure upon his fellows to retard their search for Truth. There are two types of men, one opens the door to Truth, and the other shuts the door to his fellow men. The one stimulates his friend to self-thought, and the other imprisons his mind and body by domination.

We are constantly referred to the Wisdom saying, "As above so below," and we discover in Yoga that the physical senses have a higher counterpart through which nature speaks to us, but it is difficult sometimes to frame her expression into human language. For instance, nature's first pronouncement that we must stand alone means that we must stand alone in the Presence. This means really two things: standing alone in this world, and standing alone in the consciousness of devotion to the Lord God of Truth within.

As soon as the student enters nature's consciousness he feels the Presence, which he analyzes as love and beauty. Once this discovery has been made, he must always stand thus alone in devotion to Truth, and he will find that when he has learned to "stand alone," the Presence will be with him. The great initiate Shakespeare brought into full activity the brain center or "chakra" between the eyes, which registered the source of his greater expression. The world conquerors of old had developed the brain center in the region of the navel, which is the register of the knower consciousness on the physical plane. (Compare Job 40:16.)[8]

In their early days the dictators, seeking to serve humanity, *knew* what they could accomplish, and after a man knows what he can do, he does not worry much about its accomplishment, if it is for the service of his fellow men. But when the personality, the lower "I" enters, as in some modern instances, the egotism becomes pronounced, and the surety of "knowing" disappears. We mention these two conditions for we must remember that the human body is an instrument which, when carried further into perfection, attunes itself to the vibratory impulses of nature and man, and Yogis possess sounding boards which register the physical impulses of nature, and of the sun and moon, and planets of our solar system.

Everything existing in nature is within man, but we must always remember that the mind is part of our physical body and our objective is to keep it going through a process of refinement, so that the great primordial light of the spirit in time will descend into our lower mind world, and eventually into the lower density of our body. All is change, constant change, towards the appreciation of Truth. Nature, as well

---

8   "Lo now, his strength is in his loins [sexual organs], and his force is in the navel of his belly."

as man, is an everlasting monument to God, but her light is rejected by the coarser fabric of creation. Nevertheless, in time all creation will become an instrument of service.

We have already spoken of the deeper densities which are below us in matter. There are lower worlds of nature which the human thought has created. The great teachers, recognizing these lower thought-created densities, have often instructed humanity through the instrumentality of science, art, music, and architecture, and by these means they have in many ways moulded the minds of humanity.

We are told, "The sins of the fathers are visited upon the children to the third and fourth generation," so certain types of jazz music today loosen into the consciousness of humanity the evil which our forefathers bequeathed to us. This type of music can evoke into humanity the knowledge of man's inhumanity to man through the curse of slavery. Thus, through music, the karmic law still exacts the penalty. In time we will come to realize this and then the world will recognize the services rendered by such masters as Handel and Wagner.

CHAPTER SIXTEEN

COMING POWERS

There is a new disclosure to be made by nature, dealing with the environment which exists within her, and which surrounds man. Man does not realize that when he is surrounded by the consciousness of Truth, which rests within nature's keeping, he possesses a protective force—a bodyguard which nature gives him.

In all of the divisions of nature there are directing impulses which move man to harmonize with her, and, if he can do this, he becomes immune from the pressure and onslaught of other minds. Man should try to realize that the stronghold of mind upon his environment constantly misdirects his normal attitude of thought.

Hence it rests with you to discover how to protect your mind and environment from the activities of the thought world about you. The secret of power in man is how to be immune from, yet still actively acquainted with, the thought world about him. So the student must marshal his own powers and forces of alignment with nature's powers and forces. In order to do this he must assume his real responsibility, both in nature and in his own human environment. Consequently, he must apply nature's laws for self-government.

At the present time man has little realization of the relationship which can bind him to nature's intelligence, for he has isolated himself from her; hence, he has practically no knowledge of her law. His first step towards power is a realization of the fact that he has lost his place and position in nature's environment. He still retains a faint consciousness that he can never be happy until he returns to nature and in time the urge to return will become too strong to be ignored. Hence we notice the exodus of tired workers from the cities, in order to spend some time in the country. This inner urge of man to change his environment is the faint echo of nature calling him to return to her instruction.

In Atlantean days people had memories of the nature
consciousness from which they had departed. This was the
Golden Age, when man stood in the presence of the Lord God
of Truth within. The discovery of the New Age that is dawn-
ing will be the recovery by man of that knowledge by which
he once gained nature's protection. Humanity has evolved
laws to protect itself from dishonesty and crime. Man has
discovered that if he breaks the laws of society he will suffer
punishment, but he does not realize that he is constantly
breaking the laws of conscious nature and being punished
therefor. Alas, in his ignorance, he does not realize that he
has ruthlessly destroyed the secure foundation which nature
established for the benefit of humanity and that it is nature
who is causing him to suffer the penalty.

The wanton misuse of nature's products, the willful
damage to her soil and forests, and the destruction of her
vegetation have brought dire disaster upon him. It is for us
to reestablish ourselves upon nature's foundations and bring
justice and intelligence to our minds.

When we prove worthy in the deeper states of Yoga, the
whole of nature is presented to our gaze. We look upon her
creation, and study her movements, and traverse the "missing arc of our circle." Through experience man gains a slight
knowledge of humanity, but through Yoga he enters into
other "kingdoms and principalities," where the one law of
justice prevails. On our return we sense humanity's sufferings
and its aspirations.

This world can be described as a place of torment, for, in
the eternal struggle to make a livelihood, men fail to produce
their own truth. It is only when we approach the consciousness of nature that we can regain the intelligence of the Truth
which is in us. Through countless centuries man has been
a wanderer, seeking knowledge through many incarnations
and earthly experiences. He has thus become a storehouse of
wisdom and truth, yet the average man knows little of this
submerged knowledge within himself, and is without means
to contact and use it.

Man must realize that he is a composite being, and in his body and in his mental environment he carries about atoms of intelligence which are the "recorders" of his own wisdom experience through time. In his practice of Yoga the student passes through the mind worlds into the sphere of memory, and then enters into the Presence, the world of intuition and of nature's will. Here only are all bliss and intelligence to be found.

There is a natural law of understanding, a natural law of health, and a natural law of well-being. The new discovery of this age will be to acquaint man with those laws which nature would have him obey, and the method of obtaining this knowledge. A Yogi will tell you that nature has a long memory, for after he has passed through the mind world, he enters the realm of memory. Before his vision passes life after life, he knows that they are his past lives, and he studies the laws of cause and effect. He witnesses his actions, both good and evil (ignorance). He observes their causes and their after effects, and sees periods of happiness, as well as of suffering. He realizes that as he has injured others in the past, he has so condemned himself to suffer the same injury at some future time. In this atmosphere he perceives that in one of his lives he had the desire to know Truth and to live a good life, and that afterwards, perhaps in another life, came a period of splendor and brightness, when he was able to assist humanity and leave a pressure of love behind him. He also perceives that when he gave way to his lower passions and desires, misery and suffering followed and that the effects of the evil of one life tainted his happiness in the other lives which followed. He also learns the effect of his conduct on children and youthful minds and learns how nature protects the innocent and afflicts those who injure them. He also learns the value of the love of innocent minds, which ennobles him in his quest for Truth.

While nature's realm, to mortal man, is a barrier and a "locked door," everyone possesses the key which can pass him through this barrier. When man fell into the deeper densities of nature and made himself lord of all he could possess, no longer interesting himself in the divine concerns of nature, then his faint perception of the Reality in all things was gradually extinguished and he no longer sought union with the Lord God of Truth within. His desire was to stand apart and hunt and fight and conquer all he could. It has been said of this pretentious ape that one day he cried, "I'm going to be a man and stand upright and hunt, and fight, and conquer all I can! I'm going to cut down forest trees to make my houses higher! I'm going to kill the mastodon! I'm going to make a fire!" [9] But when he did these things, his desire personality became his god, and he exiled himself from nature, and the Lord God of Truth that is within him.

---

9   From *Similar Cases*, in *In This Our World*, by Charlotte Perkins Stetson.

CHAPTER SEVENTEEN
DISEASE

Infesting the inhabited regions of the world and close to the ground there is a discordant note in the lower section of elemental nature today which is not found in the high altitudes. This discordant note takes the form of a kind of larva which endangers nature's creations as well as those of man. The constant pressure of the minds of humanity on the elements of nature has brought about these discordant conditions.

These disease germs of nature lie dormant beneath the surface of the soil and constitute danger to all life and activity in their environment. They wage ceaseless war upon each other and torment everything which they encounter. The most dangerous types are found in the jungles which have grown up over the civilizations of the past, where slavery and injustice were rife.

We should understand that these conditions were brought about by the misuse of human thought, for man must realize that thought can be destructive as well as constructive. The constant projection of the mind in anger, hatred, or malice creates a thought form which attracts others of a similar nature, until a composite thought form is built up. Nature then steps in and partly ensouls it, giving it form and being, and this thought form, if it becomes attached to the mind, often causes an obsession.

People are often attacked by these forms of hatred and malice, especially just before they awake from sleep. In some countries thought forms are built up by the human mind until they become powerful instruments of oppression and torture. There is a moorhen elemental which haunts the southern districts of England, and it is a built-up body of despair. We call it the "Moorhen," because its composite shape resembles that bird; its body seems to be of a dull amber substance, and the midribs of the feathers are strongly marked. People who are suffering from despair and loneliness attract the attention of this incubus, and it is a great danger to a sensitive mind when in despair, for its receptivity to thought covers an area of over one hundred miles. Its favorite place of residence is near the Black Rock of Brighton, and a lonely or depressed person, living perhaps miles away, is often drawn to the Black Rock, through the Moorhen's influence, there to commit suicide by jumping off the cliffs onto the rocks below. I would hesitate to state the number of people who have met their death at this place, for it is a magnet of attraction to the discouraged or distressed mind.

Elsewhere in these areas of influence and destruction are to be found conditions which revert the mind to the past, and rob the sensitive of any power to focus his mind on the present or future. It is by this means that the sadistic condition which prepares the way for suicide is brought about.

There are also demoniacal earth-bound spirits who wage wars upon living humanity and exercise a similar influence. The larvae around brothels are most dangerous when they attack disordered or innocent minds. They seek nourishment from the life force of the healthy and are very devitalizing.[10]

These conditions are very easily contacted. When men tamper with the unknown, in spiritual seances for instance, they always find their own level. A few minds together, aspiring with purity of heart, mind, and body, attract the higher elemental part of nature. Concentrating upon debased physical desires and incest, we attract the conditions of the underworld beneath our feet and bring intelligences of a lower animal nature into our atmosphere. We therefore find that disease may attack nature as well as man.

The "Wise Men" tell us that this is the result of man's own thought creations, and that it is thought which causes the evolution of those parasites which wage war upon nature and man. Thoughts are things, and man is a spark of the Infinite Great Reality. Like God, he has the power of creation and can build up forms and energies, which can either bring to him truth or evil (ignorance). It is by thought that he creates the universe within which he lives—his own thought-created universe.

---

10   Such larvae can be destroyed by use of sage, rue, benzoin, or an egg cleanse. See gnosticteachings.org

CHAPTER EIGHTEEN

YOU AND YOUR HIGHER COUNTERPART

Man looking understandingly at himself today discovers that he is a rider of his own follies. He sees himself immersed in his own world of activity, little realizing that he is being hemmed about with a world of his own thought creation.

If man will only look at himself, whether he be ambitious, healthy, or otherwise, he will discover that he is a prisoner in the environment he creates with his mind. A portion of his time he assigns to his business or profession. When he relaxes, his mind follows the pursuit of pleasure. He is seldom conscious that he is the victim and prisoner of his own thought environment. Society, with its passions, pleasures, and desires, has made him what he is, and if he were told that he must stand and live alone, despair and loneliness would sweep over him.

In the approach to the great discovery of this age the student learns that man is composed of two parts which are not separated from each other, the physical man and the natural man.[11] This higher "you," the man of nature, represents the Truth within you, and lives in the realm of Wisdom and Truth, where splendor and bliss reign. It is this being within you that has the wisdom records of all your past experiences, and his atoms are the watchers and recorders of all that you have experienced in the world of conscious nature and of man.

This natural man possesses the memory of all time, but physical man in the lower world has but the fragments of what may be called the consciousness of memory, and has little control over these fragments, for he does not possess the power to bring this conscious memory into action.

Conditions of society bring about a pressure to decrease man's power of thought, and his power to retain any memory of what he has witnessed. Try to think what you were doing at

---

11 In Kabbalah, Chesed (Abraham). In Sanskrit, Atman.

this moment a week ago, and you will be startled at your lack
of memory.

People say that memory is a gift of God, but we say that
it is a gift of the natural man. The closing down on memory
by nature is one of her penalties for the breaking of her commandments by men, but natural law originally gave men a
remembrance of nature's divine source when they left the
body, but at the present time most people only "go to sleep,"
yet is it possible for them consciously to go into the higher
realms.

We must not forget that the higher and the lower self
represent truth and ignorance. Through Yoga practice we seek
union with the higher self, the real man in man. What makes
Yoga practice so interesting is the regaining of past knowledge, for, as we aspire inwardly for Truth, the truth that we
attained in past lives begins to assemble about our own parental stem of experience, and by this we attain to knowledge.

But memory is a different thing. We possess atoms which
are the historians of our own evolution and, as we aspire, we
become conscious that anything we have known in the past,
and which we have individually experienced, can be returned
to us by these atoms, according to their discrimination. But
these atoms must work in accordance with the law of our
own real being. Even now there is a great deal of leakage of
memory from the higher to the lower self, which has the effect
of giving man intermittently salient facts regarding his own
character.

The situations in which man acted contrary to his own
conscience are the most difficult for him to forget. He
remembers chiefly the things which impressed him deeply
at the time, the humiliations in childhood, and events which
impressed themselves upon his own sensitivity. He remembers
also the noble things, the pouring forth of good to him from
others, and his moments of happiness and sorrow. If he
will analyze himself he will realize that his memory retains
many of the good things which he has received from others,
and that other things seemingly disappear. A bad man may
die, but the *good* which he did is what remains longest in

the memory of others. It is the kind thoughts arising from the memory, which a man leaves behind, which assist him through the purgatorial stages of the illusion spheres which he enters and seeks to pass through at the death of his body.

The student Yogi becomes more interested in his own self-created world than in the world about him. He seeks to know the truth of his own being within his own self-created universe, the Universe of the Lord God of Truth within. As he progresses he attains to periods of wisdom instruction, and truths are made known to him, for intermittently the great avatars and prophets make disclosures to humanity.

Through Yoga practice there is to be found a diagram or chart within man, marking the ascending and retrograde movements of his past into the consciousness of Truth. This chart shows his attainments in power, as well as in weakness. It shows the periods when he became strong and powerful and a leader in the cause of justice, and the time when he came back to be absorbed again in the herd when individual expression seemingly ceased and his environment overcame him, a time when he almost reverted to those lower animal types through which he had evolved. Here he seemed to become lost in the darkness and oblivion of time. But patiently his man of nature watched over him, stimulating him to self-thought and urging him to light again his torch, so that he could pass out of the darkness of night.

The Yogi, regarding nature as a mother merciful to her children, realizes her love never departs from them. No matter how far away they stray from her guidance, she forgives them for their past ignorance, when they again seek to return to her instruction, which she broadcasts just before the dawn.

Humanity today seldom seeks to "listen in" at that period when nature pours out her grace and bounty to humanity. Tired with the day's labor, man misses the most beautiful moments of the day. He admires the beauty of the sunset, but he misses the more beautiful sunrise, when nature seeks to redeem man from his periods of error and give him instruction most needed for his deliverance.

There is much wisdom in the old Arcadian expression, "Heralds of the Dawn," for it is at this moment that the consciousness of beauty may be known by the human mind. As these heralds proclaim the coming of a perfect day, so a great chain of initiates is assembling in the four quarters of the globe, and they are about to chant a mantra to disperse the worry and fear which is attaching itself to our human minds. It will require a great effort to dispose of destructive political machinations, so that the human mind may seek wholeheartedly for the Lord God of Truth within to abolish the slavery which today encumbers their lower mind bodies.

Already there are a large number of people in Tibet who are seeking to bring peace to the nations by their intercession to God, that his purpose may be made manifest. So it is hoped humanity will come to contact the natural man and walk in the truth and wisdom of his teaching.

CHAPTER NINETEEN
THE DAYSPRING

In nature there is an intelligence which broadcasts inter-mittently instruction and aid to those advancing into the temple of their Innermost and we pay our respect and devo-tion to the Truth which is so made manifest.

History is replete with the messages of those forerun-ners who gave humanity an upward movement towards the goal of happiness. They cleverly hid in words the glorious Information Period which nature gives to those who have progressed in aspiration for Truth, but the nature of this vibration has been little discussed.

Science has recently discovered a new vibration called cos-mic rays. To the alchemist of old, and to the occult student, it was known as the *Dayspring* [12] and this vibration manifests whenever a New Age is to be brought to birth.

Intermittently the Dayspring of Youth vibrates through humanity, bringing about a new vitality to stimulate and guide men towards deliverance. If we accept it, this vitality supports us in our desire for knowledge; if we reject it, it returns us more deeply into ignorance. It brings about a rush of new thought and stimulates the mind to a greater eagerness for Truth in all walks and occupations. It seeks to raise man above his former level of self-thought and conscious action towards a finer and more ennobling environment. It marks the beginning of a new movement in time and history; it marks the beginning or the end of religions and epochs. It brings to humanity a new type of information which will stimulate the younger minds to seek Truth.

These movements bring about developments such as occurred in Greece, when its manifestation came in the form of beauty. In Egyptian times it brought the grandeur and auster-ity of God to the people. In Chaldea, Assyria, and Babylon it brought about the knowledge of astronomy, astrology, and numbers. In the present era its first vibrations were perceived about three years before the Great War. Its message was:

---

12   Job 38: 12; Luke 1:78

"Devotion to carry through that which man undertakes, simplicity and austerity of life, and devotion to God, in order that nature may reveal herself to the human consciousness."

What does this message of the Dayspring hold? It symbolizes the union of nature with man, and of man with nature. These are two kingdoms to be married, and marriage (in the occult schools) means the perfect union of two opposites with the creation of an equally polarized result. Thus it is consummation of a union with nature's consciousness, to be effected in conformity to nature's law. In other words, it symbolizes the union of the human man with his natural man, who exists in the higher and finer vibrations of matter—his higher self—the man whose will is the will of nature (God).

The student, during his development, is possessed with a force and power which is similar to that used and manifested in the man of nature. The worker of miracles is one who is unified with his natural man. Thus, according to his degree of development, he is given command over nature and her kingdoms. We read in history of these men of God, who performed miracles and did things impossible to the ordinary man, and we must realize that a physical body was necessary in order that the higher self, by union with it, could fructify into expression. Yet we observe in history that if the body of the healer had been injured or scourged (as in the case of Jesus), the higher power could not act through the physical vehicle of the human man. For this reason the Yogi tries to bring his body to such a state of perfection that it may become a worthy vehicle of his higher self—the natural man.

The student soon comes to recognize the pressure which is intermittently brought to bear upon his physical vehicle and its densities by what he at first senses as outside vibrations. Later he learns to tune in and harmonize his body with the different vibrations which he discovers in nature's consciousness. He discovers that there is a difference in the vibrations of the higher planes and of the lower submerged worlds beneath his feet, and he learns to tune in on either as he wishes.

Man, whilst he is insulated, does not realize the force and power of vibration flowing through him, yet when he makes contact with the earth he instantly receives a shock and is exhilarated. In time the student trains himself to visualize what is going on within him in these different states of nature's consciousness.

It is quite easy to see spirits, the inhabitants of the mineral kingdom, and other earth-bound entities, but it is another matter to perceive the inhabitants of air. This can be brought about only after long periods of thought and aspiration for Truth. Man also has the power of liberating the imprisoned consciousness of trees and can communicate with them. This is a higher type of clairvoyance experienced in the wonderful voyage of discovery, the search for knowledge and truth.

This higher type of clairvoyance gives the student the power to see through material objects, in the same way that super-criminals, by using an instrument, can see through the walls of a room. This instrument is similar to the X-ray, and they can see through a thick wall, as though in a fluoroscope, the settings of precious stones, coins, and minerals. There are schools for criminological invention, just as there are schools for the honest, scientific seekers of Truth. These schools also exist on the higher and lower planes of consciousness.

A man under hypnosis can often distinguish what is in one's pocket, or identify a card which an assistant produces in a crowd. Likewise in Yoga practice the student becomes equipped with a "third eye," which can see through appearances and can register the vibration of another person's mind. We do not at first realize when we aspire for knowledge and truth, that we are receiving direction and guidance from our natural man, that the Lord God of Truth is within all, and that within us there exists the Kingdom of Heaven.

The union of the human and the natural man comes through the aid of the initiate teacher. Those teachers who have attained, have the power of bringing down this higher attainment into others, just as John brought down the higher man of nature into Jesus. These initiators first bring down a period of illumination to the human mind, and afterwards the consciousness of nature—the natural man—the miracle worker.

Every great teacher to whom God Realization has come, has attained this state through the aid of some great initiate. We read in the New Testament of Jesus' initiation by John (the voice crying out in the wilderness), and in Nepal we may see the cave in which Jesus received his initiation[13] from the great Chinese initiate.

The secrets of nature, which humanity most desires, are to be found in nature's keeping, and are evidenced in history. From this source we are taught that there are chains of initiates stretching from the remote past into our day and time, and from thence again into the remote future. If we are worthy, and have been searching for truth through many lives, there will come a time when certain of these ancient gurus will make themselves known to us, and from that time onwards we become interested in God's work, not man's.

The student finds the school of initiation a very difficult one. Initiation acts as an extension of consciousness and it is only when we become true to ourselves and others that we can be initiated. I will give you one instance from my own experience early in life. A lady once came to my studio in which there were many distinguished people. My intuition told me at once that she had need of my services, but when she left, my friends gathered around me and said that they all disliked her appearance among them, and a dear friend told me calmly that if this woman came again, she would not visit me. In my weakness and lack of courage, I did not afford this unfortunate woman my protection and aid at the moment when she most needed it. She had been dragged through the divorce court and the case was much advertised in all the newspapers. Through the bribery of witnesses, she was looked upon as a moral leper. Years afterwards she was exonerated by the honest confessions of the bribed witnesses. This is one of the greatest crimes I ever committed. It was lack of courage, but it served one good purpose, for it taught me to act at once, regardless of personal or public opinion. When you discover your personal responsibility you are beginning to form your character of expression and, if you do not act when your intuition prompts you, your natural man will bring a picture of

---

13   "Initiation has been defined as an extension of consciousness."

your "unfaithfulness to self" to your mind, and it will become a regrettable incident in your life and cause you suffering.

We must always remember to let the head govern the heart and the intuition govern the mind. Below the sternum or chest bone is a great "brain center," the solar plexus which registers our emotions and desires, and we often find that emotion governs our hearts when our clearer wisdom teaches us not to do that which our heart impels. A great doctor was in the garden of some friends when a man approached his host, asking for a job, telling a very piteous tale. The man was given a dollar, but the host wished to give the man a job. "Do as you wish," the doctor said, "but he will not prove to be of any use to us," and this later proved to be correct. This doctor was known as a man whose intuition was always correct, and he was a great puzzle to his acquaintances. He was known all over the world as a great natural healer, and one of his assistants said that of all the men he had ever met, the doctor had the most uncanny intuition. His directions were often opposed by the medical staff at the sanatorium, but it was invariably discovered later that he was right. Once, when a supposed thief was brought before him, he said, "Let the man go, he is honest." When asked how he knew, his answer was simply, "I know." He has never yet formed a wrong judgment. Even in buying so simple a thing as a motor car, which he had never seen before, his judgment was correct.

Devotion to God brings about a singular merit, for it marks the beginning of nature's efforts to forward man's development into the consciousness of his natural man (nature).

According to Yoga teaching the greatest evil in humanity is lack of devotion to the Lord God of Truth which is within us. The average man believes that God is outside of himself in the heavens somewhere, yet all the great masters have taught that the Kingdom of Heaven is within, and that the Lord God of Truth dwells there.

We seldom take the time to question ourselves about this Kingdom of Heaven which is within, but if we persevere in our aspiration for Truth, nature will provide us with the key, for the great beings within nature always stand in the presence of

God; their will is God's will, and their law is the law of universal nature, the knowledge of which sets men free.

In order to depart from old associations and ideas, we must strip ourselves bare of prejudice and, like children, begin to associate ourselves with the ideals which service to nature (God) will implant in our hearts; then instinct, intuition, and nature's will can be returned to us. In Yoga, this is similar to passing from an old state into a youthful condition of enterprise. The things which were dear to us and the possessions which we admired and loved, lose their attraction and we desire of this world only those possessions which our service to humanity and God bring us. When this change of mind comes, old conditions pass away and we seek union with our higher self and the knowledge and illumination which the Lord God of Truth within confers upon us.

Thus we acquire detachment from things. This does not mean that our interest in and love for humanity is swept aside, but we are taken into a plane of understanding where the knowledge of *how* to serve broadens within us, and a greater consciousness of love for those about us manifests. It is attachment to people and to things which causes us most suffering.

When I eventually met my teacher, I found kindliness, patience, and a loving heart. With some seemingly unknown power he stimulated me to talk about myself, and he afterwards brought back to my mind every detail of the conversation, so that I could analyze everything that I had said. After this first meeting I realized my supreme ignorance of myself, my mind, my body, and my higher self. Although I was, as I thought, physically fit at the time, I had to go through a year's hard training in physical culture and had to study dissection. Later I realized, when I passed through my second step, or phase of development, that I had need of all the physical vitality and stamina that I had built up in the previous year. It is not easy to discipline the body to prepare it to be nature's sounding board, and I must acknowledge my teacher's patience for, like a child, I had to be taken and shown the world as it is, for the first time.

As an aid to the higher perception, you are first taught to perceive the things which are going on around you. Few people today can give you a clear and accurate description of the entrance to their own house. The greatest aid that can be given humanity is to teach it to perceive what others pass by unnoticed, or accept as commonplace.

Should you meet a Chinese gentleman of the caste of intelligence, he will take a quick glance at you and meet you on your own level. He will perceive at once whether you are of the animal, mental, vital, or spiritual type, and when he goes into society he observes things in men of which his fellow men still remain ignorant. This training in perception gives the student the power to perceive the genius in the world, and it is his duty to assist by every possible means the light bringers to humanity—nature's children.

There are people who are strongly linked with nature. The man who is inspired by his natural man is he who produces great works. The instructors in nature's consciousness make no difference between any of God's children, and the real Yogi, whatever his color or caste may be, does not separate himself from his fellows.

One great stumbling block in the development of Truth is the attitude that a student may take towards people of a different race, color, or creed. This caste distinction is brought about by ignorance or the customs and habits of different races and creeds. A Mohammedan sage once said to me, "Christianity has not yet begun in your race. Look about you and see if any real Christians are to be found in your creeds. As long as a man believes in Allah, he has a seat at my board."

Nature's children come from all races and all creeds, and saints of the different religions answer the prayers of humanity, regardless of what creed they profess, for all creeds can end in God Realization and a knowledge of God's purpose in all things.

As there are egotists in humanity, so we find them in the different religions. The wine is the same, but the different creeds quarrel about the shape of the grail, and the day of the week, and much good wine is spilt. Where there is ignorance, there is also intolerance and injustice; but in Yoga, when we come into the Presence, we find only love, intelligence, and bliss, and we long for our union with the Presence.

While a suit of clothes makes no man's body purer in the presence of Truth, the ignorant must have these outward trappings. However, God can be worshipped through the love and devotion which man puts into his work, and those trappings, which bring beauty and loveliness to the mind, are worthy of the craftsman who made them. Whatever one does should be with the ideal in his heart, that it be something worthy of God's acceptance.

Seeking the presence of the Lord God of Truth within hastens his Presence into the atmosphere of the human man, and eventually the student will feel the Presence, which he at first only discovered in the deeper states of aspiration. Our higher self rests in an atmosphere of peace and intelligence, and we seek, through alliance with nature, to bring this Presence with its healing, into our everyday life. As children we have been told to love God, but how many people ever think of loving nature, which is expressing God!

Yoga practice teaches that what you give you get. Often the gift was not what was desired at the time, nor do you get what you think you want, for usually it is something which turns out to be better. The Lord of Wisdom within knows what is best for conscious man.

In many ways simplicity of life means returning to nature. In order that the spirit in nature may manifest within the human being it is necessary to clarify the body and mind, so through his union with his natural man, man provides a vehicle through which love and beauty may manifest, and then he can "walk with the gods in the morning."

People nowadays consider themselves civilized, but in reality the most advanced members of human society have reached only the fringe of true civilization. The Yogi student finds culture and refinement in those places where it would least be expected by the advanced mind. Personally, I consider that the three most cultured beings I have ever met, and in whose society I felt most happy, were people who eat their food with their fingers, yet there was such culture and refinement in their hands as I have never seen at the tables of so-called epicures in old titled families. These three great souls had attained God Realization, and were working for humanity. One of the three had his home in the desert, and I still remember his hearty laugh, and his atmosphere; there was such happiness, such peace, such realization, such compassion, such humanity! In speaking to them I felt that I was speaking to the whole world but, to tell the truth, there was no need of physical speech on my part, for my sentences were answered almost before they were formulated. In these men, especially the one from the desert, you seemed to see the rise and fall of civilization, the experience of God.

It was as if each had different attributes. When I spoke to one of them, he impressed me with the devotion of the world in which he was working. The other showed me a changed Europe, where many of our present cities were in complete ruins, and people were seeking nature. There were small self-supporting communities, and the country was divided so that the different races occupied their own divisions, and those of each creed likewise, yet all were working in harmony. But what a different map of the world was this one of the future! Over all there seemed to brood a peace and the consciousness of the spirit. New lands had been reclaimed, and there were climatic changes, but you saw the darkness over what had been thickly populated industrial centers such as Pittsburgh, where now there was nothing but a framework of steel ruins. In England also, along the Thames Valley, were ruined frameworks of buildings, and grass was growing in the courtyard of the House of Parliament, for the people had migrated away from the cities. I also seemed to get the impression of volcanic ash, and a return of hyperborean conditions.

The great discovery of this coming age will be a secret which nature will unfold to man for his "becoming," in order that he may stand in her presence and know God (Truth). Our hyperborean ancestors, returning from a long voyage of discovery, will operate the lever of knowledge upon the fulcrum of nature and bring again to man his ancient heritage.

The laws of nature are just, and she will give to our minds that which our merit deserves, for, when man earnestly aspires for God Realization, nature's purpose will be known to him, and he will be plunged in ignorance no longer. Although weakened by toil and despair man shall gain victory over the overlords of nature and receive his recompense, for man was created to have dominion over the angels. The dust of ignorance thrown into a man's eyes blinds him, but the torch of Truth will bring him out of his darkness.

CHAPTER TWENTY

MIND DEVELOPMENT

Considering the average man of today, we find that a great proportion of his time is spent in the mind world, for during the process of evolution he has developed his mind far in excess of his other faculties. The occult student learns to gauge the different degrees and ways by which natives of different races advance their evolution into the consciousness of mind. He discovers that a group of Chinese intelligences are living in a mind world far in advance of his own. At an exhibition of Chinese art in London in 1936, the atmosphere which surrounded the finer types of their art produced a composite atmosphere which had a singular effect on sensitive minds, for they perceived an atmosphere foreign to their own, which took them into a world of imagination and beauty.

The average man of eighteen to twenty-one years of age goes through a phase when his bodily passions and desires wage war upon his mind world, and he is prone to seek so-called happiness and pleasure through physical, rather than mental enjoyment. The Chinese caste of intelligence learned that the gratification of their mental passions and desires was far superior, therefore the power of the physical body was held in check and governed, in order to make possible a still greater mental indulgence.

Since our minds have evolved more rapidly than our other planes of consciousness, we have not properly balanced our instinctive nature, and it is this development which is coming into manifestation through the aid of conscious nature. It is a return to, and an alliance with nature's will, so that in time man will become a creature of intuition—nature's man. Then he will apprehend nature's laws and will obey them.

This return from the unknown to the known will bring about the Golden Age of man's discovery, and an alliance with nature will bring to man his own truth, long hidden from observation within the treasure house of his own self-constituted being. Through Yoga practice man will enter the precincts of nature's manifestation, where he will become conscious of beauty, real beauty, for the first time. Then the overlords of nature, the angels mentioned in our sacred books, will show themselves in their glory, and the consciousness that truth and beauty are one will manifest in his mind.

The instruction and the emotion of man's thoughts, when analyzed, will be clothed in the beauty of what we call the spirit, and beauty, like a surging tide, will become so enthralling that it will nearly overwhelm him. He will have to be on his guard against sinking himself completely into this bliss and intelligence, for his sensitivity will be heightened and his longing to be "at one" with the consciousness, or spirit, which is within this surging wave of beauty will be increased.

This conception of beauty places before the student a new realization, and he will sense the ideals for which all things have been created. Then man will receive information from a kingly deva and learn that the light, which the devas reflect, comes from the Presence in which they stand, that their world is a wonderful world of beauty and very different from that which man knows as his world. In the devic consciousness the student views this world through devic perception, and illusion passes away, the mountains, hills, and buildings all disappear, and standing in the Presence, the student contemplates the ideal.

But there is one thing which will remain. The aroma surrounding the works of artists and craftsmen does not vanish. It is that indefinable aroma which we sense about a work of art which causes us to realize the aspiration of the craftsman towards beauty.

In this connection it is interesting to note that the gnomes speak of distinguishing different precious stones and minerals by their odor. They are like many animals that have developed the sense of smell far beyond that of sight. Man has developed his mind far beyond his intuition.

Some of the great musicians have been able to register in music the vibrations of fire, earth, water, and air, an example of which is Wagner's "fire music." Musicians can also register the "keynote" of a great city. It is interesting to notice the effect different types of music have upon the child mind.

Take the "Barcarolle" from *The Tales of Hoffman* and ask several children what it means. They will very often say that it is not good, or they may say that it is like boats floating on water. Then give them a selection from the *Gotterdammerung*[14] and try to gain their impressions. They will often prove most instructive and refreshing.

Nature has her keynote and man his sounding board, and through sound invocation we can attune ourselves to nature's vibration or keynote. When we tune in to sound vibrations of a higher nature we evoke the finer forces of nature using the normal key, but when we lower this key we attract to ourselves the atoms and intelligence of nature's lower counterpart.

By aspiration for Truth we attract the notice of the higher intelligence of nature, for in aspiration we do not force our personality into these divisions of nature. We leave our lower personality behind when we aspire for Truth, but when we meditate upon Truth the "I" is always present. In ceremonial magic the ignorant desire power, and they evoke the reflection of their own nature, be it good or evil. This lower personal I is the danger of occultism, "I want this, I wish that, I want Truth, I want power." The real I—the "I am," is no respecter of so-called personalities, but it respects the aspiration of the lower I for Truth, for union with God, and in the proportion in which the lower I is eliminated, man can bring peace into his atmosphere and surroundings.

I have seen the immediate transformation of a business dictator, whose personality was famous. Too busy to wait his proper turn, he rushed into the presence of a Yogi, who looked at him and smiled. He became speechless and confused, but the Yogi asked him to sit down and have tea with him. The hard business man got up, shaking his head, and went into the next room, taking his rightful place in the seat he had formerly occupied.

The reader may wish to know what type of instruction is given by these higher intelligences of nature. Usually it is the doctrine of emancipation, or the power of freeing oneself from illusion (ignorance). The devas who work over the forests, or

---

14 An opera by Wagner.

the devas of what the average man calls nature, will often tune
in with you by showing you a beautiful landscape, or a forest of
trees. It is as if a panorama of nature were passing before you,
and often when your instruction begins, you are halted in a
beautiful glade away from humanity, where you are subject to
the rhythmic beauty of their vibration—a process of being tuned
in to their consciousness. Then your instruction begins.

Perhaps you are taken to a great tree which has fallen in
some dark ravine, where little sunlight penetrates. Here you
are instructed in the different conditions which manifest
among the tree people. You will find that there are disagreeable
conditions or intelligences which inhabit some trees. Some
resent approach to their consciousness, and others radiate
their benediction to you. Certain trees resent any interference
in their beginning, growth and so-called death by destruction,
or old age. Some have a quality of elemental nature, soothing
and beneficent to our minds, whilst others are arrogant and
destructive. People little realize the destructive powers that lie in
nature in the form of trees, all of which possess etheric doubles
and can pass out of their so-called physical bodies, as man does
in sleep, and these etheric doubles can press upon the sensitivity
of a seer.[15]

In humanity we find one class of people waging war upon
another. So in nature, as seen with our human eyes, there is a
constant struggle going on between the higher forces and the
lower forms of ignorance. These conditions are mostly found
where men have been intolerant and cruel to each other. It is by
sounding the keynote of nature that man can protect himself
from the onslaughts of the tree people of darkness. If humanity
could only realize what has passed in time before the dying of
a redwood tree! Before it falls and dies it has planted a ring of
successors around it, and in its falling it brings an area of light
into the center of the circle. The gypsy vagabonds of Egypt, and
some even at the present day, understood how to dominate
the tree people and use them as a curse upon their oppressors,
and we are told that the Druids, in their healing, knew how to

---

15 Read *Esoteric Medicine and Practical Magic* and *Igneous Rose* by Samael Aun
    Weor.

manipulate the varying properties and intelligence of trees, in order to serve their purpose of healing.

I have personally been shown the destruction of a Douglas fir by the devas who watch over the forest, and have seen its tall spire reaching heavenward. Then I saw it being cut down and stripped of its bark to be made into the mast of a ship, and witnessed its suffering and torture. I was afterwards shown how in the future it would snap in its upper third and bring disaster to the yacht, for it was to serve the pleasures of the idle rich. If it had been used for honest commerce, or to give benefit and pleasure to people, this disaster would have been averted, but instead of that the mast broke when the owner and his party were in a state of intoxication. The deva told me that they had caused vibrations to go zigzag up from the foot of the mast and to attack its weakest point. He added that if the possessor of that yacht had sent love into that mast, in the way that some sea captains love every stick in their vessels, it would have responded with love and strength. An engine driver, loving his engine, knows it intimately as a human being knows a friend. An engine driver once told me that in moments of distress he felt a response from his locomotive, and a sensitive barber said that one morning his razor had informed him that it was going to cut well that day.[16] Here we get the atomic response to the human mind. The devas, in the case of the above-mentioned tree, increased the vibration of the mast, causing it to crystallize from too much vibration, and thus strength was denied it.

I speak of the tree people in order to show that there is a directing consciousness which keeps them true to their species, for the overlords of nature resist all malformations which endanger the soil that brought them forth, as they say, into energy. In the evil conditions of nature abnormal elements are to be found, which terrorize the human atmosphere and energize it with discord, just as when a sensitive, psychometrizing an object, attaches himself to the vibration of, say an instrument of torture. So nature also has her cesspools of horror and darkness. I know of a tree on a ducal estate, which has cast its spell over the family for generations. In the early days of Christianity

---

16   Automobile drivers should realize this.

many inmates of monasteries were strongly linked with nature and her lore and they often, by magical art, put curses on families who had oppressed them or destroyed their habitations.

Trees, and indeed all nature, can be either beneficent or antagonistic. There is a tradition that in Hyde Park, London, there is a tree beneath which tramps and other unfortunates never sleep, for if they do, they never wake up. There are many places in our public parks where elemental nature is antagonistic to man. Children are sensitive to this and they keep away from such places; dogs also often turn around and go the other way. I could relate many personal experiences of contacting places of horror in nature. There are certain places where people's physical and mental bodies undergo a quick change. They become dense, as it were, and no longer reflect the finer essences of the spirit. We often find such places close to our most holy localities. "Out of the body," I was once taken by my teacher to a very holy spot in Tibet, where the "Holy of Holies" was separated from the most evil of evil only by the thickness of a single brick. In this connection, we must repeat again the old saying of ancient science, "Where the light is brightest, the shadows are darkest."

A Yogi perceives at once when his feet tread holy ground. The early Christian Fathers usually built their churches and places of refuge on the holiest spots where pagans had worshipped, for a group of people aspiring for Truth start a vibration which continues long after their places of worship have been demolished. There are places of holy vibrations on the earth today, where the mind is drawn nearer to God and his peace, and you also find these vibrations in holy images, be they of Christian or pagan origin.

In days of old people fasted and bathed, and provided themselves with clean garments to come unto the presence of their idols. How many people today would think of going through such a ceremony before entering a holy place! Nature is most sensitive to the attitude of thought by which she is approached. Purity of aspiration is recognized by all the denizens of nature.

In nature there is a trinity of three vibrations, which can be traced in all her movements:

The creative vibration, which means the bringing of light and life.

The destructive and distributive vibration. [17]

The protective and collective vibration. [18]

---

17 The dissolution of form, and release of light and life.
18 The preservation of form, which consciously uses space in producing intelligent effects.

CHAPTER TWENTY-ONE

STEPS TOWARD PEACE

We give our help to all who seek their own ancient wisdom records, so that they may strive toward the fulfillment of their promise to God in the beginning. We surrender all that we have that God's purpose may be known to man. Freely, for the asking, we give of what we possess, if the purpose is to surrender to God's will. Amid the shame of the world we seek to discover those about whom a new framework of creation may be established, that wisdom may thereby enter their minds and the illusions of the world be dispelled. It is better to be true to yourself for a single instant, than to be one of a crowd of blind men seeking knowledge in the dunghills of illusion, seeing not the light which is to be found within.

The devic creation moulds the destinies and fortunes of men, and systems of development are at work within humanity, which stretch over a long period of time. Yet men are often unconscious of the events taking place in their own evolution.

There are movements in nature which advance man's mind into spheres of intelligence, but there are also retrograde movements. This is brought about through the law of cause and effect, or karma. Karmic laws from the remote past move backwards or forwards, according to the character of the individual. There comes a time in the student's development when both the advance and the retrograde movements are energized and summed up into a concrete whole.

As man's consciousness changes, he experiences alternating movements, for there is a wonderful rhythm back of beauty's shield of strength and gentleness, back of the phenomena of male and female, positive and negative, good and evil.

Always there are two forces, which may be expressed as the good and evil of man's nature, brought into contact with one another and the supremacy of the one dominates and enslaves the character of the other be it good or evil. The dominating power is released from its component whole, and engenders man with his true character of expression, be it progressive for the attainment of Truth, or retrogressive towards ignorance and evil. At the summing up each man will have attained the expression of the wisdom of Truth and the wisdom of evil, and both these conflicting conditions are good for him, for he thus gains a knowledge from experience of the good in evil and the evil in good. When he becomes conscious of these two powers through Yoga practice he seeks, through wisdom experience, to be neither good nor evil, for then he aspires to pursue his path (having these rudiments of knowledge at his command) without being drawn into the experience of either. When this is realized he places himself for the first time consciously upon the middle path which unites the unknown with the known.

At this period man passes out of the conflict of his emotions and seeks to redeem himself and unify his consciousness with that of nature, with the Lord God of Truth, which is within him. Conflict may be going on all around him, but he walks through it unharmed, for he has found peace and from henceforth he cares not what may assail his environment.

People little realize the torture which minds can undergo. There is not only the conflict caused by the thoughts of anger, hatred, and malice which they themselves have thrown out, and which return to bombard their mental screen, but there is also the conflict of the lower side of nature. By unguarded speech certain contacts are made between themselves and earth-bound spirits of evil and despair.

Man makes himself a magnet of attraction and repulsion and, in order to negate such conditions, he must radiate peace through finding it, and to find peace is to find the Lord God of Truth within, which is a process of *knowing oneself.* Always remember the titanic forces which exist in earth, water, air, and fire, for in each of these elements we find one phase of the nature of our own being, be it constructive or destructive, and we must never forget that man is a universe in himself, having all the qualities within him which he sees in nature about him.

There is the thunder and lightning, there is the fire of the universe, the air and its winds, the water with its turbulent titanic forces, and the earth with its subterranean tremblings.

How ignorant is man, not to know the powers which are within him!

Did not Jesus say that he who has faith, even as a grain of mustard seed, can move mountains! This is a Yoga precept, and Yoga also teaches us that faith is energy applied to action. "A small drop of ink, nourished with thought, and expressed by action produces that which makes millions think." Elsa Barker's poem, *The Call of the Frozen North*, was the lash behind Peary in his dash to discover the North Pole, and his second telegram, after he reached civilization, was to Elsa Barker, saying that he had left her poem at the North Pole.

Thoughts are things, but few people are able to put a Titan's power into a single phrase to inspire men to a greater reverence for God. We find this power, however, in Lincoln's *Gettysburg Address*, which symbolizes the soul power in man. Thus the great lords of nature seek to implant ideas in the minds of men, in order that those who come after may be stimulated and carried on the tide of evolution towards the Truth.

The devas would have us exalt nature, and attune our consciousness to her sounding boards, so that she may apprise us of her movements and periods of instruction. We must glorify our great creator and all things in nature and in man, and seek union with the Lord God of Truth within, for each day's good. The loveliness of the dawn should be the topic of our day, and the beauty and goodness in mankind our theme. We should seek to transfer into the mind the glory and splendor of the immortal work—Truth.

If there is merit in a book it will tend to dispel illusion from the mind, and to generate in the reader some redeeming quality. But alas, man is most interested in the literature of crime and sex. He forgets the beauty of the spirit which underlies all creation. Beauty is to be worshipped in all things, for where she plants her feet the flowers of remembrance cling even to the soiled garments of our minds and bring to birth a greater desire to know real beauty unadorned.

Evil can be so clothed in beauty that she enslaves us, but no adornment can veil her true nature. An artist friend of

mine was so entranced by the beauty of face, figure, and
costume of a noted courtesan that he fell on his knees before
her in adoration. Yet there was another side to her nature, for
she brought poverty and family dishonor to many innocent
people, yet she possessed the power of recognizing in an
instant the good in others. Once, when a Yogi passed down
the street in a well known African town, the ladies of easy
virtue, very lovely to look on, hid their faces behind their veils,
for they recognized the saint.

The Yogi of today, even as the anchorite of old, is often
tempted through sheer love of beauty, for there is no period in
life when evil, clothed in beauty, seeks not to enter through a
weak spot in the character, and the really religious man is the
most prone to be ensnared by evil in her white robe of ermine.

I have watched Rodin, the sculptor, run his fingers lightly
over the neck of a princess, and then pass his finger over
the marble in its nearly completed state, and I have felt the
strength of the Titan's hand behind the lightness of his velvet
touch. When she had gone he turned to me and said, opening
and shutting his hands, "For many years I was a cutter of
stone, and my things were rejected. The collar, which my sit-
ter's Pomeranian had on today, was fashioned by the cunning
brain of Laleek, and was set with semi-precious stones. The
value of that would have given me and my sweetheart a year's
freedom from poverty in the days of my strength to carry out
the creations close to my heart. But now I am old, and it is
difficult to throw up a full life-sized figure." Then he went on
to speak with enthusiasm of the Boston gentleman, his first
real patron who gave him, as he said, his first real freedom.
Perhaps that was the reason he was always kind to American
students.

The Yogi, through his powers of observation, realizes
what is going on in his own time, and seeks to aid the artists
and sculptors, who have found their own moment in their
own time. Rodin, seen from the standpoint of Yoga training,
appeared as three different beings, and at times there stepped
into him a beautiful Greek youth—his natural man. At such
times his powers of suggestion were ripe, and he would mould

a child's foot so that it seemingly appeared in its complete-
ness. The toes were only massed together in a wide sweep, yet
you felt that it embodied the complete whole. Details came
afterwards; when it was the movement he aimed at, he seemed
a giant in whom this beautiful Greek was working. By the
movements of his hands you *felt* the creation that he had built
up, and sometimes he would look up and say, "There is no
need of speaking or talking, you know what I am after!"

Alas, Rodin stands alone in his time, and sculpture has
advanced into another period, for Truth has an ever widening circumference, as beauty unveils her face. It is a great
misfortune that Rodin never completed his statue of Nijinsky
dancing in the character of a faun. When Nijinsky produced
his masterpiece, "The Afternoon of a Faun," to the music of
Debussy, he brought a new note to the notice of civilization
which will stand out, as Rodin's work did in his day.

Sometimes in Rodin you saw the lower, almost peasant
being—the passionate and brutal stone cutter, but back of
it all you felt his power of attack, which his well-groomed
clothes could not cover. Then there was his finer nature of
expression, which suggested to you the movement of form in
a solid block of marble—something to be released in stone.
For the reflection of light, he told me to study Rembrandt's
reflected light, in his own portrait. Rodin always wanted to
reflect light from his surfaces, as Rembrandt reflected light in
his pictures.

A wonderful thing is the power of energy—the power to
search out Truth. Beauty uncovers her face only to those who
seek her promises. We are vagabonds in time, wasting our precious moments, until suddenly there comes to us the gleam of
the far distant star. That gleam comes from our innermost, in
its ancient citadel, where Truth reigns. From this source, hand
in hand, come love and beauty to enlighten this darkened
world.

There is a morning and an afternoon of remembrance
when the Dayspring enters our consciousness. Then is given
the message of our ancient periods, when we vibrated to
the call of nature and sought to register its directive energy.

Arcadian days of remembrance—beauty's morning—when
everything was aglow with the spirit! Then there was peace,
and the happy laughter of children, the lowing of the herds,
and the sound of the billowing of the grain. Then, above all,
there was peace and goodwill towards men.

The afternoon of remembrance takes us into the time of
the agony of this world, when there is intolerance, oppression,
opposition, and darkness, as if the spirit of all love and light
had retreated into the darkness of despair. All is seemingly
lost, but over the horizon there appears the rainbow, the symbol of God's promise to man; and in the midst of this struggle
and torment we hear a quiet voice speaking from all eternity
saying, "Though the world be shaken to its foundations, I
come to bring peace to all who seek to know the sovereign
Presence." The voice seems to echo down the corridors of
time, bestowing its beneficence on all who seek to know the
holy name. "Peace be unto you, my children, for I bring you
Truth, and remembrance of what you are to become, nothing
more." All is silence, yet there remains the memory of the
peace and quiet of the Arcadian pastures of our Lord and
King, the Lord God of Truth within.

CHAPTER TWENTY-TWO

CONSCIOUS NATURE

During our Yoga practice we pass inwardly through the mind world into the world of memory, and it is on this plane of consciousness that we first contact the memorials of the devic creation.

Beyond the consciousness of memory there is the world of conscious nature. The objective is to find a means of communication between the intelligence of the deva world, with its devic consciousness, and our mind world. This communication is established in our memory world, on the plane of conscious nature.

The Yogi finds that it takes some time before he can find a means of communication between the higher devic creation and himself. The first rule in seeking communication with the finer forces of nature is to purify the mind, and aspire for Truth, for then the objective personality, which we carry about with us, is not projected into this finer state of matter and intelligence.

The devas then instruct us by means of a process of observation, placing before us a pantomime of movement, similar to the pictures we see on a screen in a cinema. Our thought world of mind intelligence, and the world in which the devas live are far apart, and at times it is difficult to communicate with them. Hence, we meet them at the halfway station between the world of thought and the world of intelligence.

Having to step down, as it were, into our consciousness, they present themselves to us in the beginning by taking us rapidly through natural forests and scenery; through wild woods, over mountain tops, and through vistas of time where we watch the wonderful panorama pass before us. Often they will halt us before some titanic tree and show us its manifestation. Yet always we have to attune our minds to comprehend the means by which they communicate their consciousness to us.

Under the devic instruction, for instance, a tree will give us an impression of its characteristics, showing us not only its anatomy, but the qualities of the minerals and essences which have been taken from the earth to make up its fiber and bark. We get an analysis of what it absorbs for nourishment, and what it stands for in nature, and the qualities of its will and aspiration. We learn that it has taken iron out of the earth, transforming it to make up the strength of its body. It will show us a symbol of what iron means to us (strength) and then it will show itself as having the characteristics of iron, but the iron has become flexible and subtle. This is because the tree must have flexible strength in order to move from the roots upwards. It will then show us the qualities of quicksilver (mercury) which build up its atmosphere of intelligence, so that it can respond to and become conscious of the different varieties of intelligence which other trees radiate.

The devas impress on the student that there is a constant conversation or interchange of intelligence between the forest trees, and that really the forest is a sort of talking machine and is seldom silent. The trees can pass communications for a certain distance, and they sense the approach of man by the vibration of his atmosphere, which they analyze and pass on to their surroundings over a wide area. They also analyze the character of the man who approaches them, and pass judgment upon him according to his worth.

Although the ordinary man thinks inanimate things are dumb and speechless, the Yogi knows by experience that everything is endowed with mind, but it is only by going into the world of memory that we can bring about a means of communication between the devas and ourselves.

The devas say that when you rise above your lower mind and enter into the consciousness of its higher counterpart you meet the consciousness of nature on a common level and find a common meeting point, and that common meeting point is love.

I once knew a beautiful soul, who possessed a most wonderful natural garden in the Scottish Highlands. I always knew when she entered her garden, although I might be sitting over half a mile from its entrance, for there was a movement from all the plants and trees that she loved, telling me that she was being welcomed. When she was sent away during the World War to tend to dying soldiers in a hospital, she led me to certain flowers and plants and said, "Whilst I am away, please talk to them." She was one of those heroic Highland mothers, a descendant of the Bruce, who had entered deeply into nature's consciousness and we used to call her Demeter.[19]

During the World War, when a lad appeared to be dying in the hospital the doctors and surgeons discovered that if they could get his mother to him, her atmosphere and mother love would do much to bring him through the crisis. They soon found out that this "daughter of the Bruce" could also give these boys that comfort and mother love which wrought miracles. The doctors did not hesitate to send long distances in order to bring a mother to her stricken son and the Government was most generous in providing financial aid for this purpose. I knew one case of a peasant woman arriving with bare feet, but she brought her son through the crisis and the nurses provided her with fitting raiment.

As we have said in another book, Mother Nature is the great healer and she longs for the return of her children from their long voyage of discovery, that she may heal them and bring them into the consciousness of her Truth.

Nature throws her cloak of protection over youth and, until boys and girls mature, they are looked upon as innocents by nature, no matter how destructive they may be. Often, unknown to humanity, nature protects and guides youth when lost in her domains, but from the time of puberty they must fight their own battles and stand upon their own feet.

It has been foretold that science will in time be able to measure the push of nature and her elemental kingdoms. Elemental spirits certainly have the power of propulsion, especially in wet weather, being partly ensouled by nature's coordinating forces, they may become destructive agents, bringing giddiness to the brain and illusioning the mind to such an extent that their pressure can bring the individual to self-destruction. Often, people looking down from a height of less than three hundred feet, will feel a strong impulse to jump. As they ascend to a higher and

19 Also called Ceres, the mother of nature.

clearer atmosphere, where the lower elemental nature forms
cannot reach, the impulse will disappear, for the grandeur of
God and his creation take the first place in their thoughts.

The student will be very much interested when the deva
takes him into the forest and shows him the huts of the modern anchorites and initiates, and their places of retreat. The
great American initiate, although working among the master
minds of commerce and politics in the thick of humanity in
times of great crises, is often found in one of these retreats
where he may be seen manipulating the titanic forces of nature,
in order to bring about the emancipation of struggling humanity. I once asked a student if he would like to go with me on a
trip "out of the body." I took him across the sea into the wilds
of North America, and the initiate left his abode among the
tall trees to meet us. The student exclaimed, "He is an Adamite
man. Do you see the light about him?" Then he suddenly
turned to me and said, "Do you think that Cynthia loves me?"
With that we came back to our bodies, and he had missed a
most golden opportunity to bathe in an atmosphere of peace
and intelligence.

These hermits, who live at times so close to nature, often
return from service in the world showing traces of suffering, but
the light of realization is in their eyes. One must remember that
although there are different degrees among these students of
nature, when you meet them in the different capitals of Europe
and other continents, they always speak of their longing to get
back to nature. I am thinking now of a great soul, a scientific
benefactor whose statue, erected by loving hearts, adorns a
public place in Paris and he sleeps among the illustrious dead
in the Holy of Holies of France. When I first met him, I felt his
cultured distinction, but when he began to speak with authority
about things of which I was ignorant, I thought that perhaps
he was a "crank," yet I can never forget the look back of his eyes,
the look of realization and sacrifice, nor the atomic link of love
which can never be broken. I was young then, and so ignorant!
It is the memory of these great souls, who have made so many
sacrifices for the world, which helps us to be patient with all we

contact. We have to learn by experience to reverence the living, and not wait until they are dead.

What wonderful specialists some of these noble men and women are, who have asked nothing but light, but who give their services unselfishly that youth may more easily gain knowledge. The teacher who has gained the knowledge of one slight division in nature can demonstrate that truth. Idle talk is not becoming, humanity desires manifestation. As an American said, "If you have got the goods, give it," but few people realize the persistence and struggle which is demanded of one for a simple demonstration of an additional degree of consciousness.

The story of Moses and his master, Melchizedek, is related in the Koran. It should be read by every searcher for Truth and every occult student, for it teaches that the Kingdom of Heaven can only be taken by energy.

There are times when whole nations are plunged into darkness, when guidance and direction are denied to their political leaders. This is the beginning of moral decay and, until the united people seek direction from the Lord God of Truth within, their lawgivers will not attain the consciousness of intuition. The lords of nature scourge and afflict man until he appeals to God for right direction, which nature can bestow upon him.

What did the worthy ideals of the League of Nations amount to? Nothing, because the whole body served not in united movement, for a weaker member destroyed the united effort of the whole group. People must realize that there is a law of cause and effect and that as you do unto others, so you will be done by. Nations like individuals, must suffer for the wrong and suffering they have caused. The persecuted of the past are today persecuting those who wronged them. People ask why they should suffer for the misdoing of their fathers, but in reality they are suffering the penalty of the wrong they themselves did to others in past lives.

It is far better after a fight to shake hands and sit down and become friendly, for when disputes are heard from both sides in a friendly fashion it is invariably realized that lack of understanding in the beginning has brought about the disagreements.

Humanity has gained nothing from the past great war, except the prospect of the next.[20] Perhaps someday we shall realize the wisdom of our prophets, and listen to the words of the wise men of our own time. Someday people will realize that their souls demand freedom and love, and the opportunity to create. Then they will know that they must first remove the beam from their own eye, before they can be of real service to others.

The student must know that man is only four-sevenths developed, yet he has a universe within himself and possesses the power to become at one with his creator. Imagine yourself, through Yoga, leaving the world of man, entering the environment of a great forest, and listening to a redwood tree! It can relate to you, like a historian, the movements of nature. Perhaps it was born and first appeared above the surface of the earth in the year of the Nativity and has witnessed the setting of the landmarks of time. It has seen the rise and fall of many nations, and its atmosphere is vibrant with history. But until you are in tune with nature you cannot hear its message.

---

20   An actuality since this was written.

CHAPTER TWENTY-THREE

INITIATION BY FIRE

The higher counterpart of fire is *intense coldness,* and the vibration through which some Yogis pass, known as the intelligence of fire, is a vibration of coldness. An advanced Yogi will often evoke this higher counterpart of fire, which has a physical manifestation and can be seen with the naked eye, and he will lead the student into this element. Here the good and evil of his nature are presented to the student. If the good predominates, he can enter this flame without harm, for its consciousness is that of the *knower* (to know a thing without thought), the world of intuition where nature's will manifests.

When the student faces any of the lawgivers of nature they evoke in him his true characteristics, be they good or evil, and these higher evolved beings who have never incarnated in human form, always stand in the Presence and although a man may fool himself, they are not deceived.

In the initiation by fire, one of these hierarchal beings will often join the circle and pronounce his judgment of the Law. Then the pupil sees a mirror of his true character and sums up his own evil (ignorance) and his own good and, if the evil predominates, he is afraid to enter the circle. This is one of the minor initiations. What a change for good would blossom in this great land of ours, if the mirror of Truth could be held before every man and woman! These higher devas give to the initiated what may be termed their gospel of the world of mind. It is the gospel of emancipation, the gospel of freedom, and we discover that all the great religions and creeds of the world are but fragments of a still greater book of truth.

Although man knows it not, the desire of his world is to become at one with its Creator, the Lord God of Truth within. In this Presence these higher beings stand and it is becoming to give reverence to these lords of nature, who inhabit the principalities and kingdoms of these inner worlds of being. The Christ is one of them that taught through the Master Jesus, and the recognition and worship of these overlords of nature long antedate the Nativity.

In every man there exists a fragment of these forgotten truths. The devas desire us to recollect and manifest truth, and thus become the instruments through which the fullness of man's nature may be revealed. The devas reflect into our consciousness the seven different attributes of nature.[21] The greatest of these is will or power, then comes love and compassion, and then intelligence or knowledge. Do you not realize that bliss and intelligence are always about you! Seek inwardly for its true expression, that you may be able to recognize it, and whatever you draw out from the framework of nature, seek to build into a habitation in which a deva may dwell. Whatever you attempt to create with your mind, do it in devotion to the gods who have watched over the material with which you fashion for them a dwelling.

When the crude Irish peasant enters the abode of a friend, he says, "May God come and dwell in this house," and it is delightful to hear them say it in their deep, rich brogue. If you ask Pat why he says it, he replies, "I must make a clean place into which to put my foot."

Before the Egyptians went to their temples they cleaned and disinfected their houses with natron and bathed and put on fresh garments, in order to be clean in the presence of their deity, and it is said that among them the average age of an honest man was 120 years. The scientific studies of bacteriological conditions in our sacred edifices have proved so startling that we might greatly profit by adopting this ancient custom.

The purification of the sacred vessels and of the priest and of his vestments is but the echo of ancient pagan rites. Proper incense is a barrier to the approach of entities and elementals from the underworld, and so are the vibrations of music and chanting, for they harmonize man with God. Most of the ceremonies of the early religions were based on the scientific principles of nature. Activity of purpose and power is the stimulation which nature gives us, in order to bring out the hidden wisdom from within and thus unify man with his Creator. The objective man is the reflection of his own thoughts. Where we place our thoughts, there we are. Intelligence comes from the

21   Seven vowel sounds of nature, the seven-branched candlestick, the seven liberal arts and sciences, the seven human senses.

Lord God of Truth within and we should place our thoughts within the temple of this God when we search for knowledge and the place of understanding. Man's search for knowledge has been misdirected and he has not made contact with that dynamic power from within, which brings realization of God's purpose. If we review the experiences of the day just past and analyze its happenings, we discover a minute amount of wisdom gained, and from that experience we should learn what not to do tomorrow. This should make us more alert to avoid the same mistakes in the future, and it is this process of observation which will build up a stronger foundation for our character, and a finer expression will result. We must get out of the herd and become ourselves, and learn not to be destructive to our fellows.

What a wonderful change comes over the student when he begins to analyze the happenings of each day, seeking truth and right conduct towards his fellows! It is said that when this happens the lords of nature stoop down and lift one up and, in time the Yogi discovers that wherever he is placed there is a lesson to be learned and an experience to be gained.

When he learns how to assist those in his environment, no matter how irksome it may be for him, he is immediately given freedom from that environment, and that is the law.

By sacrificing ourselves and giving of our best to the work we are doing, we discover a way to assist those about us, and thus we gain release from our prison. Take a man who is in business; he may be unhappy in his environment and worked to the extreme limit of fatigue, but if he looks about him and studies his environment, giving his best to the firm and working to assist his weaker brothers he earns a sudden and quick release, and later he will thank God for the experience which he has had, for he has gained wisdom. Should he ever again be placed in a similar position, he has learned the power of pushing his way to the top and the power of command and, in this position of power, he will be better able to serve those beneath him.

A weak man is taken advantage of and mistrusted by his fellows and underlings, and is not appreciated in this world or any other. My teacher once said to me, "You must bring light to those at the top." It is easier to bring light to the materialists in commerce and business than to those on the lower rungs of the ladder, for those at the top are seeking light and a way out. There is a doctrine of the heart and a doctrine of the head, and there is the Wisdom Teaching of the ages.

A business man once came secretly to my rooms in Paris to meet a Yogi student and he told me he had found peace for the first time in years. He came every day at 11 o'clock for two weeks, and then returned to America. I asked him if he would mind my seeing into his past and present, as I saw he was a master mind, and had thousands of men working for him. He then informed me of his executive position in a great trust. He was seeking a finer outlet of expression for his strong character and, after his return to America, he wrote me that he now controlled all the breweries around his works, and that since the breweries controlled the saloons, he also controlled them, and was cleaning them up and making them more of the nature of clubs. He was not giving them so much alcohol in their beer and he hoped to bring about better conditions by working from the top.

The wise employer is he who interests himself in the welfare of his workmen and seeks to make the surroundings attractive, and to give his employees a sense of freedom. The workman today little realizes that he should be honest and faithful to those who employ him and he should look after the interests of his employer. Unfortunately in Europe, caste conditions obtain in trade, and the workman seldom comes in contact with his employer. It is not so in America where the employee has easy access to his boss, but the caste system in Europe makes it difficult for the lower grade workman to be accepted in a higher grade environment. Each caste is suspicious of the caste above and below, and suspicion breeds contempt, therefore the lower forms of Socialism, called Communism, become powerful in this atmosphere.

Traditions and principles of honesty differ in different countries, hence it would be a good thing if different countries understood each other better. A business deal considered honest in one country is judged dishonest in another. You will quickly discover this if you travel through the countries bordering on the Mediterranean, where honesty has its varying degrees. It is the lack of understanding of the customs of other countries which brings so much disaster to the world.

I know one country intimately where two persons who are friends socially, will think it very clever if one of them can best the other in a business deal. The old New England canon of doing business by word of mouth has passed into obscurity, although there are great giants still in business whose word is their bond. Yet many who pride themselves on adhering to the highest standards of honesty in individual transactions, fail to realize that. Nature's great overlords step in and interfere to bring dishonor to the man in business who robs humanity.

CHAPTER TWENTY-FOUR

DEVIC CENTERS

The devic creation, the overlords of nature, have established their stations remote from humanity, in different places in the world. There they intermittently focus their minds. In a remote valley in America, on a raised plateau, which divides a river into two separate streams, there has been built up through time a composite elemental sounding-board. It is comprised of the thoughts, aspirations, and wisdom teaching of the races which have migrated from the regions of Brazil to far Northern Alaska.

This elemental dome-shaped form records the history, the migration, and the attainments of the different civilizations which have swept over the Northern Hemisphere. It is the depository of the learning and culture of these races, and from it radiate vibrations, potent to shape the future progress of America. Yet this great dome-shaped body is the depository of the so-called forbidden knowledge.[22]

Mountain tops covered with snow are often the site of these devic principalities, and distribute to the surrounding areas a message of truth and culture. Think of the ancient Druids with their wonderful knowledge of jurisprudence, healing, statesmanship, and art! From whence did the Elder Brothers who built up Druidism get their knowledge? From whence did the alchemists of old gain their knowledge of the so-called hidden laws?

When he becomes worthy, the student sometimes is taken to these reservoirs of wisdom, and after such an experience he can comprehend in some slight measure the knowledge and wisdom which will be returned to humanity when man seeks to contact the Lord God of Truth whose temple is within.

These elemental centers are hidden in secluded places, guarded by elemental nature, and it is not until the student is taken into the confidence of nature that he learns the secrets which have mystified mortal men from time immemorial. The reader may well ponder upon the secrets of Mount Everest,

---

22 Forbidden? Yes, while man remains an exile from the temple of his Lord God of Truth.

and of the Sphinx, and the Pyramids, for in them is locked the knowledge of how to use nature's providence to pass through the illusion spheres, and into the consciousness of truth and beauty—from the deep illusion to the lesser, until at last man gains God Realization and attains "at-one-ment" with the Lord God of Truth within.

Nature has many divisions and principalities, and so have the great hierarchal devas. It is terrifying to man to consider suddenly losing all that his senses reveal to him. When, however, illusion is removed from his mind the tangible things of the senses, particularly of sight, disappear and when he reaches inwardly the nirvanic plane of bliss and intelligence, all nature, as we formerly saw it, disappears. As we pass through the different densities and reach the finer planes of consciousness we realize the truth of detachment, for truth and beauty become magnified, and we long for union with their source.

There are many places on this earth where elemental characteristics of nature abound, places of magic where we pass from what we call nature into a natural and elemental world, for nature herself is going through a constant change from a baser to a more refined vibration. There are places seemingly natural to the observer, where even the very stones are elemental, and the devas will tell you sometimes that a great boulder is going through its transition stage, and will demonstrate how easily they can pass through it. The student is told to observe its characteristics of mind stuff and sense its memory, and see what the boulder can tell him about its hyperborean existence.

Before the earth changed the angle of its axis great civilizations existed at what is now the North Pole, and in some parts of Asia scientists have discovered valleys which are magical. A scientific party easily found their way into one of these valleys where they found implements of bronze beneath tertiary rock formation but they were imprisoned there for four years. All the time their native cook had known of the exit, but did not tell them.

I was once privileged to go to the retreat of some brothers, which was protected by elemental nature, but when my guide took me into this valley, he began to be afraid and told me that

he was the only son of his father, who was very old, and that he
wanted to return and cook his father's food. He pointed out the
way, but it took me half a day to cross the valley, and another
half day to find my way up the pathway along the face of the
cliff which, in wet weather, reared above the clouds. In the past
this place was easily defended, having only one entrance. It was
a place of peace, and of terrific vibrations, and the brothers
there seldom conversed in audible speech.

I found there the names of people of many nations, who
through the arts, sciences, or statesmanship, had brought great
blessing to humanity, and some who had seemingly died came
here and passed their remaining lives. There are only seven
members in this retreat and they have records of those whose
life experiences they consider to be of use to humanity and
their observations reach back into the remote past. Here I often
studied the beautiful frescoes of a great Italian artist of the
period of the Medicis, whose work was as fresh as if it had been
painted only yesterday, and I also learned some unknown things
about Rembrandt and Botticelli, and found a missing fragment
by a great artist, which has been a puzzle to the critics of today.
When you see the work of these anchorites and know of the
privations which they underwent in order to build this retreat
in the early Roman days, you will appreciate their ardor and
fixity of purpose.

In another valley, honeycombed with the cells of ancient
anchorites, I felt elemental influences which were destructive.
There I met a shepherd with a strange dog, and I recognized
that the soul in that dog was human, and felt its agony and
despair, its horror and suffering. As I sent it love, it flashed
this message to my brain, "Do not go into this valley, it is evil;
the monks were murdered." I shall never forget the horror and
suffering seen between the eyes of this great dog. It was as if this
human soul, imprisoned in a dog body, had been the cause of
the horror of this place in the past.

You get a reflection of the same type of horror from those
animals which provide the vaccine for the cure of rabies, and
which live suffering torture. You also get the same horror in the
eyes of men and women who are possessed, and if humanity

were only allowed to see the possessed and obsessed men and women generally hidden from the public gaze in asylums they would seek purity of thought and honesty in their actions. If you listen to the cries of a maniac possessed of an evil spirit crying out for help, you realize to some extent the conditions which are evoked through magic and the wrong use of nature's gifts.

But the ordinary man heeds not, sees not, and cares little what is going on about him, unless it interferes with his immediate life. The devas of nature penalize the wrongdoer, if he heedlessly takes life for the sake of pleasure.

A friend of mine, a gnome, once came running to me and asked, "Why is it, I am told we are denied immortality?" He was born in St. Edmund's time, and had been taught by some monks of that period. He wanted to know why they, who never injured anyone, were denied immortality. He said, "We hear the little people of the fields crying out in their anguish and suffering to God." When I asked what he meant by the little people of the fields he said, "The rabbits in their burrows which have been injured by men, and yet the men who have injured them are not denied immortality!"

I had to explain to him that "from God we came and to God we return," and probably some day he would be a man possessed of a soul. He was very learned, and he told me the Saints' Days as he had been taught by the monks, and sometimes he would bring me an earthbound spirit in distress and ask me to pray for him. I did so, and got the responding chord of music, which comes when an earthbound spirit has been taken through the lower illusion (purgatorial) stage. The next morning, when I least expected it, I found him standing by my side and with enthusiasm he said, "The Lord be praised, he has gone."

He told me that the monks, in the early days, had little trouble in communicating with him, and evidently his friends knew much about magic; hence the spell which he said they had cast over him, and which he asked me to remove. You learn to love these little fellows, pompous and egotistical, but this gnome surprised me with his knowledge of the observances of the Roman monks of St. Edmund's time. He used to weep at the cruelty of men, and the sufferings which they cause the animals.

Animals have a power of clairvoyance, for they see elemental places, as well as earthbound spirits. For a short time after their death animals can appear in their astral or spirit form and converse with anyone who has developed his higher clairvoyance. A person who bestows his entire love upon an animal lowers himself into the animal nature and consciousness, but naturally our instinctive nature makes us fond of all animal life, because of their reliance on us when taken out of their natural state; therefore they should not be disregarded by man.

CHAPTER TWENTY-FIVE

TOLERANCE—A MESSAGE

Old people often trade on their age and shorten their lives by seeking to dominate their progeny. After death nature steps in and protects the children, and the spheres of communication between the living and the dead are cut off.

One often meets people of this description out of the body, unloved perhaps in life, their passions and desires still hold them to the densities of worldly illusion. Failing to realize that they are dead, they demand that the living carry out their wishes.

They want love, for it is love that links the living and the dead, but if they have limited the finer expression by attempted domination of their progeny they must pay according to the karmic law.

Unless the children have the power to escape or to sever the parental domination such parents place square pegs in round holes, and round pegs in square holes. The really strong soul can never be caged by authority and usually the boy or girl who leaves home is the support of the parents in old age. All souls without exception desire experience, and those relatives who are without tolerance are most pronounced in their effort to shape that experience into their own preconceived plan.

Men preach to and converse with relatives and friends, but are they tolerant toward them? Ask yourself if you are tolerant of your friend's opinion, when it differs from yours, and do you love him as much.

The total disregard of other people's opinions, when you differ with them, creates a maelstrom in the stream of life where there should be peace, happiness, and contentment.

Man's inhumanity to man when he seeks to dominate the personalities of others, is injustice to nature. This is not serving the purpose of his creation. It is a means whereby one seeks to perfect his own experience, but is heedless of and disregards others whom he wrongs. Could such an one step into the presence and greatness of all time, he would see the shadows that he has cast behind him. He would feel the remorse and despair, the quenching of the happiness and joy of the innocent that he is responsible for. He would see himself as others had seen him and if he could return to the illusion world, he would seek to remedy the shadows and darkness that he had cast upon the faces of others, else he would hide himself away from his kindred.

The doctrine of emancipation, which brings man into the consciousness of the Reality, is the Yoga gift to humanity. You should try to find it in the hearts of other men, as well as seek it in your Innermost.

Every man carries about with him a torch lighted in the fire of his elemental nature. When this torch is ignited by nature's truth, it will enlighten the horror in the world. When men carry this flaming torch of Truth, they acquire an understanding of nature; then the "lost voice crying out in the wilderness" will lead men to divine truth and inspiration.

In the Yoga teaching, when the student taps the consciousness of the lords of nature, he can analyze their austerity and the justice of their edicts, yet he can never perceive individuality of expression. He is conscious that the lords of nature are separate entities working together in harmony and union under the law which directs their environment. He discovers that the elements of air, fire, water, and earth are working in harmony, yet distinct from one another and in their atmosphere he always perceives the Presence, which also exists in the deeper states of Yoga.

Not only are there many exalted beings of the devic creation, but there are similar less powerful beings that group themselves about these more powerful intelligences of the higher elements. These beings make themselves known by sending an appropriate symbol to attract one's notice. Association with these higher elemental forces brings new perception of the wonders of nature to the human mind. One deva, for instance, gives a vision of tiny brooks and rivers, and of water emptying itself into the great ocean. It may say to you that these brooks, streams, and rivers are the vital system of nature and that they, like the human body, have their periods of activity and rest.

Water, with its nourishment, brings activity into all nature, giving life and vitality to all growing things, but when it returns to the ocean, its mother, it has periods of rest; then it is again caught up into the clouds to refresh nature once more. The devas inform us that nature, in her "giving" to man, must have periods of rest, so that she can regain her normal strength. When man, in ignorance, works nature to exhaustion and does not allow the soil a fallowing time to regain its strength, nature steps in and penalizes his greed by using her forces of destruction.

Through ignorance man is a destructive force in nature. When he will not be guided by the wisdom of science, and the knowledge of his forebears, nature scourges him through droughts, pestilence, and famines, blotting out those civilizations that have destroyed God's handiwork. The engineer atoms, which formerly fertilized the ground and brought forth abundant harvests, no longer carry on their labor, and they become discouraged by the introduction of alien agents into the soil, a practice which brings about abnormal growth, and activities entirely foreign to previous lines of direction.

Just as this is true in agriculture, so the human form is being developed to conform to the plan of the *nous* atom of the heart, and thus man's form is constantly being brought from a lower to a higher tension of activity.

The *nous* atom, which is in the purest section of the blood stream, has legions of builder atoms serving the upkeep of the physical vehicle, so nature has similar atoms in the subsoil, to keep it true to its original plan. Similarly the devas keep the animals, trees, and plants true to their species. Hence you seldom find hybrids in nature. When man, in his ignorance, introduces seeds foreign to the soil's natural element, he encounters the opposition of these atoms, which seek to render the new introductions harmless to the soil.

The mixing of other races with the native inhabitants of a country brings about a deterioration in the original native strain, for the parental stem is changed by the introduction of a foreign element, hence the progeny lack the stamina found in either species.

As we have indicated before, the lords of destruction scourge the world when men no longer call upon God for direction. The devas will show you land in its natural state, prepared for those who dig and delve in the field, with babbling streams and groves of trees and they will impress you with the happiness that exists in nature and her movements. Then they will show you the heedless cutting of trees and you witness the parching of the soil, and the drying up of the streams until all is an arid waste, and thus it remains until nature again promotes growth in that district.

There is a division of nature, enacting justice among outlaws in humanity and nature. The penalty of wrongdoing brings about a karmic effect, for karma is the law of cause and effect. When a man dies, although his crimes may have escaped justice, he must be tried before the bar of nature for the crimes which he has committed against her. But nature is just and places him in that environment which balances his wrongdoing, thus giving him the power to ascend slowly to a finer environment by right action.

The children of nature weep over man's destruction, but their sorrows are hidden from mortal eyes. To them a tree is a work of God to be worshipped. The Chinese artist portrays symbolic clouds, which to the Western mind appear strange, but to them the clouds represent symbols of great hierarchal intelligences. Modern science says that the Chinese must be shortsighted, or they would not veil distant mountains in mist, but it has yet to discover that those artists never place the human form out of its place in a landscape. Always they place him in his true relationship to nature, and in his true position among the different elements. They express the sensitivity of a mind similar to that which the handwriting of a person may express.

Chinese handwriting, like a painting, stands alone in expressing the thought put into it, hence the careful observer can recognize the grossness or refinement of the writer's character. The artist also becomes so skilled with his hand and arm that the hand instinctively follows the thought. In the finer lacquer work the Chinese will say, "Run your thought ahead of your line, and your brush will follow your thought."

It is the same with a great violinist. His technique is so perfect that his actions obey his mind instantly. If you present a rose properly to a Chinese lady, she will present herself to you with the thought emotion which the rose had evoked in her mind, just as some of the early Russian dancers unconsciously responded to the character of expression which their mind had formed; for instance, their response to the thought of happiness or fear. When Coquelin, the great French actor, portrayed the gross and bestial man, all his movements were entirely different from those which he used when portraying the part of courtier. The true nature is shown in the manner people greet each other and in the way they shake hands.

The Western habit of shaking hands is a very bad one, for physical contact is an exchange of both good and bad conditions on the elemental or psychic planes, which can be transferred or taken on by the weaker person. I once knew a man to be obsessed for three days after shaking hands with a man who practiced the darker side of experimental magic, and it took some time to completely remove the condition. We were in a doctor's office when the condition was removed and the financier, since dead, said, "I have been in hell for three days, for I have been dragged around by another intelligence; my real self I always found standing outside of me. Probably I appeared normal, but I was not myself. I found myself following my body, which was occupied by something else."

The Chinese do not shake hands, they bow instead, keeping their hands clasped, which prevents the entrance to their body of anything of a psychic character. George Washington knew the value of this, for he always tried to avoid shaking hands with people, and after meeting his teacher he was known to smile only once. He learned that nature's first pronouncement is that we must stand alone.

The student must seek to detach himself from all contacts harmful to the well-being of his natural man. In the Golden Age of Chinese civilization nature instructed their adepts in the wisdom teaching. Today, alas, Chinese scholars are not always clean in their clothing or persons. Like the hermits of old and the Bohemians of the Latin Quarter, cleanliness with them has ceased to be a godlike virtue. The sylphs are very drastic towards the student. Before he can enter the element of air, he must bathe two or three times a day, eat no animal food, and purify his mind, for he must obey the laws governing their realm. He is asked to observe and not ask questions until the proper time.

As the instruction is given, questions are answered by visions. Once, when I was living in Italy, I was wondering what the plague looked like, when suddenly three shining beings appeared. They looked at me and smiled, their shining raiment disappeared and they showed me how the plague looked in its three different stages on their nude bodies; then they resumed their shining garments.

This manipulation of mind stuff matter is most wonderful to behold, and in beauty of color, feature, and figure a beautiful sylphid can be so lovely as to be a veritable torture. If any impurity is allowed to enter the mind she vanishes, although her loveliness will increase in proportion to your love of purity. Here you gain the secret of Botticelli's unreal reality of the human form, for a sylphid can show you her foot as Botticelli would paint it, her canons of art can be contrasted with those of Aphrodite by Praxiteles, and with nature's bracelet just above the ankle, which you see in the masterpieces of the great Greek sculptors. She will show you a normal ankle and then, as she would have it. She will adorn her foot with various sandals of the different stages of Greece, or of the Roman period of Augustus, with bejewelled enrichment, and then back again to nature, with nature's delicate rose tinted feet. In this display is loveliness incomparable! The rippling intensity of the smiles of a sylphid, the adornment and enjoyment in their walk, and their power of transforming themselves to show you the different types which abound in their realm is very marvelous.

Alas, it is this same beauty which often leads the student from his quest for truth and beauty! These contrasting beau-

ties of the elements; the undine of water, with her pink pum-
ice colored skin, and a certain heaviness which you do not
find in the sylphid of the air, and her power of borrowing and
absorbing from the student's atmosphere. She is apt to lower
the student's vitality for a period. The sylphids, from the writer's experience, do not do this. They merely express the joy of
living movement and rhythm. They have a steel-like mentality,
brilliant, but very compassionate, if sadness enters the heart.
To my mind, their manifestations of love can best be analyzed
as steely sweetness. Seemingly they have no kindred, and no
patience with the love affairs and sex attraction of youth, and
they do not forgive any dishonesty toward themselves. As one
of them said to me, "Dishonesty dims the mirror of Truth."

One must remember that there are different degrees of
intelligence among the sylphs. In Tunis, there is a marabout,
or Mohammedan priest, a miracle worker, who is married to
one of these sylphids, by whom he has three children. People
in the Mohammedan countries of Egypt and Northern Africa
come very closely in touch with the elemental kingdom of
nature, but in the West it is difficult to live a life close to
nature, for these finer forces dislike man's lack of consideration for nature and the sordidness of human creations.

Some of these lords of nature are terrible in their aspect,
especially those found in the element of fire, for their mental
pressure seems to speak through the entire universe, yet you
are conscious of their infinite understanding and power. They
can enlighten the mind in a flash and intelligence is in their
words, for they can sum up in a single sentence the essentials
of a situation which will enlarge the scope of the mind. They
challenge your intelligence to *think,* and guide your thought
in one direction only, until a large amount of information is
acquired. One word leads to a train of thought, which seems
to have no end, and a sentence is like a resounding thought
which seems to extend through all the world.

Many human beings, who are strongly charged with the
element of fire are quick thinkers, and are apt to be intolerant
and always run ahead of the other fellow's thought. In a word,
you may sum these people up as Titans of thought.

All the different elements and their divisions are classified by a token or symbol. Each of their symbols, vibrations, and sounds have their higher counterparts, but these symbols are given to the student only when he is worthy and when he seeks to know God through his manifestations. We can attain union with the flame (light) by means of worshiping God through the element of fire; hence we get the word *Chohan,* one who seeks God Realization through the element of fire. We have always been impressed that beings, chiefly elemental in their bodies, will one day return to nature worship and adore God through nature's consciousness. Even today some people are unconsciously nature worshipers.

There are many ways of approaching God, and this is the natural way. It was called paganism by the early Church, but every man must find his own path, which will be discovered through his aspiration to *know God.* We find "books in the running brooks, sermons in stones, and good in everything." Mohammed has said, "To its own book shall every nation be summoned." A sylphid once said to me, "Do you not realize that great teachers come to our spheres, as well as to yours, and that God is never apart from His creation?"

In dealing with this subject I do not wish to discourage anyone, whatever his religion may be, in his quest for Truth. I only wish to give out knowledge gained through Yoga practice, in order that a better understanding between man and nature may result. There are saints of many grades and religions, who work to bring about better conditions in this world of illusion. They are noble men and women who, in this life, have gained "at-one-ment" with the Lord God of Truth within—God Realization. In their desire to help the weaker members of humanity, they remain behind to assist in the enlightenment of their younger brothers.

The Yogi, in the deeper states of consciousness, often comes in contact with these great workers for humanity and by personal observation I have often witnessed their answers to the appeals of humanity, sometimes within a few moments. We learn to love these saints, who are constantly working in our midst toward their sovereign goal, both in and out of the body. It is only by our finer perception, which we have attained in our quest for Truth, that we can recognize the saint when we see him in our midst, but through the higher clairvoyance we recognize the "light" of these saints and seek to be of service to these little known members of humanity.

Those who have sunk the spirit deeply into their mind bodies are able to recognize those who seek service in the name of Truth. Often the perception gained through Yoga practice gives the student the power to *know*, and he is able to be of assistance to these future saints in their childhood.

It is one of the first duties of the student, after he has met his teacher (one of those enlightened ones), to render service to these innocents that their bodies may be well nourished and their natural gifts not too quickly developed at the expense of the physical body. Light comes to the Yogi student through unselfish service for the good of others, without regard to religion or creed. These enlightened ones are met in all classes of society, and in many creeds and religions.

Those who have received their first illumination have knowledge of their own limitations, and of the plan and activity of their lives. Those who really know their own limitations will not interfere with the affairs of others, and will work within a certain range of experience, which they know is their work and mission while on earth.

Some day, the great doctrine of emancipation, which is the gospel of nature's consciousness, will be given to this world, and the world will then experience nature's great healing powers. A great avatar, who lived long before the advent of Jesus, through sacrifice of himself, advanced our Iron Age nearer to the consciousness of nature, so that her truth and wisdom knowledge were made known to man. We must remember the information given to us by a great teacher, which brought happiness to many. He said, "Great souls foresaw the advent of Krishna, and they incarnated as common cowherds, in order to be with him. Krishna played on his flute, and danced throughout the night for them, in order to advance the Steel Age and this present Iron Age in which we are now living, taking on himself their karma, in order to advance it into a newer, cleaner age again." The great avatars have also sacrificed themselves in order to enable humanity to enter more quickly into the presence of Truth.

CHAPTER TWENTY-SIX

REGAINING OUR LOST BIRTHRIGHT

In the deeper states of Yoga we are not conscious of having any form, but we are like the intelligences around us and are similar to the reflected light cast off from a pin's head. The advanced seers tell us that our ultimate form will be globular.

When we become acquainted with the esoteric side of Chinese and Japanese art we discover that to these Orientals the devas took upon themselves the shapes of dragons. In the pictorial representations of a great Emperor Initiate, known as the Dragon Emperor, because he was fathered by a dragon, the artists always show him with his attendant dragon. Our great initiates, wise men and philosophers, were often fathered by one of these lords of elemental nature. Merlin is an example, and we have spoken about him in a former book.[23]

Those people who have a natural inheritance of both the human will and the will of nature are miracle workers. The children of such unions are called the "twice born," and their mission is to bring spiritual realization to the world of the mind. They are the messengers of *Stilbon of Arcadia*, who is symbolized with a rod, bringing the light of the spirit into the mind world. In other words, the children of these unions are messengers who stimulate the mind to the realization of Truth.

When considering nature's powers, we must remember that on this earth there are also lords of the mind from other planets, who respond to the mantric call of the student and bring him into an entirely new mental atmosphere. The sun, moon, planets, and stars which are about us, all have their part in our schooling and evolution, for they have their receiving stations in our human body.

We realize that we must tune our receiving set to receive a clear response from a broadcasting station, and we must likewise attune ourselves to receive nature's instruction. We must also realize that the vowel sounds have their higher counterparts which, when sounded, attract the atoms of other planets

---

23   *Comte de Gabalis.*

into our atmosphere. When we call upon nature to bring atoms of intelligence and purity into our surroundings, we clarify our atmosphere and by this means we bring health and understanding to the minds we contact. This illustrates the power to be found in nature's laboratory.

One of the great discoveries in Yoga is that man can become conscious of the different vibrations which flow through him from nature. He learns to distinguish between the vibrations of Mercury and those of Jupiter, just as he distinguishes between the sound of the vowels *a* and *e*. He becomes conscious of the law and love back of the Jupiterian vibration and discovers that Mercury clarifies his mind, giving him the power to commune deeply with things which are of worth to humanity. He sees the struggles and endeavors of mankind, and the avenues which are humanity's means of escape to happiness, and he understands the difference between deep intelligence and keen and witty intellect. He analyzes the forces which would pull him back into the depths of his past, and the forces which would enlighten his mind towards God, where seemingly thought no longer exists, and he begins to *know*. We speak of these things, hoping to stimulate the seeker to aspire for love and beauty and, when we think of love, we think of Truth as well. It is difficult to speak with authority regarding these things, but it is a natural urge for every man to speak from his consciousness of Truth, and in nature's consciousness it is becoming that we should speak with authority as we do.

Man is composed of atoms. These atoms are minute bodies of intelligence, possessing the dual characteristics of nature and man. They have a discretionary power which speaks the truth to dispel the illusion of the world. In time the student will align himself with the intelligence of these atoms, which he has assembled in his own self-created universe.

When preparing to contact any intelligence within or without his body, the Yogi realizes that he is like a wireless instrument combining both receiving and transmitting apparatus. In meditation, as he aspires inwardly for Truth, he sees what is going on within himself. He discovers that he has an engineer atom which can establish for him contact with any state of consciousness he wishes. He discovers also his instructor atoms, which are the depositories of knowledge of the experiences which he has passed through since his beginning on earth. In time, as he aspires for true union with the Lord God of Truth within, he finds that the engineer atom contacts him with these instructor atoms and he receives that information which is best for him to know. Sometimes he will be given a period of instruction, which may come from unexpected sources, and in surprising ways.

This is similar to a man having a book full of interesting information, such as Burton's *Anatomy of Melancholy*, on a high shelf in his room. It has been there all his life, but he has never known its contents. Suddenly his eye and hand are guided to this volume, and thus our engineer atom has made contact with periods of instruction and opened the mind to new worlds and vistas of discovery.

Although the volume may awaken memories, the knowledge comes to us through the "natural man" returning us to our birthright, which we had sold for a "mess of pottage." The reader must not be surprised to find the Yogi conversant with the past of this world; very often he will pause a moment, and suddenly place before you the life and activities of people of a bygone age. Perhaps, after having discussed ancient Egypt with him, you may suddenly feel as if you were there as an observer at that period. The Yogi has attained to the consciousness of nature, in which her plan—past, present, and future—is unrolled.

Sometimes we wonder why the great ones do not avert the terrible wars that create so much suffering and distress. Knowing the plan and purpose, they do their utmost to alleviate the pain and suffering which the dark forces would visit upon the world, conditions far worse than that through which it is passing now. Yet always they know that man will continue to suffer, until he does unto his neighbor as he would his neighbor should do unto him. Since a terrible war is one means of teaching this lesson on a large scale, to avert it would delay fulfillment of the plan. It is true that there are people who have perfected themselves in one life, so that they are not obliged to return to this world of ignorance, tumult, and despair. The end of all true Yoga is to bring God realization to humanity which is union of the lower self with the Lord God of Truth within.

This book is written to make man realize that he is not apart from his fellows. It should awaken him to the need for new institutions and laws, and stimulate youth to self-thought and a deep appreciation of the true, the beautiful, and the good. If it shall serve "To interest by the True, to move by the Beautiful, to persuade by the Good, and to illuminate by the Intelligence," the blessings of the great discovery will be more quickly realized.

Nature awaits man's discovery of his power to reclaim his own lost birthright, the gift of the spirit. This lost birthright, when man seeks union with his Innermost, brings a greatly expanded consciousness to his mind.

He then recognizes that there is one edict of nature which cannot be written about. It is passed down through the ages only by word of mouth. It is the "spoken word" of Jesus, Mohammed, Buddha, Krishna, Bau, and others down through the long chain of avatars. It is the most precious thing that can be given to man, for it is the light which illuminates his torch.[24] This key unlocks all hidden things and is the Truth which brings immortality to the soul. It administers justice to all things in the deep night of circumstance, it is the voice which proclaims the truth to the elders of our race. The book of the universe is known only to those who have served in the fulfillment of its purpose, and beyond that, it is the torch of Truth which unites the sovereign purpose of man with his creator—it is the Law.

The angels of nature open this book of the Law and read it to those worthy of its instruction, but beyond that we know not; we only know that everything is formed and shaped in the image of the Law.

Many have been given this commandment in the Western world, but their lips are sealed. To them we bow our heads in reverence, for to them has arrived the understanding of this sacred word—the word which Jesus and Buddha spoke. The great devas bow in reverence, as the word passes down through

---

24   This secret was revealed beginning in 1950, through the books of Samael Aun Weor.

the different densities of matter, to ascend again and stand in the presence of its giver, the Lord of all Light, that which is above and that which is below—the Sanctuary of Peace, and the light of all becoming.

Since man really lives in seven degrees of consciousness, the little "I", the man as we know him, only occupies a small portion of this universe. For instance, we use our conscious mind, but we are told that we also have a subconscious mind, that each little man has within him a world that he knows very little about.

Note on Symbols: We have spoken about Stilbon of Arcadia, one of the lords of the mind world. Nature's instruction gives us the symbols of the vowel sounds of nature, by which we attract finer and purer elements into the density of our mind world. We are like people in a moat of ignorance, looking up at a being of splendor and brightness on the bank; if we call out to him and we are worthy, he will assist us in our desire to attain Truth. So serve the saints, who have remained behind to assist humanity up to their own level of consciousness. We must knock, in order to gain their attention, we must ask in order that we may receive instruction, but the key or password to their services is our aspiration to *know God.*

CHAPTER TWENTY-SEVEN

NATURE'S HIDDEN CHORD

There are many things hidden in the mystery of nature which can be revealed only to those who have passed through their first phases of initiation into the mystery of her law.

In order to become conscious of them we must submit to nature's jurisdiction; then, intermittently, we are given suggestions as to her beneficent work for humanity. I have been permitted to suggest some of the newer disclosures which nature has in store for us, but it is very difficult in such matters to explain that which is well understood by the initiates.

When we analyze the vibrations flowing through us from nature, we find a white stream of intelligence in operation, and its color informs us that it is a dominating force or power. It is similar to a clear stream pouring itself into a larger stream of muddy and befouled water. Although this white stream seemingly loses itself in the foulness and turbulence, yet its pristine color persists unchanged. Like a beautiful melody of music, clearly audible in the discord of a great city, it brings a blessing.

The student must realize that there is no difference, save in frequency, between the vibrations which are registered by man as sound, and those registered as color, or taste, or smell.

There is a vibration in nature which, when drawn upon by the student, clarifies his atmosphere and makes known to him the same impression and sensation as if a great soul were standing in his presence. Consciousness of this vibration will forge the link which will unify man and nature. In his ignorance man knows little of this invisible force or vibration, which nature bestows upon the sincere student, but it is the same "bindery note" which harmonizes his mind with the Lord God of Truth within.

This bindery note is one of the greatest forces that the mind can comprehend, and is the instrument which will attune man to his rightful place and position in nature's consciousness. Man knows little of the true nature of what he calls electricity, yet he has harmonized it for his service.

The devas call it "the third service," and say that there are two vibratory forces ranking above it. The devas regard electricity as of little importance in comparison with the other powers of nature.

When the devas speak of the electricity controlled by man, they talk of its harshness and jagged appearance, for electricity is a purely natural force, unaccompanied by intelligence, and science seeks to dominate it by the control of its use. When the devas speak of the "white cord," they talk of its softness and pliability and when man learns to contact this, it will become a great factor for healing.

Through the consciousness of nature's bindery note when tapped, one is able to attain to virtue and understanding of the primary edicts of nature. It is a lost note, a lost word which, when known and perceived in the future, will bring reward to the honest man. "As above, so below!" The prophets of old spoke of the just and virtuous man, but the meaning of the higher counterpart of virtue can only be known through the instruction and teaching of this so-called new force in nature. It is of the nature of truth and of understanding.

This age is like a workman holding a tool waiting to be instructed in the laws regarding its use. The Egyptians had a knowledge of this force, as had the builders of the temple in Jerusalem, and the knowledge has often been used by those who have received instruction from the great dome-shaped elemental globe in nature's consciousness. The presence of this force has been hinted at by the prophets of old, and it has been suggested as a force which holds all atomic life in its true place and position. Beyond this we can say very little, except to suggest that this force, when tapped, will awaken the mind to greater vistas of experience. Its collective ability will bring man's nature into closer union with his parental stem of experience, and will also bring races collectively to a central focusing point.

The Egyptians symbolized this force over the gateways to their temples, in the wings which went to make up the symbol of the creative, distributive, destructive, and the protective forces of nature—the symbol known as the "winged globe."

It is the protective force in humanity, the wings of Mother Nature protecting those who return to her source, and recalling those of her children who have strayed from her truth and intelligence. Man, in his past pilgrimage, has had the light enkindled in his heart; therefore these forces of the spirit in nature bring light to our mind world again, for it is the law that when a thing is conceived in the mind, the essence of the thing conceived thereafter links you with it, be it good or evil, light or dark, intelligence or ignorance.

Regarding the white stream, we only know that it is liberated essence from the source, somewhat akin to nature's will. Its essence is healing, in that it is the comfort which a mother brings to her distressed child, and it exhorts us to seek God through nature. Yet it is a tangible essence which will lead us to the source of all things. Then will the great discovery be found within nature's keeping, that the essence at its source is "The One." Within this essence the man of nature within us bathes; it is his guide and protector, the mother of wisdom, titanic and forceful, soft and hard, gentle and strong. It is the pronouncement, the law of all time; it is beauty (love), strength and gentleness. "Ask and ye shall receive, seek and ye shall find, knock and it shall be opened unto you."

The bindery note shakes up all the atoms of our body and assembles them about their parental stem of experience in order to bring them to its beneficent peace and understanding. It reorganizes that which has been disorganized; it gives, but it does not destroy, and to the sincere student in the deeper states of Yoga, it reveals its secret and its promise. The "word of power" which links the mind with its essences has been hidden from the student hitherto, but he must aspire through nature and her understanding to know the truth of this manifestation.

The power of hope will never falter when once we tap this essence. It is the link which will bring men and women out of their discords, so that they may acquaint themselves with the broader realm of experience, through which they have migrated from the beginning of time. It is symbolic of peace and the offspring of peace.

This power gives the saint his strength and enables him to answer the prayers of the multitude simultaneously. Great initiates have used it to multiply themselves, so that they might be seen in many places at the same time. We must remember that Mother Nature is the great healer and miracle worker. By this stream of energy, when he is conscious of it, man may conquer self and stand in the presence of his own Lord God of Truth within.

There is more significance in the initiate Paul's admonition that "The Kingdom of Heaven is within you," than most people realize, and when we seek alliance with this singular energy in nature, we can exercise dominion over our own "kingdom of heaven."

A worthy sylph has told us that man is not set apart from nature. Within himself man has the creative, destructive, distributive, and protective powers of nature, to govern which he must seek union with the Lord God of Truth within.

We must learn to heed the man-of-nature within us, and to seek to serve the purpose of the God within. We observe that nature is the burial ground of our past civilizations, in which we find very few monuments erected. Yet in her etheric substance nature has recorded the history of all these past civilizations. As we advance deeper in our Yoga practice, nature opens the history of our past, and of the nations which existed before, and to this the historians of the future will go for facts. That which is imprinted with the human thought exists forever, awaiting man's advancement in his evolution and perception.

When the student can compare the written memorials of man with those of nature's library, he will learn how truth becomes obliterated and distorted by the desires of man.

What a revelation it would be if we could read the true histories of our great prophets, avatars, and saints! "The Wise Ones" tell us that a controlled imagination is one of the greatest gifts, for uncontrolled imagination brings disorder and disaster. It was through the control of the imagination of his hearers that Jesus gave out his pronouncements, both in his parables and in his teachings.

If a man's liver is out of order he has a distorted imagination, for in the physical body the liver is the seat of the imagination. The upper third of the lungs has much to do with the mind body and, if that portion of the lungs is infected with tuberculosis, the psychology of the patient is most interesting. The majority are self-centered, indifferent to the feeling of others, and selfish. Disorganization of the digestive tract and constipation are often the cause of great depression. The average person sees no connection between the finer bodies and the physical man. But from the standpoint of the inward vision the physical man is gaseous in appearance, and there is some slight attachment of his finer bodies to his glands.

The time is not yet ripe to write of other things in which nature instructs us. Man is not yet worthy to receive it. When a student, I myself lost seven years of development through bestowing a power of nature on one whom I loved, who afterwards proved false to the keeping of this treasure: seven years of darkness and suffering! Thus nature's karmic laws teach us wisdom.

Mother Nature is compassionate, and forgives her children for their ignorance, but to lose her presence, even for a period, causes great suffering and agony to the soul. Though the world may seem dark at the present time and destruction and famine abound, yet the Dayspring of Youth brings with it glorious help, and stimulates our persistence and patience to *know*. The advanced student learns the power of his self-created universe.

Although suffering may be rife in the world, yet when you can stand alone in the Presence, there you may be in the glorious sunshine of immortal youth that is within you and through the at-one-ment perception of truth you may be of assistance to your fellows. Through this hidden chord in nature man is warned of his own true condition in time and he can discern adverse conditions by measuring the light which is shining upon him, and thus "forewarned is forearmed." This is one of nature's beneficent gifts and if only we seek faithfully, we will gain conscious knowledge of our own place and position in our own time.

CHAPTER TWENTY-EIGHT

NATURE'S TWO DIVISIONS—
DAY AND NIGHT

It is in the lower levels of humanity that the night forces of nature are most active. Man sees clearly only during a portion of the day, and he sees only in part what is coming from any direction. His organs of sight record a limited range of vibration. I have met some members of the red Indian tribes who have what is known as nine-tenths vision, for they can see clearly at night things which escape the observation of most men.

In our study of nature we learn that the weight and pressure of the atmosphere is greater on the lower levels than on the heights, and the destructive side of elemental nature predominates in this density of atmospheric pressure. We also observe that nature has two great divisions—day and night. Man attracts the true levels of his own density; if he aspires and seeks union with God, the density of his body changes and he becomes immune from the elemental nocturnal inhabitants, who have their life and activity in these lower densities of atmospheric pressure.

The great beings of light and intelligence show themselves in the sunlight, but the earthbound spirits and elemental forms must have darkness in which to manifest—hence spiritualistic seances are held in the dark. The Bringers of Light may occasionally manifest at seances, but such are not their natural habitat.

Grown people do not realize how terrified children generally are of the dark, for their sensitivity registers fear. Sensitive children should always have a night light carefully shaded. They should not be told ghost stories or frightened with tales of invisible people who will catch them. Everyone is open to the suggestion of fear, yet it is something which must be conquered. Occasionally a child does not outgrow this sensitivity and fear.

I once knew a man in Scotland who would not walk on the main road, but preferred to tramp over ploughed fields

and ground to the post office half a mile away. I once said
to him, "Jock, why is it that you will not walk in the road at
night?" And he replied, "To tell you the truth, sir, I am afraid
of the invisibles." Jock was evidently clairvoyant, for he had
described me correctly to his friends a year before I arrived
in the district, and he also described the new schoolmaster
who, he said, would arrive in a top hat, which turned out to
be absolutely true. He became greatly worried about a dream
which he discussed with me. He had seen three people washed
ashore, and his dream came true regarding two of these
persons; then he became frightened, thinking that he himself
would be the third, so he left the place. He had described the
first two unfortunates correctly, and he had an idea that the
third looked rather like himself. However, he volunteered for
active war service and met his death in Gallipoli. The shepherds in the Highlands avoid those places where elemental
fear is sensed. Some of these hauntings are caused by half-
human, half-elemental monsters, and it is extremely difficult
to bring the light to these intelligences, so that they will cease
warring against humanity. Their atmosphere is that of a soul
in hell, and they can spread an intensity of depression into
atmospheres which they contact, and can magnetize an object,
such as a book, so that it will bring depression and suffering to
any honest mind.

There are some elemental monsters who seemingly never
die. Often their activities are directed at great historical families
which won power in the past through wars and destruction.
I knew a man of magnificent character who inherited a title
cursed through many generations. Within three months, after
coming into the vibration of his ancestral home, I noticed a
gradual coarsening and thickening of his physical vehicle. I
talked to the elemental guardian of this place. It lives beneath
the ground, in a dungeon-like apartment, and it informed me
that the heads of the house had not hesitated to burn religious
houses and holy places in the past, for the sake of personal gain.

Families, who own places such as these, would be doing a
kindness to humanity if they razed them to the ground. Schools
and universities, hoary with age, cause the minds of youth to be

placed in the past, instead of the present and future, and such institutions should also be burned, beautiful as they are, for they are the charnel houses of the past. If you enter into conversation with the inhabitants of these ancient places, you will find that they talk chiefly of the past, and seldom of the present; the exceptions to this being in the scientific departments of learning.

Visiting the cathedral towns of England, we walk into the glamour of the past, but even in those places where the light has been bright, we can get only the shoddy impress of the past today, for the debris of the ages has not the intelligence of experience. It is in such conditions that the negative forces of nature exercise their greatest power over the mind of the individual.

All the great teachers say, "Be positive." This does not mean to be egotistical. When we enter into the positive side of nature we encounter what the Egyptians called "the Lord Giver of Life." Man is a solar system within himself and has nerve centers and diaphragms which register all the impulses of nature. Most people have heard of the solar plexus in the body, just below the sternum or chest bone, but they know little of the others. Man has a "moon center" between his eyes which, like the moon, reflects the solar light. The application to human affairs of this division of nature into day and night should be carefully observed by the seekers after knowledge.

Man has accustomed himself to the pressure of the normal radiation of sunlight, just as he has accustomed himself to the atmospheric pressure of which, until he ascends to a high altitude, or descends deep into the sea, he is unconscious. The student of Yoga however recognizes two essential and opposing forces in nature. The sun, with its pressure, holds in check the vital energy of the seed, until that vital energy becomes stronger than the power of the sun over it. The moon draws the vitality of a plant to the surface, whereas the sun represses it. The moon liberates the forces of nature, whilst the sun holds them in check.

The earth current, flowing to the magnetic pole, is strong enough to keep a magnetized needle always pointing in one direction. This current flows through a man's body into the ground; hence, if we kept our bare feet upon the ground at night, when we would have no protection from the solar forces to retard this flow, we would become devitalized. It is noticeable that although fur is a non-conductor, furry animals do not sleep with their foot pads on the ground at night. Chickens get off the ground to roost, and the red Indian sleeps on a buffalo robe, a bear skin, or a heavy woolen blanket.

For centuries Yogis have practiced what is known as the "cold water" treatment. It is an interesting experiment and beneficial to the health. In the early morning, run or exercise barefooted in the wet grass, or along the water's edge at the seashore, or in your bathtub. The water should never be above the ankles. You should take active exercise, running until you begin to perspire, and it is better to do this in the country, if you can. When you have thus increased the voltage of the life forces within you, then insulate yourself. Yogis and Indians sit on fur, as it is a non-conductor, but a woolen rug on the ground is also suitable.

You should sit quietly, aspiring to enter nature's consciousness. In this way you charge yourself like a battery with nature's current. Send out your love to nature in your aspiration, for this is the first step the student must take to enter nature's consciousness. At first you may be conscious of fear. This is brought about by the lower elemental intelligence in nature, which rebels at the destructive agent, man, entering her realm. But if you persist in this practice, and send out all your love to nature, you will suddenly become conscious of a change. It is as if you were in some great cathedral of nature, where you apprehend its peace, its love, and its intelligence. Then the higher beings, and the elements of fire, earth, water, and air will become known to you, and for this entrance into nature you must thank the sovereign sun.

You will find that a great change in your health will take place, if you charge your battery in this manner, and all I can say is, "Try it!" It took the writer a year and nine months of practice and hard work, living close to nature, before he could receive the instruction and be worthy of the notice of these overlords of nature. Many people wonder why ascetics and Yogis need so little food. One of the most vital men I have ever met, ninety-two years of age, demonstrated this secret.

The hermit life has its compensations and they very often come, as they did in the writer's case, after the quest has been renounced as hopeless. Nature teaches us to aspire earnestly for the light and wisdom which are within us. If we fail to gain that which we seek after patient effort, and reverently renounce the search saying, "Thy will be done," a vacuum is formed within us, and that which we earnestly desired makes its appearance in the form which the Lord God of Truth within knows is best.

The sun gives us the power to restrain ourselves, and patiently to conserve and build up power in order to break our way into the greater truth. There will come a time when we receive a knowledge of the elemental side of the sun, whose symbols Chinese initiate artists have so often portrayed, but which in our ignorance we pass by, without close observation.

The presence of the elementals of the sun, moon, and planets has much to do with the plan of our horoscopes, and the Yogi will often find a sun elemental in the form of a full grown African lion standing by his side. In these sun elementals the nose is extremely broad, and the countenance looks somewhat human.

The sun elemental has power over mind stuff matter and will often transform itself into a golden lion, which you may sometime see sitting on your mantelpiece, radiating rays of crackling, brilliant sunshine. Before the beginning of the Great War, three of these elementals walked around my bed, wearing Sam Browne belts, as humans would wear them, and they projected a picture of a well-known railway station, with many troop trains departing.

Great beings come to this earth both from the sun and from the moon to become guardians of certain nations. They appear at various places on our earth, and Yogis, and others who are highly evolved, journey to certain retreats where at times these higher beings show themselves. The great goddess of the moon, especially worshipped by the Chinese, appears at regular intervals in a retreat in China. At the moment of her appearance the Chinese hold up linen cloths to saturate them with the moisture of the moon, which is then squeezed out of the cloth. They call this the elixir of life.

However, the sun elementals are beneficent, and are of a scientific nature. They tell us of the seven great suns, of which our sun is one. A number of years ago a great adept passed away in Egypt. He had received from an angelic being information of a scientific nature, which was scoffed at by the astronomers, but today many of these pronouncements have been proved to be correct. Our physical sun has its higher counterpart, just as man has within him a higher self, the man of nature. Man also has atoms of the sun, moon, and stars in his body, so his real light and guidance comes from the sun behind his own sun.

Man has within him an elemental nature pertaining to the sun, as well as to the moon. We are told that the greatest of the wisdom teachers came from the moon, and passed into the higher realms of consciousness. From the solar elementals we learn that the seven great suns are constantly giving of themselves, in order to bring about the formation of a greater sun, the globe of arcanum.

A great Eastern nation at the present time is under the administration of the sun. In the course of a few years she has come up out of obscurity and become a world power. Furthermore, she has never been defeated in arms.

CHAPTER TWENTY-NINE
OUR HIGHER POSSESSIONS

Few people in the West have been able to pass the causeway leading to nature's storehouse of wisdom instruction. Very few have been able to tap that consciousness in nature's keeping, which is symbolized to the outside world as "the hidden fruit within nature's veil." Today we can only suggest those things to the man who is able to comprehend.

Mortal man sees through a glass darkly and knows little of his rightful inheritance. The Yogi student stands apart and alone in his quest for Truth. If he is earnest and sincere in his devotion, there will come a time when nature will lift her veil. He will then be able to enter into her consciousness.

If the student will seek for Truth only in the consciousness of nature, the veil of illusion will be rent, and he will perceive light in the midst of the darkness of his own time. Nature has her science, her obligation to the Creator, and, as we study her systems of government, we discover the scientific application of her laws. By being positive and direct in aspiration for her truth, she will give us the fruits of former harvests, long forgotten in our world activity.

Our man in nature possesses a wealth of information and knowledge, and a wide range of wisdom experience. Being ignorant of this information stored up in us, we have never sought to draw upon it. In Yoga, during each incarnation, we pass through the information periods of our past lives, so that our man-in-nature[25] can return to us these higher possessions. The Yogi seeks union with God, with the Lord God of Truth, within which all things exist, and which exists in all things.

When the student notices that the "director" atom within his body is contacting him with his "man-in-nature," he is conscious of a hymn of praise going on within him, which later becomes a paean of victory, when he forges the link with the divine guidance which is within him.

He then becomes conscious that our sun has a foster parent. Previously, the sun in our physical world was observed by him,

---

25 Sometimes referred to as our "higher self."

but now he also recognizes the sun within his inner worlds, and the difference is like the passing from heat to light. In that light there is quietness and peace and he senses the immensity and grandeur of peace. He discovers that its vibrations multiply things, and that it constantly multiplies the unseen wave which carries the consciousness of truth and intelligence within it.

In this vibration there is an ever widening pulsation, which he feels throughout his body and mental atmosphere, and in it his aspiration seems to be taken up and multiplied. The devas speak of this light as the pulsating chord in nature, for it shuts down and nullifies the activities of the lower mind, until it seemingly ceases to exist. By this light we discover that man's human mind can be purified and illuminated by the spirit of truth, which can unify the consciousness with its vibration.

In Yoga practice we become conscious of that light which is always above our mind world, from which the devas receive their directing impulses. The individual mind, while retaining identity, seems to have passed into the mind which embraces everything. One realizes this light permeates the world of mind and the world of memory. It is the brooding consciousness of light and intelligence.[26]

Here things are realized without thought, the energy that we formerly used in thinking disappears, and we absorb the consciousness which we have attained, and bask in an infinite and great reality.

Few men have been able to enter into their rightful domain, for living in an era of ignorance, we have become chained to the wheel of circumstance and must remain so until we can enter into nature's consciousness. The key to this door of knowledge is aspiration and, in order to aspire, we must have a one-pointed mind to know ourselves.[27]

Man looks about him in his own world and considers himself to be the supreme thing that has actual existence. He looks at the sun and moon, the plants and trees, as he looks upon a painting; he does not conceive that anything could have greater intelligence than himself. He regards everything as created for his pleasure and support and does not realize that he is in fact

---

26   The place of understanding.
27   The Book of Job is a story of initiation.

an exile from nature's providence. He has been driven from her domains for disobedience of her law. He thinks in his ignorance that he is greater than the cause.[28]

If man will aspire to learn and live according to the laws of nature, he will be allowed again to enter nature's consciousness and become unified with her movements and intelligence. Thus he regains his lost inheritance.

The union of man's will with nature's will brings about the regeneration of man's entire being. He becomes a man of God, and nature will give him those fruits most needed for his development.

After long periods of aspiration for Truth, the student is told to conceive of another being like himself, which is to stand beside him and be joined to him. This being he is to create or reassemble as an elemental lord of Truth. This concept will assist him in his development and help him to enter nature's consciousness. The student is like a magician assembling his own "man-in-nature," in a form similar to that which he now occupies, but with a body of truth. This bodyguard is a protective force, and contains all his pure aspirations and thoughts assembled before he left elemental nature to build up the present form in which he lives. The student protects himself by unifying himself with his own elemental thought form which exists in nature, but of which he has not been conscious until he took up this practice of Yoga.

Nature has ensouled all our purer and finer thoughts, built up through many incarnations, in the form of our guardian angel. We have also built up another thought form composed of all our evil thoughts and desires, which exists as our secret enemy. We have spoken of this in our former book, *The Dayspring of Youth*.

Nature makes known her laws to humanity, when man is ready to profit by them. When the student seeks to obey these laws and becomes subject to her jurisprudence, she will quickly remedy the natural conditions with which she scourges humanity. The simplicity of nature's laws is indicative of her greatness, and an understanding of her laws is necessary for

---

28   Read the story of Adam and Eve.

man's readjustment. We can redeem humanity only when man is worthy to resume his place in nature's consciousness, so that her beauty and understanding may be known to the common mind. Then intolerance and misunderstanding between nations will disappear, and the primordial, brooding spirit descends into our human consciousness and makes us akin to nature and to man.

The greatest discovery for any man is to find his own note and instrument in nature's symphony, and realize and understand that he is a part of her manifestation and creation. When this is discovered, its application is exceedingly simple. It exists as a harmonizing essence within nature's bindery note, which dissipates misunderstanding and contention.

If men would only sit down in harmony one with another, all differences would fade away and a natural understanding between man and man would result. Where there is peace there is also prosperity and an eagerness to acquire knowledge. This is the foundation of man's true character and expression. This force in nature is the fulcrum of the universe, and its activity and knowledge can be gained, and its harmonizing effect be perceived by all men.

It is this force that will unite the lion and the lamb in peaceful contentment, for it will abolish fear[29] and give the power of discrimination, which is the power to stand alone. It is said that Yogis who receive large gifts of money from their disciples lose the power of discrimination, for the donor so gains power over the donee. It has been written that money is the second power in this world as wisdom is the first, hence the power to stand alone in the Presence is difficult to attain.

In Asia, on the boundaries of Tibet, there is a place known as "Heaven." It is the supposed abode of the immortals, the men who never die. A friend of mine, a great traveler and teacher of Yoga, went there with two companions and tried to enter the place. When they arrived at its natural wall a being appeared and spoke to them in perfect Sanskrit, telling them that they must not try to come further. One may well ask if these, through great tribulation, are not now perfectly attuned to the bindery note of nature?

---

29   Fear is an invitation to suffering.

CHAPTER THIRTY

THE DISCORDANT NOTE IN NATURE

We have mentioned before that plane of consciousness which intensifies pleasure and, when tapped, enables our minds to understand its gratification. Few people in the West have been able to tap this power which is akin to nature's will and is far greater than electricity. This is symbolized as "the hidden fruit within nature's veil." Running parallel to this consciousness is a vibration in nature which can be called the discordant note. These opposing vibrations exist even in the light rays. Thus, most men, knowing little of their rightful heritage, "see through a glass darkly." But to the earnest Yoga student nature will lift her veil and receive him into her consciousness.

White light can be broken down by means of the prism, the colors of the spectrum analyzed, and the existence of destructive colors demonstrated. Here, as elsewhere in nature, the destructive factor is controlled by its fellows, so that its destructive force is neutralized. For instance, the color green is the bindery note in light, and it exercises control as a policeman controls the traffic in the streets. There is much significance in this when we consider how the vegetable kingdom consummates its aspiration in greens of various tones.

Science informs us that other colors in the spectrum control and make harmless its destructive member. In like manner nature seeks to control her destructive factors by negating their activity, but when we draw upon these destructive forces with our human minds, we bring their intensity to birth within ourselves. These forces are Jupiterian in their influence and intensify destruction. But the beneficent higher counterpart of these forces is also Jupiterian and thus stimulates our creative faculties and powers of expression. If we harbor hatred and malice in our hearts, these forces work our own destruction. Hence, each man is master of his fate. It affects our minds according to our true merit. Consideration of this may throw light on "the good of evil and the evil of good."

The younger musicians of today are an example of the working of this Jupiterian force, for very few composers have made their jazz music beautiful, whereas the original jazz played by the negroes of Africa, in their natural surroundings, had great beauty and dignity. The radio is introducing into the sacred precincts of our homes certain forms of the lower jazz music in which this false note in nature is found and accentuated, and such music, intensified by working through the lower instincts and uncontrolled imaginations of our jazz composers, causes us and our children to suffer.[30] The white race, influenced by the spiritual music of the negroes, has become degenerate and the minds of many composers have been overshadowed and intensified by this false and destructive note in nature; the devas say, "by a wrong use of mantric rhythm." We must not forget that the use of this rhythm by a beautiful mind can intermittently bring real beauty to birth in the minds of listeners. Some of Irving Berlin's compositions are comparable to some of the best music of the negro race. It has been through music that some of the initiates have molded the minds of humanity. The Cingalese music would assist greatly in eradicating this false strain from jazz music but man, in his ignorance, distorts noble things, and through the radio he forces them upon the seclusion of our home life. In Debussy's compositions we find the influence of the Cingalese music, which he first heard at the Paris Exposition.

The higher counterpart of destructive activity being Jupiterian, its justice is distributive. For instance, rather than allow some member of a family, in which there is discord, to be inflicted with the clan consciousness of the family, it separates him from them and sends him out into the world.

The Egyptians symbolized the destructive and distributive powers in nature by placing the "swelling asp" next to the sun. We must remember that we become what we aspire to become and it is only aspiration for Truth that will unfold a knowledge of nature's laws to us. Science is also constructive when controlled, but destructive when uncontrolled. Aspiration for temporal power has brought about poison gas warfare

---

30 All modern popular music originated from this lower "jazz."

and the most destructive forces which the scientific mind of man can conceive. Thus, when destructive forces are placed in the hands of the ignorant, they endanger the peace of the whole world. Again, the conquest of the air was quickly cursed by its use in demolition warfare. A great discovery becomes a danger to all humanity and to our own civilization, when not used for the good of mankind. Atlantis perished through the wrong use of things designed for good, and nations that use beneficent discoveries for evil purposes will follow her example.

In the book of nature we read of a great discovery which is to be made known to man. It is something which, if used by man for the good of others, will ennoble him to selfless purpose, but selfishly used it will cast him into oblivion. Nature, the lawgiver, has an exact science to give to humanity and this new "lightbringer" to our world of darkness has already arrived over our Eastern horizon.

When man recognizes that his physical body is a vortex of all animal instincts, but that he has been endowed with a creative and controlling mind, by the exercise of which he can resolve all discordant conditions, he will have gained the right to enter into this land of discovery, which is so near. No matter how ignorant he may be now, he must take steps to *know himself*, in order that he may consciously mingle with the gods, and God's promise of emancipation be realized.

We must not forget that on the causeway to nature's consciousness there stand two elemental lords of nature. One is beneficent, the other forbidding.[31] The destructive and the distributive elements of nature, analyzing our character of expression and aspiration, would seek to turn us back until we have perfected our hearts through experience in the world and fortified them by the analysis of our experiences. When we approach the beneficent guardian we are challenged to show our credentials and, if worthy, through right conduct and action towards our fellow beings, we are welcomed into nature's consciousness.

---

31 The elemental advocate and the dweller on the threshold.

In order to enter nature's consciousness the student must
have three times the energy of a normal man. He must conserve
his natural forces[32] and evoke physical, mental, and spiritual
power through developing the latent energy within him. For
instance, in this world we see by means of our physical eyes,
but in the finer states of matter we see by the "third eye."[33] This
third eye, while distinct from, functions in conjunction with
the pineal gland, and gives us what is called higher clairvoyance,
for it is the higher counterpart of our human eyes, and sees and
visualizes things in a manner quite different from them.

Linked to this higher clairvoyance is the consciousness of
the *knower,* which is within. By aspiration, and a Yoga process of
breathing, this clairvoyance is quite easily attained, but there are
certain laws regarding its use.[34] This higher clairvoyance is an
instrument which is quite difficult to attune to the atmospheres
with which we are constantly associating and there are certain
things we cannot see in the early stages of development. As one
seer has said, "It is difficult to see for that person whom I love
most, and in whose atmosphere I have passed most of my life,
but it is easy to see for any person with whose atmosphere I am
not familiar."

It is seldom that the great souls can see for themselves, or
know their own fate. It is only just a little while before the seer
departs from this earth, perhaps a year or two, that this knowledge is made known to him, and Yogis often foretell the day and
hour of their departure, which they refer to as "birth into life."
Jesus was such an example. At the death of a true Yogi there
are manifestations which show his pupils the exact state of his
development, especially if he had gained union, or God realization while in the body.

Always the student must be careful in projecting his mind
to another person for, as you enter that person's thought
atmosphere, your mind is carried along the pressure lines of
his thought. A friend of mine, who is a Scotland Yard official,
spends much of his time tracking down offenders against the

---

32 At the time this book was written, it was forbidden to reveal the precise
nature of these "natural forces."
33 A center of atomic force between the physical eyes.
34 Described in *The Dayspring of Youth.*

law. I have met very few people who are as quick in their observation of things around them. He will enter my room and surprise me by noticing the absence of any article which has been removed from it since the time of his last visit. When I think of him, I see him at work. Perhaps he is disguised as an immaculate butler, or as a tramp, but I follow the pressure lines of his mind and pick up the conditions where his mind is placed. Thus I not only pick up atmospheres of evil and ignorance, scintillating with the brilliancy of minds of criminal instincts, but I also pick up the horrors of the elemental conditions around these people. I see the lower forces of elemental nature, twisting, writhing masses, obsessing forces, powers of titanic strength, seeking human expression. It is very easy to contact these conditions so that they enter one's atmosphere. My friend is seemingly immune, but I always feel that they may get the mastery of him someday, if he is not very careful.

Therefore we must be careful in our thoughts towards others, for many ignorant people, in trying to assist those who are evil in thought and deed, have taken over their evil obsessions. Of this I have had personal observation for I have known people who, through trying to assist others, have brought on themselves conditions of hell and despair. Strange to say, I have found these cases among the amateurs of Christian Science. Therefore, great is the mind that can let every other mind alone, but greater still is the mind that has learned to stand alone.

Many families have suffered the torture and misery of having the habitual drunkard in their midst, not only while he was living, but afterwards when supposedly dead. You can pick up conditions where your thoughts are placed; therefore man, with a one-pointedness of mind, should seek the kingdom within and should not let his mind become a mental highwayman, seeking to interfere with the mental activities of others.

People in the ecstasies of so-called conversion sometimes band together for the express purpose of bringing mental pressure to bear on others. This is a most unwarrantable interference in other people's affairs, for our attitude towards the beliefs of others should be that of love and tolerance.

When you respect men, men will respect you, but when you try to prevent a soul from gaining the experience for which it incarnated, you bring upon yourself the enmity of that soul. The soul desires freedom above all things, and particularly freedom of expression. In the commandments of nature you are told the things that you shall do, and the two commandments of the Master Jesus were, "Thou shalt love the Lord thy God with all thy heart and with all thy soul, and with all thy mind, and with all thy strength." This is the first and great commandment. And the second is like unto it, namely this, "Thou shalt love thy neighbor as thyself."[35] If you love your neighbor as yourself, you will not try to interfere with his freedom of body, mind, or spirit.

We cannot assist others until we can stand alone; not only must our motives be good, but our actions must not be wrong, else we shall be like Tom Hood's monkey, which felt it was so wrong for animals to be caged that he sought to liberate them, beginning with the lion. However, by the time he had unbolted Nero's cage, Nero had "bolted" him.

35　Mark XII:30.

CHAPTER THIRTY-ONE

THE YOGI'S DISCOVERY IN NATURE

In the practice of Yoga we often make discoveries which startle us. Seeking union with nature the student begins to make contact with those fixed principles which exist in nature's environment (natural law), and he discovers that when he aspires for union with the Lord God of Truth within, his "natural man," through the consciousness of nature, begins to ally himself with his human mind. He begins to forge a link of union between the elemental man (nature's counterpart) within himself and the human individual as we know him, and he seeks to establish his sun and moon nature.

At the baptism of Jesus with water by John the Baptist, the union of the human and the natural man was accomplished, and early Christianity called this the "descent of the Holy Ghost."[36] It was by this union with nature's consciousness that Jesus, having command of nature's will, was able to perform miracles.

When we consciously travel out of our body we perceive the splendor and brightness of the light about us, and sometimes we hesitate and look back at our physical body, as we would look at a curiosity, for we look at it now from a very different viewpoint. We see ourselves as others see us, and we are surprised to realize how indifferent we feel towards our physical body. Out of the body we are free, and can travel with great speed to any place we desire. We are alive to what is going on in the different atmospheres through which we pass, but reentering our body is like passing from light into darkness and oblivion for a time. We then find, however, that we have no longer fear of death, as taught in childhood, and we are fully conscious of the elemental side of our being; but on reentering our body this seemingly disappears.

The world little realizes the brilliancy of those adepts from many nations who work out of their bodies for the welfare of their own country. At the present time there are many men, connected with the staffs of certain armed nations, who are brilliant

---

36 Jesus' baptism with fire was a later initiation.

in their work of espionage. Out of the body they discover the hidden arsenals of a nation, and can inform themselves of the latest inventions. But there is a law regarding such activity and our world is overshadowed by the great immortal beings who watch over its development. They do not allow the destructive forces to crush out the well-being of the youthful inhabitants.

Yet the world must be allowed to suffer until nation shall call to nation in love. It is only through the experience of suffering that man can be brought to realize that nature's laws cannot be broken with impunity. Man, through ignorance, constantly breaks nature's commandments, until through suffering he seeks to obey her great command to "Be honest, with yourself and others!" Until man practices honesty between man and man, he will suffer the scourge of nature's flail upon his flesh.

The Indians were far wiser than the white man, for they did not recklessly destroy. The early white settlers exterminated the buffalo, and dug up the buffalo grass to plant wheat. Today nature has taken her revenge, for famine and drought have ensued, owing to the transference of alien wheat into alien soil, which nature had intended to be planted with buffalo grass in order to conserve water. The roots of the buffalo grass went 18 inches deep into the soil, and thus found nourishment through dry spells, while wheat penetrates only about four inches and is destroyed.

Men of science have prophesied that unless something is done, parts of America will be a desert within two hundred years, but they do not tell us how to avoid this. The answer must be found by contacting nature. When we aspire to the God of Truth through nature, she begins to build around us a shield of protection, and this brings about a union of consciousness between nature and man.

The Yogi is aware of the fact that he is a part of nature, and that she lives, moves, and has her being within him, and he slowly comes to comprehend her movements and intelligence. There is more than most people are conscious of in the phrase, "close to nature." The man who lives close to nature is the natural man, and when we meet him we find that he possesses something which had hitherto escaped our observation. These men are gentle, yet strong, contemplative, yet active in their movements, and there exists in them a harmony and a natural understanding of things which the city man does not possess.

We also find these characteristics in those who live on or near the sea. I have found culture in the hut of a Cape Cod fisherman, and among the shepherds and weavers of the Highlands of Scotland. Often these people are a challenge to one's intelligence.

As a boy I lived in the farming community of Concord, Massachusetts, gathered mushrooms in Emerson's front yard, and listened to the friends of Emerson and Thoreau relating anecdotes. These people were dear, cultured men and women of nature, living in an atmosphere impregnated with thought. As a boy I once told my uncle that I had read Thoreau's books, but could not understand how he could possibly live on twenty-five dollars a year. My uncle answered that when he went on Sunday afternoons with Emerson to see Thoreau at Walden Pond, they always took him a basket of good things. Thoreau was an example of a man who had partly unified himself with nature's consciousness. Walt Whitman was another.

CHAPTER THIRTY-TWO

ADVENTURES INTO TRUTH

Within the Yoga student there is always the spirit of adventure which comes, not as a pioneer exploring uncharted seas and land, but in the form of an approach to the uncharted seas and lands of knowledge. In other words, he is a pioneer or explorer into the realms of Truth.

As the student progresses in his study and in his quest for knowledge, he is given access to a newer type of information. He becomes conscious of a progression of thought which carries him into the solar intelligence, and he finds that he is able to advance into the consciousness of the future. In his instruction periods of observation the student often is shown the things that are to be.

The student sees nature's movements and manifestations in the form of a pronouncement, a something which IS; and he is shown the development of a newer type of individual which is becoming. The future man, responding to his aspiration for truth and knowledge, will become a being whose mind will be individualized according to his worth, as viewed from the consciousness of natural law.

At the present time each human being is judged according to that degree of physical perfection to which he has attained, yet man as an individual is to become a standard of the "sun" type, and the collective forces in nature are even now uniting humanity into groups and forms suitable to their natural expression.

When a man dies his individuality allies itself to his own true nature and mind, but also, amongst the living, nature's collective units are working to unite man to his true collective group expression. Seeing into the future, the Yogi measures and analyzes the intelligence in these different groups. Face to face with people of a similar nature of expression to himself a man is either tortured or stimulated by his environment, because it is similar to his own nature. If man seeks knowledge and aspires for good, he will find himself upon his own level of aspiration, and his associates will be similar to his own nature. Thus men of knowledge associate together, and those in ignorance associate with those who do not have the knowledge of good.

In this way nature rewards and punishes mankind, for it is her intention to reveal to man his own true relative expression in nature. If man indulges in his evil instincts, he gradually loses his freedom and comes under the jurisdiction of a dictator, whom he must obey. Since happiness is the ultimate end of man's evolution, he eventually realizes that happiness can only come from freedom of individualized expression.

Poor pigmy man, standing alone in his ignorance of the law of karma! In the years between 1666 and 1766 the British alone imported into British, French, Spanish, and American settlements above three million slaves. A quarter of a million died on the voyage. Between 1766 and 1860 the total can hardly be credited. But by the law of cause and effect the people who enslaved these negroes must bear the penalty of being slaves to other minds, for nature is the lawgiver and her penalties are according to the law. To profit by her teachings man must make alliance with nature and recognize her intelligent overlordship.

In his ignorance man knows not that nature is urging him and that myriads of eyes in nature are watching him. Like the ant he is building his mounds in nature's thoroughfares, where they are bound to be trampled down by the feet of time.

Thus nature, in her march, is administering justice. Man is getting meted out to him the treatment which, in present and past lives, he has meted out to others. In similar manner, the justice of God is sifting the stars, enlightening some and clouding others. The spirit thus enlightens the minds of some, while darkness closes in on others, so that in them even greater ignorance of the law prevails.

CHAPTER THIRTY-THREE
CONSTRUCTIVE AND DESTRUCTIVE FORCES

The devas who work for the good of humanity are constantly opposed by the titanic forces which exist in the lower levels of consciousness.

The atoms of these Titans within the earth constantly seek liberation and they find their way into the higher levels of our atmosphere. Moisture becomes clouds, the electrical potential becomes overcharged, and the breeze becomes a gale. Then these titanic forces are gathered into a unit of manifestation. In their return to the lower counterpart we get thunder and lightning, wind and rain. The enslaved energy in these atoms is the cause of the destruction caused by the lightning, the wind, and the rain. When manifesting as destructive elements they constantly work against the constructive efforts of the devas. These titanic forces are enslaved by the attraction of the earth which causes them to return to their proper spheres. Then it is that they seek to destroy what is beneficial to humanity, so the lightning becomes a bolt, the rain becomes a deluge, and the gentle wind a hurricane, bringing disaster in their wake.

Here we see the forces of the underworld in nature, and its rivulets of energy accumulating in the form of lightning, wind, and rain, flow back to their original source. Atoms attract atoms of similar nature and, their accumulated forces once unleashed, become seemingly uncontrolled energy, but eventually they must return to their prison house.

There is intelligence in everything and all atoms have intelligence. These Titans in nature are no exception and like the denizens of earth, air, fire, and water, they can communicate with the Yogi. Science today imagines that eventually it will annihilate the atom. They can photograph its radiation and measure the energy it throws off, but they have not yet been able to photograph the atom itself. Science tells us that it gives off radiation as the sun does, but science has not discovered the third power in nature which we have spoken about, which, in many ways, is the higher counterpart of what we call electricity. When scientists discover this, they will learn much concerning those powers which exist at the North and South Poles of our sphere, and also the arc of radiation which exists around the belt of the Equator. Science knows little of the titanic forces of our earth which some day will be discovered and analyzed. We know that man has evolved into spheres of consciousness above the animal, and that in the finer states of matter beings exist who have evolved beyond us. Beneath our feet is the subhuman world, where there are beings whose nature ranks below that of the animal kingdom, beings with faces of the color of lead. When great evils, such as war, manifest upon the earth, these low intelligences become extremely active, for whatever happens upon the earth radiates into lower as well as into higher worlds of being.

Upon leaving the body in full consciousness we pass through three belts of illusion which surround our earth, inhabited by the astral forms of men and animals. Spirits will often ask us what is going on in the world above them, and sometimes we are accompanied back to our bodies by discarnate beings who have reached a higher state in the knowledge of Truth. The spirits of the lower sphere will fall on their knees in reverence to these bringers of light. Sometimes the student will see groups of these earthbound intelligences, and their spokesman, clad in a Georgian costume, will ask, "Whence comes the Light?" Sometimes these bringers of light who accompany us back to our bodies will answer their plea and remove the more trying of their earthbound conditions.

It is quite easy to analyze a man's true nature when he has passed over, for he then expresses his true character which he had so cleverly hidden in his earth life. In the lower levels beneath our feet where evil dwells, the student encounters beings which have an evil beauty, the intensity of which they can magnify.

In these spheres the intensity of evil is easily measured and studying these conditions teaches the student to recognize the evil nature in the faces of mankind, which would not be perceived by the ordinary observer. It teaches him the marks

by which an evil man or woman may be recognized at a quick
glance and he finds many, especially in the younger generation today, that are consciously or unconsciously en rapport
with the great submerged evil beneath their feet. He learns
to understand the "Pan" type in men and the "faun" type in
women, which some people call changelings. They are types of
good and evil—male bodies ensouled with feminine instincts—
female bodies ensouled with male instincts.

Just as the student recognizes that the middle zones of
nature consist of that material through which man appre-
hends Truth, so likewise the higher deva creation use it as the
medium to communicate their desires to humanity.

It is like the quartz in the early wireless crystal sets, which
adjusted the higher vibrations so that they became audible. In
time the student harmonizes himself with this zone in nature,
which is the natural "sounding board" between gods and men.
In Yoga practice, by a process of breathing and aspiration, the
student adjusts himself and changes his own natural note and
vibration into that of a higher octave, and if he is fortunate in
the perfection of his own instrument, he can present himself
to, and register the Presence.

This brings to him a nirvanic state of bliss and intelligence.
Just as the wiser members of humanity watch to discover
youth in whom they can discern signs of genius, so likewise
the higher intelligences in nature watch over humanity, and
recognize the "bright lights" immersed in darkness. When the
student gains his higher perception of clairvoyance, he is able
to recognize in children and in the younger members of his
environment, those who radiate the peculiar light above their
heads. These children are looked upon as the bright lights in
nature, and the Yogi student in his apprenticeship, discovers
that it is his duty to care for the health of these children, and
see that their psychic vision is not too rapidly developed at the
expense of their bodies.

In one instance, a teacher suggested to a student that he
should go down into the slums of a great city and find work
to do there. He was to remain there until he realized what his
mission meant. For two weeks he wandered around in the

mud and cold till one day behind an old church, a little girl
came up to him and said, "I am Grace, I want you to meet my
mother." He *did* visit the mother that evening and he found
that the girl's nickname in the neighborhood was "St. Grace,"
and that her presence in the schoolroom always brought
about orderly conditions among the other children. Her
mother was a widow, refined and cultured, working as a sales-
woman in a shop, and the little girl did most of the household
work. He found that the child was developing clairvoyance,
and spending too much time in seeing things invisible to the
normal eye, and he saw the earthbound conditions which
presented themselves to her atmosphere. She would say,
"Here is my princess." It was not a princess but a dancing girl
belonging to a temple in India. This student brought about
conditions which made the life of the mother easier and more
remunerative, and "St. Grace" was provided with proper food
and a more beneficial environment.

This is the type of work through which the apprentice
gains much experience, for he learns to rely upon his intuition
and not hesitate. He learns to act at once when called upon
by the higher beings in nature and the guardians of youth,
for the gods say, "It is difficult to find human beings who can
tune in with our vibrations." Much pressure is often brought
upon the student in his early years to make him minister to
the welfare of the bright lights in humanity, and it is by close
relationship with these children that he learns in time to
recognize the marks of genius which many human beings possess and when, with proper help and instruction, they would
be of service to their race.

In middle nature, there are beings and powers which
oppose the constructive work of the devas and also watch for
these bright lights in humanity. As they have power over mind
stuff matter, they often seek to capture and take possession
of the bodies of these "bright lights" to drag them down
into their sphere of consciousness. Many of these promising
children, especially those living in rural places, disappear, and
their bodies are taken over by the beings of this lower middle

world. They are often slightly deformed, as are the children wherein the animal world beneath our feet has incarnated.

In the same way that the student discovers the "bright lights" in humanity, he also learns to recognize people with human bodies who are really elemental beings under their skin; they are educated in the atmosphere of this world, but they intermittently live in the world of "fey" people. They show great inventiveness in whatever they do, especially in painting, decoration, and sculpture. In all their work, an unreal reality is portrayed. They love to portray pucks and fauns and other beings of loveliness from the world of "fey." They cannot help putting into their work the fairy elements of nature, be they good or evil. Unfortunately these people are often exploited by the men of commerce, for they are too sensitive to drive hard bargains, and do not recognize the value of their creations. They should be allowed to work out their own destiny in their art and creation. If some wealthy philanthropist would only provide for the necessary care of these changelings, the world would suddenly blossom forth in artistic creations of beauty, the source of which is now so often extinguished by poverty.

Poverty as a rule goes hand in hand with the young artist and painter. He often spends many years in the struggle to acquire mastery of his craft, and yet is often forced to make hencoops for a living! From the "middle" region in nature these changelings often bring over into our world traces of their far distant gleam, but the world denies them their opportunity to *become,* and as they live in two places at once, the world of inspiration and the world of "dog eat dog," they are denied the power to bring their creative genius to fulfillment.

There is always the commercial man who seizes upon and picks the brain of the genius, thereby gaining great fame, honor, and reputation. A famous Continental artist, known all over the world for a certain painting, stole the composition of one of his pupils and painted a picture from it, and the student afterwards committed suicide. There are many changelings who are inventors and they seldom have any business instinct, but we are told by the great teachers that in the future the State will protect these people.

Children will often tell you that they have been conscious of being taken out of their bodies, and that they were frightened at the time. They say that they prayed earnestly to God in their fright, and that beings came and took them away from those who were carrying them, and returned them to their homes. This generally happens after a child has been given a hot bath, for the warmth of the water makes it more easy for it to leave the body, and usually this occurs when the child is not being watched by the mother or nurse. These journeys and the return to the body are never forgotten by those who have had the experience. Many sensitive people disappear and take up their residence in that "middle" region of nature's consciousness. These so-called humans often appear to and are seen by the student, and they talk to him about their work and activity, and speak of their loved ones whom they left behind.

There is a great deal of evidence regarding the vanishing of people into this region of the "Siddhe" and the shepherds of the Celtic races (when you know them) will often discuss these beings of the "middle" realm, who appear clad as they wish to be seen.

We must not forget that after a building has been destroyed, its plan form or astral counterpart exists for a long time in nature, and that often a place which has physically passed away remains in the etheric plane. These places are often infested with earthbound conditions, just as houses are haunted by beings who have passed over, but have failed to physically realize the change. It is like people who love to return in memory to a room that they have been fond of, and visualize the place again. It is a thought projection of ourselves to the place, and we often cause a projection of ourselves to be seen by any sensitive who knows us, for we must remember that *thoughts are things.* As we think we often project our thoughts into the atmosphere, thus making "thought forms," which can clothe themselves with astral substance, and a sensitive person can see the thought formations of his friends which are projected towards him, and recognize the person by the color and form which his thoughts take.

The stirring up of a multitude of people in hatred and anger and the surge of conflicts attract "thought forms" of a like nature from all over the world, and build up in humanity a battery of hatred, malice, and envy—all of which is an ignorant use of good. The very crust of our earth may be shaken by their forces, and this stirs up other energy lying dormant beneath our feet, forming avenues of escape for the entities of the underworld of man.

Nature finds today no security anywhere in mankind, who in time must learn her law and render her tribute. She gives of her plenty to man that he may not starve, yet humanity heedlessly drains her nourishment from the land, changes the channels of her streams, denies her plea for water, and abuses her bounty. Man brings confusion everywhere in her orderly manifestation, and nature's intelligences appear to the seer and weep over the destruction which man creates.

Ungoverned passions and desires bring misfortune and desolation to the innocent and inoffensive population of a land. The policy of nations has been to conserve and build up energy preparatory to a course of action which will bring future desolation, poverty and despair. Nature looks on weeping at the formulation of these plans, and deplores the desolation which has come over her land, where the sun should shine and the voice of peace be heard. When this present period passes humanity will call again to nature for her support, and expect her to begin again to bring forth the fruits of her soil. Man takes no account of the injustice of his treatment of nature; he cares not, and hardens his heart, and he yet expects nature to give and withhold nothing.

Crime beneath us, crime about us! Where is there a man today who will serve mankind? A man who will speak to the multitude, and give them understanding of themselves, and be their apostle of justice?

Man's own "man in nature," when unified with his objective mind, becomes the prophet, the sage, and the lawgiver. Let us seek union with our higher man within, the real man, the real lawgiver, the prophet of peace, that no evil may spring up in the minds of the speaker or the listener, for man can only find his own living God of truth within himself. Such a man who finds his living God of truth will live and have his being in nature's finer essences, and will obey nature's will and commandments. The objective man who seeks his Lord God of Truth within, will harmonize his "natural man" (nature's man) with his objective body and mind.

CHAPTER THIRTY-FOUR

THE LAW OF MAN AND OF NATURE

The student should study nature and follow her example. The great smiling mother will give bountifully of her products, for she knows the future trials and needs of humanity and she prepares ahead that which will supply her children when drought or distress is to follow.

A few years ago she gave her abundance to the people of the United States but humanity, instead of storing the wheat and building warehouses for its keeping, ruthlessly destroyed her bounty. By government order mounds of grain were destroyed by the railway tracks, while there were hunger marchers in Washington. Millions of little pigs were killed and their flesh burned. Then came pestilence and drought, the wind blew away over fifty thousand acres of alluvial soil. Man had destroyed the abundance which nature, knowing the calamity to follow, had provided for him.

In the days of his prosperity and plenty man should not spend his abundance foolishly for pleasure, but should store away a portion of his income for the lean years. He should then be following a law of nature, for when he has abundance it generally foretells lean years to follow. If he provides for them he will not become a burden upon the thrifty members of society, for the years of plenty are Nature's warning to him to warehouse her products, and she penalizes those who waste her gifts.

Experience teaches that eventually the surplus products of the soil are used up, for Mother Nature is mindful of the necessity of the human race. It is man who, in his greed, seeks to corner the markets of the world and upsets the balance.

In Chicago, when speculators forced the wheat market to a dollar a bushel, there was starvation in Italy. The world should seek to form lanes of distribution to meet the law of demand. London, for instance, through modern distribution, is provided with fresh fruit the year around. Within the keeping of nature is that Book of the Law of Conservation, which will eventually be revealed to man. Our religions and the teachings of the great avatars are but fragments of this forgotten truth, excerpts of nature's secret doctrine which, if carried out, would bring freedom to the races of humanity. The fulfillment of nature's command is realized when truth is recognized by the human understanding.

This book is a pronouncement of the law of nature, in which the higher self lives and moves and has its being. It will be given to the Yoga student when he arrives at the realization of Truth, which is justice, and the author has been promised that his book will be given to humanity in the way in which humanity can best receive it.

It is differences of opinion among the leaders of humanity which have brought about disorder and intolerance. Races differ, as individuals do, in their understanding of the law. When the steam engine was invented the ecclesiastical courts pronounced it the work of the devil. The Church persecuted the inventor of the telescope, and made the publication of the discovery of nature's laws a risk of torture. It was not realized that all depends on the use we make of God's benefits.

One of the advantages of the science of Yoga is that when one has attained to an expansion of consciousness, he also knows when his fellow man has attained it. There is no disputing the fact that the attainment of this consciousness advances the student into happiness, and the Knower's realization of Truth.

Many people think that in the pursuit of Truth the Yogi is running away from life, but he is really running into it. He immerses himself into everything which is going on around him, until he becomes a part of it, without separation. He begins to learn what is going on in his own time and sees its effect upon the world. Lincoln warned of the evils of the present day, besides writing about the tendency of his own time. He was concerned for the individual liberty of the citizen.

In the West the little self-supporting communities no longer exist, and many people wonder whether folk were not happier formerly than they are now. Yet city congestion has necessitated hygiene, and through the advance of hygiene man has been able to prolong his life. Thus, by reason of congested living conditions, man has learned one of nature's primary laws; that cleanliness next to godliness is a virtue which brings its own reward.

CHAPTER THIRTY-FIVE

DEVIC GUIDANCE, A KEY TO NATURE

As you seek union with the Truth, think also of the devic creation, with which you have had much intimate relationship in the past. This is a composite form of intelligence which, if you can bring it into your atmosphere, will devitalize the opposition that may come into your presence.

In seeking union with a deva, remember that you are endeavoring to contact the intelligence of an angelic being that exists in an atmosphere or vibration quite foreign and in opposition to the sovereignty of your own place in the physical and mental divisions of your world.

Few people are able to assimilate the devic consciousness, for its power is tremendous and disturbing to the human atmosphere. Seek always to glorify God through these beings or intelligences, for they represent all the nobler standards and ideals to which few men can attain. Therefore, watch that their presence may be known to you, for in the beginning you will get intermittent vibrations from their plane.

These devic intelligences can give you the deeper truths which lie behind the foundations of all society. When you feel such a vibration, let nothing disturb the tranquillity of your mind. Seek union with God through these vibrations, for there is a great need for such union with your man-in-nature. The deva itself is not always conscious of your approach, and you must seek to absorb as much of its consciousness as possible so that a bindery link may be formed between its consciousness and yours. This will open to you certain divisions of your nature, with which you are little acquainted, and remember that within its atmosphere is the brooding spirit which unifies all things in nature's creation.

This is a discovery to which you must attain, for without its power it would be hard to assume any position of real importance in the world. This has been symbolically referred to as "the herald of the dawn" to this new age of discovery into which you are awakening. Your world is foreign to the devas' nature, which has a high standard and witnesses the illusion which man fails to perceive.

To those who have the potentialities for reading and understanding the book of nature, the doctrine of the spirit will unfold itself. The great book of emancipation is given to those who can read, assimilate, and understand the real nature of their being.

The devas, in an age of corruption and wrongdoing, are composed of those atoms which are witnesses of the Law. They understand how wrongdoing developed in humanity, and witness things which cannot be perceived by the human mind. When the student allies himself with nature's understanding he will have a vision which is threefold. With reference to the nature of its being, he will see the beginning and the emergence of a thing into the truth. He will perceive the law of cause and effect operating through it while in being, and will realize that there is also a power which will retire and disintegrate it.

It is necessary that you should unite yourself with the "middle" kingdom within your nature of being, for here the deva can assimilate itself with the outer covering of your atmosphere, so that its presence can be felt, and the activities of its spirit be known to you.

In other words, that which is above unites itself with that which is below, and that which is below unites itself with that which is above; thereby a common ground of understanding is made known to your human consciousness.

You must take a great deal of care in seeking to enter and analyze the nature of truth on its plane, and you must endeavor to sense the relationship which exists between this world of being and that of your lower counterpart, which is the world of humanity at large.

Remember also that this division in nature, symbolized by the devic consciousness, exists in parallel within the finer nature of your being and, in order to unify yourself with this consciousness, you must travel inwardly towards the source and center of your being.

You must also realize that you have within yourself this great emancipation book of the Universe, and when you wish to bring its material into the light of your day, you must aspire inwardly for its manifestation. To enter into nature's consciousness, you must seek out the inner things of the spirit, and not cast your thought outwardly into the atmosphere of so-called conscious nature, which you behold and analyze with your senses.

Deep down within man are those streams of energy which bring to birth in humanity fountains of expression through the voice of literature.

There is one thing which you do not realize, and that is, with the aid of that instrument in nature which you have in your keeping, you have a part and place in the reorganization of human conduct. This power is given you so that you may be able to discriminate between that which is false, and that which partakes of the truth.

Through devic guidance man comes to realize that the cell life and atoms which are to be found in his composition have their corresponding positions in the seven divisions of nature, and that he corresponds to nature's embodiment and is a part of her manifestation. Man, in his waking consciousness, has little realization of nature's divisions of consciousness.

At so-called death, however, man makes the discovery that he is a part of nature, and he passes through a period of being reborn into her consciousness. This is why people who have passed over find it difficult to adjust themselves to the new environment. After the age of seven years, when boys and girls merge themselves deeper into the consciousness of this physical and mental world, nature withdraws from them, although a few people retain their link with nature's consciousness during their human life.

This is a point we wish to emphasize; when man passes from this earth plane at death, he is slowly reborn into that plane of consciousness through which he had passed before incarnation. We also find that the more developed aspirers for Truth pass quickly into the nature of their being, and that is why they seldom communicate with their loved ones on this earth. Humanity in general is not aware that when we pass out of our body in sleep we can, if worthy, associate in the finer spheres of nature with those whom we love, but when we come back into the confusion of this world we do not retain, unless trained, the memory of our conversations with those who are now evolving in the finer states of consciousness.

When the ignorant person, with a strong passion and desire nature, concentrates upon the loved one who has passed on, he is unconsciously creating a line of communication as in earth life. He is breaking a law of nature by this desire, for with the force of his longing and desire, by personal domination, he is pulling the departed back into the density of our world atmosphere.

Often by concentration of desire upon a beloved one, who has found peace and tranquillity in the finer essence of matter, he is drawn back into our world of tumult and disaster, perhaps into the family atmosphere of self-pity and sorrow, and this will cause acute suffering. If the chamber house of memory could be entered by the ordinary mind, there would return to us memories of those spheres from which we came, memories which usually disappear within seven years after birth.

The little child in his pram can talk to the Yogi by telepathy and often, in the presence of a baby, you are listening to the inarticulate utterances of a wise man or woman. I have often felt myself in the presence of a sage, whose soul was imprisoned and bound in the inarticulate body of the child. We are often asked by the unborn child to inform its mother what food it needs for the deficiencies of its body, or the type of books its mother should read to it. It will sometimes tell us when it was last incarnated.

These unborn babies will often converse with you in the tongue of their last incarnation and one said to me, "Tell mother that my body will be deficient in a certain property, which swine's flesh fed on acorns will give me." It spoke in old English, and it told me that it wished to be named Alfreda.

These unborn babes will also inform you of the things which should not be done to the child as a baby, because of prenatal shocks. For instance, a pregnant woman got a chill from the water being too cold in her bath. This sudden immersion caused the unborn child to suffer. After this child was born, the mother, forgetting this incident, squeezed a spongeful of cold water over its head in its bath. The baby became hysterical with fear, and she then remembered the warning.

Sometimes when the child passes on at birth, it will ask that the mother should be given the message, "I will try to come again." The Yogi often converses with these souls who are to incarnate, and he becomes quite attached to them, for they are whimsical like the "little people," the fairies in nature, and bring a purity into his atmosphere. We seldom see these children seeking incarnation in the atmospheres of men and women of evil nature. In such atmospheres we see half developed and half human entities, which seldom show themselves more than a foot above the ground, crawling in the slime of a dank and fetid pool. These are denizens of the underworld who seek an entrance into our spheres of consciousness.

Often we see malformations which can be applied to the human frame; creations consisting of a combination of the human and animal of the lower elemental worlds. These forms often inflict themselves upon a sensitive man on waking. They seek to becloud the sensitive with their atmosphere and try to influence his personality by contacting him with some other character, which is not of the nature of his being.

An evil man, who died a leper, brought his atmosphere to impress me with the vision of what was once his face, and asked my help. When such an one asks for help it should be given freely. In time you will learn to love these poor monstrosities, whom disease has malformed, as you observe the slow awakening of their bedimmed consciousness. They tell us that there are very few who will love and help them, and that many drive them away. The Yogi often finds himself speaking to vast audiences in those spheres where the light is dark. I know a lady who is very much of this world, but "out of the body" I have listened to her orations to great audiences, in a world where midday is like a London fog. Many people, unrecognized in this world, are working out of the body in the deeper states of consciousness to bring the hope of peace to these people of the underworld.

One of the severest trials of the Yoga student is the conquest of fear, for when he has attained to a slight degree of consciousness of the light, the moths of the underworld see it, and flutter about his candle. Many sensitive people, suddenly seeing these apparitions, have suffered shock. The less cultured members of society who loved coarse jokes, when earthbound, like to try their jokes on sensitives who can see them. They are like boys who hide behind trees and jump out with a shout upon some lovelorn swain to give him a fright. Their antics resemble the sadism which most boys display at about the age of fourteen. So we find these jokers dressing themselves up as pirates or highwaymen and trying to frighten the sensitive.

Whenever you see an apparition of this kind, quietly send your love to it, and then it will reveal its true nature, whether good or evil. I was once privileged to sleep for six months in a hut in a churchyard and my work, each night before going to bed, was to go through the churchyard to break, when merited, the linga sharira thread which held the astral body to the corpses.

The clergy in the Protestant churches know little of the science of liberating the soul from its tomb, but in the olden days the sonorous intonations of the mass and the tolling of the church bell brought this about. This is why cremation should be advocated, as this releases the astral body from the corpse.

When a man died in the early Christian days, if the priest considered him worthy, he could be helped out of the body and piloted through the three purgatorial belts of illusion which surround our earth. Among the death scenes I have witnessed I find that the seemingly devout Christian fights for life. He is afraid of death, which should be welcomed. If a man earnestly aspires for Truth there is nothing to fear in death, for it is an awakening into those spheres which his just deserts merit.

People will dogmatically state what they expect after death, yet, because they never take the trouble to observe things about their physical plane, they know little about life. If people realized what emanations of a lower elemental nature arise from churchyards, they would not bury the dead in the midst of the living.

Sometimes ill people are taken into hospitals or nursing homes and placed on a bed in which a person has recently died. The room may have been used for some time and magnetized by the thoughts of the former occupant. A normal person placed on that bed for a minor operation, if sensitive, may take upon himself the atmosphere which his predecessor left behind. The room may have been properly cleaned and disinfected, but a person who has passed out in a state of delirium seeks to return to his old bed, and it is difficult to remove such an atmosphere.

In my travels I have often found a bed which I was to sleep in, already occupied by the passion and desire body of a being who would ask me what I was doing in his room. He did not realize that he was dead. Also, I have found supposedly uninhabited houses haunted by old people who have passed over. It is their passion and desire body, known as a spirit, which remains behind.

We find also through clairvoyance that the astral form of an old building, which has been pulled down, still exists, although another house may have been erected on that spot. This astral form is often inhabited by a spirit who may tell you that there is a bag of sovereigns back of the skirting board behind the washstand, even although to the normal eye there is no washstand. Clairvoyantly, however, we could see a fragment of the old room, with its green washstand and when we mentioned the green washstand the spirit (an old lady), in great excitement said, "Yes, it is there." She had been a miser and did not realize that another building had been erected upon the site of her old home. A miser is difficult to help.

Sometimes we also talk to the gnomes, an elemental people whose habitat is the mineral kingdom. They may take you to a very old ruin which, to them, remains as it was in its days of prosperity, for its astral form still remains intact. Perhaps they will show you where things of value were hidden in the past and are often surprised that you cannot see things which they register.

They may show you treasure which to them remains intact, as well as treasure which our living friends may possess. In Scotland one of these friendly gnomes accurately described to me the treasure chest of an old Scottish family, and when I went to see this friend and told her what the gnome had said, she got the chest, which she said had not been opened for two and a half years. We found that the gnome had been accurate in his description. He had particularly described an ornament that had once belonged to "the Bruce." In speaking of my friends he would say that their bodies were made up of precious stones and certain minerals.

I wish that humanity in general were as honest as my friend, the gnome. While he could magnify the qualities of sincerity and honesty, the charming thing about him was his enthusiasm over everything which was going on around him. He had the wisdom of an old man and the enthusiasm of a child, and he had the power of foretelling whenever I was going to travel into the land of the fairy folk. He could tell me where the elemental conditions were good, and where they were evil, and he also told me to beware of the gnomes that had pot bellies and legs like frogs. His great interest lay in the Christian religion and its observances.

He knew a great deal about the secrets of levitation, which he called a change of vibration, or the bringing into the student of a vibratory arc where the lines of vibration converge to one point to counteract the pressure of the earth traveling through space. He did not speak of gravitation as we know it and I asked him if a man standing at the North or South Pole would be blown off the earth. He replied, "That force which is back of the vacuum pushes the earth along."

He told me also that this force which propels the earth will propel the airplanes of the future, and that the Atlanteans of old knew this secret. He said that the future airplane, when it gets this "push" from that which is back of the vacuum, will propel itself and that its design will be quite different from that of today. He often spoke as if the earth propelled itself through space. I do not know if he is correct, for I have never investigated the source of this information. This gnome was educated by the monks in St. Edmund's time and had access to books which have passed beyond our ken. He would often bring these books to me, and putting on a pair of spectacles to appear wise, he would read me what the ancients had written.

Whenever I told him that I was going to Ireland, he would dance with glee and go through a pantomime showing the pains and sorrows of the poor people there. He said that the gods walk there in the sheltered places at daybreak. He is cosmic in his happiness, as well as in his sorrow, and his consciousness seemingly extends over a long range of time. Although he is fond of bedecking me with ornaments, and will suggest certain qualities and virtues which he wishes me to attain, he also brings a touch of sadness.

He hopes that I may attain to the Light which is back of all creation. He sometimes gives me a blessing as if he were a prelate, but I cannot analyze the kind of a prelate that he wishes to express, for his costume was of a period which I did not recognize. It was rather like some old Celtic priest, then he changed to the period of St. Alban. When departing he always shakes his hands together.

CHAPTER THIRTY-SIX

DEVIC DOORWAYS TO TRUTH

The student, as he travels from the North towards the
Equator, and from the East towards the West, passing from
one country to another, will notice a change in elemental
nature.

The devas assume a costume of the nature of the division
in which they have taken up their habitat. The costume in
which they clothe themselves when appearing to a student
is most pleasing. As each country differs in character the
devas clothe themselves in color, and each costume differs.
For instance, to the artist the devas, especially the three great
ones who are working over Ireland, portray themselves in a
deeper range of color from that which we find in England or
America.

The Irish devas show themselves in a color which is of
a strong metallic hue, such as we see in early stained glass
windows, and the greatest density is at the bottom of their
robes, where you see the metallic blues and greens, which
decrease and become lighter as you approach the head. The
high lights of the folds of the costume are of a pinkish gray.
We sometimes get this effect in fabrics woven in two colors
like in shot silk, the folds appearing gray when the two colors
are complementary.

The devas in Ireland impress you with the depth of their
knowledge of the present, past, and future. They show you
their work in bringing peace out of disturbed conditions, and
they will impress you with the conglomerate foundation of
races, which they divide roughly into two divisions, classified
as Good and Evil.

They will show you good influences in races, nullifying
disturbing ones which the "dwellers in darkness" have left
behind them. They will show you the Golden Age long before
Christianity, and also the renaissance of that age in the early
Christian days.

Ireland today is still a place of pagan worship. At the side
of its holy wells are to be found bushes and trees hung with

strips of clothing from the diseased bodies of those who pray for help at these shrines. Later Christianity invariably built churches on holy places of pagan origin, for the early saints knew the efficacy of these sacred places.

At the Rock of Cashel today stands an ancient Druidic altar, on which the Munster Kings were crowned. Placed on it is one of the earliest Christian crosses, on which the figure of Jesus is clothed, as is always found on the earliest crosses of Ireland.

The Irish devas are the storehouse of great wisdom knowledge. They instruct the student how the lower knowledge of "the Four Masters," the manipulation of nature's elements, came into the hands of the early monks, who were interested in ceremonial magic. Through the book of the Four Masters they gained scientific knowledge which the renegade monks practiced secretly. In time this book was withdrawn by nature, for its knowledge was used illegitimately. The devas say that instead of becoming a bringer of light, it became the curse of Ireland. Few people know today that these renegade monks could put a curse upon the people who had plundered their seats of learning. These curses have lasted to the third and fourth generation. In such manner good may become evil.

There is a similarity between the lower counterpart of the Four Masters and the Four Horsemen of the Apocalypse. Thus Druidic knowledge filtered into early Christian minds.

The devas say that a great poetess will be born in Ireland, a liberator of the mind of the world, and that her music, strange to say, can be heard today rising out of the earth; this poetess will descend deep into the earth to bring back the gods of wisdom and understanding, like Orpheus and his lute. One of the devas often makes his appearance holding a child in his arms, a girl "who will once again bring music to this land."

In the Highlands of Scotland the devas show you strong men leaving the land and going across the sea in many directions, like militant beings with sheathed swords. They will also show you ancient maps of Britain and Ireland bound together to the continent of Europe, and they impress you with the brooding of the spirit over Ireland, Scotland, and

Wales. In England they impress you with the heel of the
Roman law and scales of justice. But the scales they show you
are not yet balanced.

In America you find the devas working through the youthful minds of humanity, and they show you symbolically a
handful of grain being thrown over the land, and then the
finer kernels are gathered together and sifted, each kernel
according to its stature and strength, and then the sun is
shown shining upon them, symbolizing the sifting and gath-
ering together of the more advanced types of youthful minds.

The moon has a great influence over the treasure house in
nature, for the beings who came over from the moon passed
rapidly through the densities of matter and progressed into
states of consciousness far beyond mankind, but they left
their wisdom records behind them in nature's treasure house.
It is from this chalice in nature's keeping that the devas can
draw information for the Yogi, if he will live according to their
standards. If he does not so live, this wisdom knowledge of
nature is forbidden to him.

Surrounded by illusion and ignorance, the knowledge and
comprehension to which we have attained is very small compared to the knowledge and comprehension of the devas, for
those sentient beings stand always in the presence of truth.
The student quickly discovers this when he can enter into a
higher and finer atmosphere by going inwardly towards his
own kingdom of heaven.

You can feel two divisions of comprehension when you
place your hand upon an ancient Druidic altar which has
not been defiled by modern man. Its vibration separates you
from your own time, and impresses you with a splendor and
brightness alien to our age. You discover vibrating through
you a perception which carries you beyond ordinary realms of
thought, a cosmic consciousness that God is not apart from
his creation—that God is within everything that our senses
register.

We reverence the learning and perception which the Druids
derived from nature. We are told that much of this information is about to be revealed through the younger members of

their torch, and early Christian chivalry symbolized by King Arthur and the Knights of the Round Table will acquire deep significance.

The man in the street little realizes these changes that are intermittently going on around him, or that he is undergoing a change. He must learn that nature changes rapidly and that evolution is not gradual, but intermittent.

Geologists have discovered that ore deposits, especially copper, which thirty years ago were passed as low grade, have suddenly become first class. The alchemical drawings stress the Four Winds, East and West, North and South, and in the Yoga teaching, though veiled and hidden, great stress was laid upon these "winds of heaven." In the physical transmutation of baser metals into gold, great stress was laid upon the recognition of these movements in nature, and of the moment they began their operation. The Yoga student, through observation, should know when to tune in to these currents, in order to attain to their moments of instruction.

Nature revealed her instruction to the alchemists of old who were less worthy, and they knew the grandeur which surrounded them when they sought to harmonize themselves with nature and God. It was from this source that the great alchemists were able to perfect their art, for in their Yoga practice they were able to receive that instruction which brought them to God Realization. They were taught how to see into a thing and realize its activity and position in nature's movements, and by perceiving the spirit, which works through all things, the realization came.

Few people question themselves as to the meaning of life, and as to where we are all going, and why we are chained to this world of illusion. But the student should take notice of what is going on around him and find out toward what goal all things are striving.

The sage says, "Go and seek knowledge; for the attainment of wisdom is the end of all things." Does the student realize that moments are precious? Does he ever consider that this world is but a school room of experience? Some are eager to know the truth, but many allow it to pass unheeded.

There are many doorways leading to Truth, but each individual must find his own and learn how to knock thereon, and how to ask admittance, that he may receive the realization of Truth and attain to a finer perception.

There is a doorway to nature through which the student gains a wonderful realization of the Truth which is in all things. To enter it he must seek to know himself, to be true to himself, to be honest with himself, and he must also be honest with nature and with his fellow man.

The bringers of light, who are within nature, will always stimulate the student to aspire to his "sovereign gold." He must pass through their door of honesty before he can stand in the presence of those upon whom Truth shines. The student is not ready until he seeks truth and honesty in all things. Aspiration for Truth gives him the power of perceiving the truth and falsity in other people. He must face the world in the attitude of a child, seeing and seeking the good in all things. Through his perception of truth he has learned that most of his own sufferings have come to him from his own spoken words, for as he brings himself into a closer union with his own Lord God of Truth within, he becomes doubly sensitive to the things set in motion by his spoken words.

In moments of anger, therefore, the student must learn patience and carefully to guard his speech. There are many invisible powers in nature which direct a man, and he may receive aid from those more evolved. Sometimes four or five people will enter a person's life, in order to bring him the right contact which will bring greater assistance in his higher development. This is a thing learned in Yoga. You may have great admiration for the work a certain person has produced and you feel intuitively that an invisible link is drawing you towards him. Then watch for contacts and, if you are patient, you will find invariably that the meeting of a number of different people will be the means of contacting the friend of your desire. But if you are impatient with the contacts that you meet, you disorganize the work of nature, and probably the soul that you were seeking is not contacted.

A person may be listening to the performance of a great
musician, and may turn suddenly to a friend and say intuitively, "I am going to meet that artist some day." If the student
is sincere in his practice, he will contact those who will assist
him in his quest for knowledge and the greater wisdom.

A man came hurriedly into the home of a student who was
busily engaged on his own work. The student lost his temper
and was not as patient and as courteous as he should have
been. That night a great teacher visited him and suggested
that he had been most impatient that day, and that the whole
career of his visitor had changed, for he had given way to his
lower nature when he found no help coming to him from the
student. To make up for this the student labored for over a
year to assist that man, but the man knew it not.

We are not conscious at first of the instruments which our
higher self uses in nature to assist us on our path, and that
constant devotion to God and Truth brings us the protection
of nature's higher counterpart intelligence. We must remember that great light has been brought to this world through
these intelligences in nature. The Koran was transmitted to
Mohammed from the Lord by the angel Gabriel, that he may
establish those who have believed, and as guidance and glad
tidings to the Muslims; and it is also written, "It beseemeth
not a man, that God should give him the Scriptures and the
Wisdom, and the gift of prophecy, and that then he should
say to his followers, 'Be ye worshippers of me as well as of
God;' but rather, 'Be ye perfect in things pertaining to God,
since ye know the Scriptures, and have studied deep.' God
doth not command you to take the angels or the prophets as
lords."

The inspirers of our great poets and writers have been
beings of nature. They have left symbols in humanity which, if
properly used, will contact these different spheres of a higher
and lower inspiration. Each man has within him a mandala,
or chart, which is a symbol showing his place and position in
nature and resembles the map of his horoscope.

The Yogis of the East, with their clear vision, will present the student with his mandala, or symbolic chart of his

acquirements and his position in nature's consciousness. This marks a point in the student's initiations, and people who have acquired the art of drawing from their superconscious self, often draw their own symbolic charts.

We often see these mandala symbols in Tibetan paintings made by the initiated. However, the working and operation of these symbols is closely guarded by nature's administrators of the law. It is a globe of consciousness of the past, present, and future. In other words, it is a means of linking an atomic filament or line to the student, through which he contacts the intelligence in Nature with which he is desirous of communicating. The reader must remember that the symbols we have here on the earth plane, when properly used, are energized by the intelligence of its higher counterpart symbol, and then the student knows that the line is in working order. Each great nerve center in our body has its own symbol, and is a receiving and transmitting station through which we contact nature. These centers are all linked up with our human brain.

The making of his body receptive to these finer vibrations is always difficult for the student, and the law is that you cannot speak about a thing unless you can demonstrate it. Until one has attained to the knowledge of how to run his motor car, he cannot teach another the intricacies of its operation.

When we pass through the doorway into nature's consciousness we must remember our littleness, for this is the doorway of the bringers of light into this world of little perception. War is going on now in Europe and in China, all the nations are arming, and the people are already burdened with taxation after these centuries of experience. Look you to what little perception man has attained!

But nature's intelligence still vibrates her chord, and some day man will be at peace with his fellows and no longer destroy human life. Nature is severe and shuts down on man's power of perceiving the True, the Beautiful, and the Good, until he shall witness and revolt at the horror of his own bloodstained hands. Avarice, hypocrisy, and greed are at his elbow, while his arms are burdened with the weight of his sword. Therefore, let us each assemble ourselves to become the instruments of peace.

We have read about the dark ages of the past, and in the future people will read about the dark age of the present, when man was a destructive agent, warring against his sovereign, the Lord God of Truth within. Where are the poets to sing again the ideals of chivalry and righteousness among men and nations? Suspicion and jealousy do not dwell in an honest mind, or in an honest nation. Nations should follow the edicts of nature, which are:

That men or nations should stand alone.

That men and nations should be honest and truthful.

That men and nations must seek earnestly for the Lord God of Truth within.

When men and nations follow these precepts they will feel the strength of those great laws of creation at their backs, and they will not, through wars and bloodshed, pass into oblivion.

Poets, as stimulators of our ideals, should not forget that the pen is mightier than the sword! When Harriet Beecher Stowe, authoress of *Uncle Tom's Cabin*, met President Lincoln he said, "So this is the little woman who caused this great war!"

Before a thing is destroyed, something better should be put in its place. The sovereign purpose of nature requires that man must first have the ideal of self-perfection before he will be able to perfect himself in his heart, mind, and body. He must have the aspiration for justice (truth within), before he can become truly just.

He must remember that truth is the sword of justice and that he must first find it within himself, in order to recognize it in others.

He must ever be prepared, without hatred and without malice, to strike with the sword of justice when the cause of right demands, guarding well, however, that his stroke be ever short of vengeance, or oppression.

CHAPTER THIRTY-SEVEN
DIVISIONS OF INTELLIGENCE

When the student has perfected his body and mind, and has been able to pass through the door into nature's consciousness, he becomes aware of the powers and properties which exist within her keeping. In full consciousness he works through the lower levels into the higher spheres of intelligence and, if he is worthy, he comes rapidly into the presence of these higher intelligences.

The wise men of the past have mapped out these higher divisions and have handed down secretly from generation to generation the scientific application of the power, by the use of will and imagination, to contact these different divisions of intelligence. If the student aspires for Truth, and for the light which is within him, he will, when worthy, receive recognition from these overlords of nature, and be given instruction by them. As he develops there will be placed a mark of approval upon him, for when he aspires to the Lord God of Truth within, the infinite and great Reality, he becomes conscious that there exist, in these inner worlds, beings who are evolving into the consciousness of the Reality, and who are regents of the great law of Truth.

Dwelling in a region of light they make themselves known to the student by clothing themselves in elemental matter and appearing to him, just as in the same way the more highly evolved souls can be perceived by the higher clairvoyants clothing themselves in mind stuff matter, so that we can register their appearance.

The same being can show himself as a youth, or an old man, but they generally show themselves in a costume which registers eternity to our minds. A Yogi once showed me a vision of three ancient avatars under whom he was working on tracing his descent. The student is instructed in the use and construction of a symbol, and if its operation is perfect, its higher counterpart is returned to him as a living elemental ensouled entity, of the sphere of intelligence that the symbol represents. If the student is seeking the higher knowledge which is within the keeping of those beings who stand in the presence of the light, he listens in to receive the illumination period of instruction, which is poured into him from this sphere of splendor and brightness.

This science of the use of symbols may be called an absolute science, but knowledge of the practical operation of nature's forces can be given only to the seeker for light. The symbol of the "winged globe" over the doorways of the Egyptian temples contained in its essence all that man needs to know. When we approach nature and study, for instance, the oak tree, we realize why the ancients dedicated this tree to Jupiter, and when man studies it, its atmosphere and character of expression, he gains the courage to face the world and stand upright. It symbolizes much to the seer, for in one way it is a "half-way house to God."

If we look upon virgin gold, its character appears to the student entirely different from gold as seen from the commercial point of view. The student never looks upon it as a commodity. He meditates upon it for the essence of the spirit which it contains. In the vegetable kingdom we look upon the oak tree as having something of the nature of the higher counterpart of gold. The Druids of old recognized this, and with the Greeks, approached it with the greatest reverence, and they also worshipped the mistletoe, which came into its keeping.

At the equinox, when the sun passes into Capricorn, new life passes into the sap and it begins to flow upward in the oak tree. At this time the sacred mistletoe was reverently cut with the golden sickle of the priest and caught on a linen sheet. It was too holy to be touched by the human hand, and from its atmosphere came the prophecies for the New Year.

Men who live among oak trees assimilate their atmosphere of strength, courage, and protection, and take it out into their world. The nation that worships and protects its oak trees becomes like the character of the tree, and is never defeated.

In some future day, scientists will study the type of people which nature's environment produces, and they will recall what has happened to the races which cut down and despoiled their trees. Those nations which have cultivated the oak have withstood the toil and struggle longest. When a country destroys its oak trees, great strength departs from the land.

There are certain shrubs and trees in nature whose atmosphere forms a universal flux, which is allowed to pass through the atmosphere of other trees. They have a power and speed which other trees lack and, when directed by thought, they become messengers of the gods. The hazel rod, the wand of the magician in nature, has an atmosphere similar to the serpent fire in man, and is allied to the third power in nature, the hidden power of which we have spoken, which in man is found below the navel. It is that hidden power which the adepts in judo use to overcome an attack. Judo practice is the power, on the physical plane, of overcoming one's enemy by softness. It is that which is gentleness and that which is strength and, when developed, it is unconquerable in man or nature.

CHAPTER THIRTY-EIGHT

THE WORD OF POWER

In so-called judo, or jiu-jitsu practice (knowledge brought from the hatchet men of China to Japan), the initiated, after two years of intensive training, suddenly shouts the word, "Kaia." Although the student uses this word from the beginning, it does not become a real "word of power" until after two years' training, when he can bring its true vibration from his seat of power in the navel area. The initiated can look at a bird on a branch, shout the word of power, and the bird seemingly paralyzed, drops to the ground. The vibration of this word of power drawn from the navel, when used in combat, causes an opponent to blink and in that moment the enemy is taken unawares.

This is the principle of mantric sound invocation. Even if mantras were written in English and evoked by the student, he would have little chance of gaining their power, unless the sacred knowledge had been handed down to him by an initiated teacher who could demonstrate these things.

The manipulation of sound values and the use of symbols is the basic knowledge back of all real magical ceremonies, for every organism and inanimate object in nature exhibits its own vibratory note, and the student, by higher perception and constant practice, seeks by sound invocation to tune in to these different vibrations.

The devas, and all elemental creations of the different spheres of consciousness, have their vibratory note, and a deva, if we are worthy, will give us its symbol and mantric sound by which we can contact its consciousness and attention.

Some of the spiritual beings which exist in nature have never borne human form. A great avatar has said, "Man was born to have command over the angels." This is true, but the student must know that we do not have command over these beings who have lived on this earth and passed into higher states of consciousness and truth, but, if we are worthy, through compassion they will sometimes minister to our aspirations for God Realization.

A great many of the younger generation today have read books of magic and met experimentalists who have placed before them the idea that "man is greater than the angels." Therefore, through magical ceremonies, they seek to gain power and dominion over elemental beings and spirits, in order to compel them to act as they desire. This is done through mantras and the use of symbols, for spiritual beings have their own rate of vibration, and this secret is often discovered accidentally. Such experimenters may also evoke the lower elementals and spirits, whose abode is in the submerged world beneath our feet. They bring them into their magical circle and seek dominion over them to make them their servants. Unfortunately these magicians usually desire personal power and evoke intelligences of their own nature into the atmosphere of humanity. This is looked upon as black magic.

It is not easy to contact the beings of light who stand in the presence of Truth, but it is very easy to contact the lower natures beneath us and bring them up into our world, where they become a danger to the experimenter and the community, and I advise none to experiment along these lines.

The student can often follow the character of those people who have striven for power by means of magical performances. As we said before, the cleverest magicians on the "black" side of ceremonial magic are those incarnated animal souls brilliant and seemingly human in appearance, who have been liberated from the submerged spheres beneath our feet through magical performances.

Their physical bodies generally have some deformity and, in consulting with their "higher self" you will discover invariably that they have been magicians in previous lives, working contrary to the law. It is easy for them to evoke the denizens of those spheres from which they themselves were evoked into human form.

The denser the atmosphere, the easier it is for the lower clairvoyants to perceive. In Yoga practice it takes discipline of body and mind, will and imagination, to contact the intelligence which exists in the light, for God's messengers appear to the Yogi in full sunlight, but the intelligence of the darkened seance is usually of a low order.

Some mantras, when uttered, bring into activity the different nerve centers of the body, and a real mantra is a preparation for entering into a closer relationship with the Lord God of Truth within. There is a higher counterpart for all physical vibratory enunciations from the human body; that is why in judo practice it takes two years of higher aspiration to gain knowledge from the higher self before the word of power can be properly enunciated.

The world today little realizes the number of people who are engaged in magical practices, often seeking contact with the higher powers in nature but constantly, in ignorance, evoking into our world streams and hordes of undesirable characters, which seize upon and influence such human vehicles as they can find.

These are beings that have a hatred for humanity, beings who have been tortured during their former experiences on earth, and they wage war upon us through those that they can influence. Our prisons are full of such pathological cases. They have some malformation of their psychic structure, for they have left openings through which these entities are able intermittently to obsess and possess them. In magical circles you will often find the operator surrounded by these denizens of the underworld and, instead of their being controlled and subjected to the will of the operator, they often break through the circle and possess the magician and his neophytes.

We have an example of this in certain religious cults. Through singing and vibration, they arouse themselves into a state of ecstasy and for periods become obsessed by outside intelligences and speak with foreign tongues. These obsessing forces are often spirits of the red Indians of the plains, or negroes from the Congo forests. Unguarded emotionalism provides an opening for the lower elemental forces of nature and discordant spirits, and these people have awakened themselves into a state of positive ecstasy.

The Yogi, when he seeks to enter into the presence of
nature's consciousness, is alert and vital in mind and body,
with all his nerves centered upon the aspiration for Truth.
Most people believe that Yoga practice is the shutting down
of the lower mind and body, but the Yogi's first approach
is one of alertness, and the quickening of all his powers for
union with Truth. This positiveness pushes him through the
spheres of illusion to the goal, until he becomes conscious
of the Presence. In the finer spheres, within and without, he
gains knowledge and intelligence; a knowledge of mantric law,
a knowledge of what he should seek and what he should dis-
card, and he realizes the teaching of St. Paul that the kingdom
of heaven can only be taken by force (energy).

A friend once said to me, "Yoga is a process of 'gate crash-
ing' to heaven. I shall sit down and let heaven come to me."
Looking at him I answered, "Where your mind is placed, there
you will be. At the present moment your mind is upon a lady
in Congleton." This may be his particular heaven for the time,
but I do not see it lasting, for he was most attractive to the
fair sex, but back of it all there was a greater desire for Truth.
He was a sailor in a distinguished position of authority. He
had that clear atmosphere which the sea gives to man, as
distinguished from the muddy atmosphere of the city. These
men of the sea have a clarifying atmosphere and are able to
look deeper into the truth regarding nature and man and you
perceive in such men the long ranges of experience through
which they have travelled in their search for knowledge. They
build up in their imaginations positions of power and honor,
but they often illusion themselves in their self-importance,
and they seldom admit that they are wrong.

The right use of mantras in magic leads to freedom, but
the wrong use of them causes one to be ensouled and bound
by the powers the magician evokes. This is the so-called good
and evil magic.

When privileged to meet one's teacher, great stress is laid
upon the care of the body and the use of the imagination, in
order that the body may be strong and healthy. After meeting
their teacher most students do not have enough patience in

the development of the physical body. It is the storehouse of all strength and, although a man may consider himself physically fit, he little realizes how very fit, alert, and reliant the body must be, in order to meet the demands that will be made upon its structure.

Anyone who takes up fencing or judo will understand this. An alert body gives a man the joy of living and, when he begins to feel this, he is ready to take up the serious practice of Yoga and the development of his finer forces and faculties, especially if he has the desire to know Truth. It makes great demands upon him for a time, for he slowly undergoes a complete change of his nature. There comes a time when the light within him is lifted up from its seat in the body and placed between and above the eyes.

We often see pictures of the Buddha in meditation, seemingly looking at the tip of his nose or at his navel, and at first we wonder why these statues of the saint are found in this attitude. The real secrets of Yoga cannot be put into print, but we can suggest certain things which may make the minds of readers of books on Yoga more clear.

The nose is a director, and when a man aspires for Truth and closes his eyes, with his imagination he looks at the tip of his nose, and then following the direction of his nose upward, he discovers that he locates a place between his eyes. His mind stops at a certain point and he does not go further upward. The imagination, the instrument which the soul uses, stops at this certain point where the two channels of the sympathetic nervous system nearly unite. Below the second rib, near the sternum, or breast bone, is the seat of the Lord God of Truth within man, that divine spark of the Reality. As the Yogi, in his aspiration for Truth, follows the direction of his nose upwards towards its root, he lifts up this spark of the infinite and great Reality to this point between the eyes, and he aspires and meditates for Truth, holding the fire at this point, until in time he perceives a radiant spark of light.

Normally you cannot see two objects at the same time, but when you lift the soul up to this point between the two channels of the sympathetic nervous system, a miracle hap-

pens—you can see in two places at once; for the first time you
can see this spark of light, and at the same time you can see
just below the navel.

In the Golden Age, when we obeyed the will of God and
had not developed a personal will, our atoms were of the
likeness of the Golden Age, and as we pass from the Golden
Age into the Silver and Copper, and then into this Age of Iron,
we still retain in this section in our body those atoms of our
Golden Age. A man may possess a steam engine, the boiler
may be filled with water, and fuel placed under it, but it will
be silent until flame is kindled in the firebox. So likewise our
human body must be purified by fire, and from that spark
of light in the forehead, we must bring those golden atoms
within us into a molten condition, until they begin to trans-
mute the coarser element of silver into their own likeness, and
after that the still baser metals of copper and iron.

When this is accomplished, a voltage like static electricity flows upwards and, if controlled, brings life and activity
into the nerve center of the spinal column. As this center is
awakened, a greater voltage is produced, until at last it rises
up through the nerve centers of the central column, and out
through the door of Buddha, or Jesus, at the top of the head,
and our highest aspiration is realized.

When this happens, the student has found freedom and
the soul is no longer a prisoner; it is free to unify itself with
this greater reality. The development of this power should be
undertaken only under the instruction of a competent initiate, one who himself has freedom. Under his guidance the
development is brought about by the proper use and control
of the breath.[37]

Man little appreciates what is going on during the day with
regard to his breath. When he thinks intently, he will discover
that he is shutting down on his breath; he is shutting down
the body from interfering with his process of thinking. "As
above, so below." By aspiration for Truth, man attracts into
his lungs atoms of an entirely different nature than those
which he usually attracts from the environment in which he

37   I.e. pranayama, as taught in the books of Samael Aun Weor.

lives. In time he attracts the finer types of atomic life into his blood stream, as a magnet attracts iron filings, and as the soul desires freedom above all things, man will enter into a new world which was formerly hidden from his vision, for he is now aspiring for union, and seeks earnestly for Truth.

When his body and mind are ready for the higher instruction, then a great soul makes his appearance, and by personal contact gives the student that power for his initial effort to *know himself.* Few people are aware that what a great soul has achieved, he can bring to birth in the less evolved. We see this in the history of the life of Jesus, but very little is known by the uninitiated about those great souls who were prepared to receive him, and carry out his mission in the four quarters of the globe.

CHAPTER THIRTY-NINE

MAGICIANS — WHITE AND BLACK

After the student has sincerely worked at his Yoga practice, he is aware that there are great souls working for humanity, for he becomes conscious of their vibration. For instance, I know of two students who suddenly and simultaneously exclaimed, "A great soul has just arrived at the Ritz." A student can be conscious of the general location of a great soul in his own country, or place of residence, and that he is watching him.

The student often longs to sit at the feet of these great ones and in the early days of his seeking he has often been helped by them, although they never revealed their higher individuality. When he begins his meditations, he seeks to pick up their vibrations and, if he is worthy, he receives communications from these great souls by a system of wireless.

After reading philosophical and theosophical literature regarding these advanced men and women, the student is apt to be shocked at first meeting with them, to find that they are most human and childlike. Sometimes he does not at once realize the summits they have reached, for these men of the Western world live and dress very simply, although they may be connoisseurs of the best of the world's art.

I remember having lunch with one of them. We had soup, but when the second course of fish was to be brought, he turned to the waiter and said, "Give me a double portion of fish, and afterwards some fruit, that is all that I shall require." I looked at him, and he answered my mental question, "I find it better never to mix my meats, and to eat a little less than my normal appetite desires."

He told me of an adventure in his youth with a man in Buenos Aires. Sitting in his office, he could look across the street into the park opposite, and one day he saw a man seated on a bench who interested him. The next morning he walked through the park, and seeing the man in the same place reading, he sat down beside him and spoke to him. The man's clothes were clean, but very much worn, and my friend said to him, "Excuse my inquisitiveness, but may I ask what you are reading?" "Certainly," the seemingly poor man replied, and he handed over a small book, on the title page of which there was an inscription in the author's handwriting, showing that it was a presentation copy. The author was Maurice Maeterlinck, and he had written, "To my dear friend X——, in appreciation, Maurice Maeterlinck."

My friend, who was a clairvoyant, said to him, "You have a rupture." "Yes," the man replied. My friend took out his card and wrote on it the address of a surgeon, and a short note asking the surgeon to fit this friend of his for a truss. Two or three days afterwards he met the man seated in the same place and he asked if he would accept a small gift of money, as he seemed undoubtedly very poor. He was thanked but was told that he had no need for money. The following day he again saw out of his window the man sitting in the same place, but then he found a telegram which demanded his presence on one of his ranches one hundred seventy miles away. He accomplished the journey partly by motor and partly by boat. When he arrived at his ranch, there, seated on the top step of his porch, was the man he had seen seated in the park that morning! He told me that it was practically impossible for any normal man to have gotten there quicker than he had.

The master who met him on his own porch is one of these great souls who are working for the enlightenment of the younger minds and their security in South America, and this great teacher has been an overshadowing protection to the great soul whose vibration we can pick up easily.

One of the thirty-two great souls working in humanity carries on the humble trade of a water carrier in Egypt. I have met Yogis who told me that they were masters, and others who said that they were mahatmas, and one even here in London, claimed to be the avatar of this age and said that he was the "master of the masters," but I am afraid that I had not the grace to enable me to perceive in these men the humanity and compassion that I have met in the unknown workers for the world. There are some Eastern Yogis in the West who are sincere and are quietly doing a great work, and they have our reverence and love. It is difficult to mix the East and the West through misunderstanding of customs and teaching, but we hope that in the future the West will have the grace of heart to listen and try to understand the instruction which the East has for the West. Likewise, we hope that those in the East may realize that the West also has something to teach it.

This is why travel is so important for the Western man, and why he should live amongst other peoples, races, and sects, in order that there may be mutual understanding for the common good.

Man should also seek to unify himself with the consciousness of nature, in order to familiarize himself with its different vibrations and densities. He should "listen in" for moments of instruction, for then he begins to realize the immensity of the universe in which he is living, and seeing the falsity around him, sooner or later seeks the path of wisdom. Man will never be happy until he seeks the sovereign good and, if once for a moment he stands in the Presence, then nothing else matters in this world but the attainment of Truth.

The control of any power in nature can be accomplished only when man gains a working knowledge of the control of the powers and forces which he has within himself. People are sometimes introduced to well-known personalities through reading their plays and books. They also project their minds towards people whose pictures they see, and whose characters they esteem and admire. Our thoughts towards such are tinged with the ideals which we form in our minds about them, and we project to them our finer qualities. This ennobles them and gives them strength, courage, and power.

When many minds are concentrated upon even an insensitive man, such as a public speaker, he will feel the pressure and it will enable him to give out a finer expression of his nature.

There are, however, other personalities who have not created favorable impressions upon our minds and, in our ignorance, our unguarded thoughts sometimes place into their atmosphere qualities and powers which reflect our feelings.

We must remember that many people who are really great souls have fallen into ignorance (evil) through the practice of black magic. These people are "halfway houses," or contacting points with the dark realms of the so-called evil beneath our feet, and those who surrender their souls into these regions are able to pass the powers of darkness into humanity, and contact people with the elemental and demoniac entities of nature and man.

Should you meet these bringers of misfortune to others, be non-resistant, and seek and speak of the good that you can perceive in them. This is a process of being negative to the attachment with which they seek to contact you. The world in general would laugh if we spoke of the great power which some of these black magicians possess, but the power of life and death is one of them.

The white magician works under the law of attraction, that which gives freedom to every living being. He makes no demands, for a demand brings forth opposition and limits freedom of expression. Love is something to be given freely, with no demands. When we give to another person, the giving brings about a karmic link with that person. In some countries Yogis will not receive or handle gifts of money from people, for they say freedom is limited and power of discretion is lacking when they receive money. Yet so potent is this second power in this world that few Yogis after all can resist its temptations.

People do not realize that the black magician, similar to the white magician, has at his beck and call myriads of forces, both elemental and elementary. There are spirits who, unknown to mortal man, follow the direction of his thought like locusts, to project into his atmosphere the so-called evil, and the so-called good.

We have seen the word "initiation" in books on mysticism and quietism. Initiation is the conscious attainment of illumination, of knowledge, and of power. It is an expansion of consciousness on the mental plane. It is a step on the rungs of the ladder to *knowing oneself.* The initiated student is like a man controlling an automobile; he can aid and assist his fellow beings, or he can ruthlessly destroy them. Thus initiation is the attainment of conscious power, whether good or evil.

Many of the younger magicians, in their circles, try to experiment, play tricks upon, and annoy people whom they hear well-spoken about. The Yogi often watches the effects of their experiments, and sees the astral entities which their minds and imaginations have created and sent out towards somebody. They do not realize that what they evoke and send out towards a person returns to them, just as a dog returns to his master. As these creations are conceived by the will and imagination of the operator, so they return to him and, if he is not careful, they will distort his imagination. Our asylums have many inmates with distorted imaginations, and the unbalanced imaginations of humanity unite and form a composite whole which, if contacted, may bring illusion to and transform a passive or a weak mind. Even doctors and attendants in asylums often tell you, "I just have to get out of here, or I shall go 'batty'."

Man should take great care always that he has a normal and healthy liver, for this is the seat in the body of man's imagination. The "livery" man is never normal, nor his atmosphere healthy for others.

CHAPTER FORTY
ELEMENTAL HELPERS

Today there are saints who can answer the prayers of humanity, and I personally have witnessed some miracles; also, there are people who have a preponderance of elemental nature in their human framework.

When these seemingly human, but really elemental people pass over at the time of so-called death, they are ministered to by elemental beings in nature's consciousness, in the same way that the average man receives attention from helpers on the other side.

I have been acquainted for some years with a great elemental teacher, who has given instruction to a friend regarding his work. When I went out of my body to meet this elemental being, it asked me not to reveal to my friend the source under which he was working. I was then informed that he was working under the consciousness of the Christ, and that his work was to pilot through the "Land of Virtues" those beings who were more elemental than human.

Fortunately, some few of our religious instructors have realized that these great elemental helpers stand in the Presence, and devote their time and labor for the benefit of those humans who are in the likeness of their nature.

Out of my body, this elemental being told me the process by which the newcomer is aided through the Land of Virtues. When the average man passes into elemental life after death, it is new to him and it takes some time before he can adjust himself to his new surroundings. He discovers that this earth has really been a tomb and, according to his development, his progress is rapid or slow in attaining again the consciousness of nature, which he passed through before he was born on the earth plane.

Around our earth are spheres of illusion, or purgatorial states, which the normal, moral man easily passes through. On this earth plane our great avatars have given us moral principles which will provide greater security for us in a future life if we follow them. There are also saints, and beings in the elemental world of nature, who answer the prayers of those human beings who are largely elemental.

An elemental being, such as a sylph, can easily enter into a religious image and cause it seemingly to open and close its eyes, so that it can be noticed by those at their devotions before it. I have seen this happen in a church in Naples.

The Yoga student often associates himself with a sylph or sylphid, and many holy men in the East have been married to sylphids. To enter into a relationship with a being of the element of air, the student must go through a severe discipline for purity of body and mind, for the sylphs quickly analyze his thought atmosphere, and will have nothing to do with foulness of any kind. In one of the ancient occult societies of the past, when a member had attained to purity of thought and cleanliness of the person, he was symbolically married to one of these elemental beings.

A sylph or sylphid will say to the student, "Seek to purify your mind, so that my vibration may pass through you." This is a most difficult process, but he must do so in order to hold contact with a being whose intelligence covers such a wonderful range of knowledge.

It is easy to carry on a conversation with a gnome of the mineral kingdom, for he belongs to a far lower range of vibration than the other elementals and it is easy to harmonize with his consciousness. When the student contacts the intelligences of air, he passes into an astounding range of beauty, full of loveliness and gentleness. These people of the air always exhort the student to pursue the quest of Truth, and to be ennobled by the spirit. Many of the great teachers of the past have found rest and peace in an association with one of these lovely beings of the element of air. By manipulating mind stuff matter, they can present themselves in any form of beauty which they think pleasing to their "loved ones." But this is dealing with that higher intelligence of air.

As above, so below! There is the same elemental intelligence in the lower realms, and there are beings of evil most wonderful to behold. St. Anthony and his experiences with these lower elemental beings has evoked compassion and pity for his sufferings.

The higher sylphids register the brilliance of intelligence and love, as well as of hardness. They have an entirely different point of view from ours. The sylphs are like children, having no knowledge of what we term sin, and they speak what they *know*, not what they *think*. They would be looked upon by certain sections of the earth as immoral. They measure people by the purity or impurity of their bodies and atmospheres. You can often see an elemental angel of death by the bedside of a dying child, and by the robe which the angel wears you can tell the child's degree of elemental constitution.

People often do not understand the types of elemental humanity about them. There are misfits in society and by their intuition they quickly recognize anyone who understands them. I know one very elemental person who has the habit of speaking the truth, and society does not like to meet anyone who speaks the truth. She told me that when she spoke the truth about herself people did not believe her.

These elemental humans have a great perception of beauty and produce beautiful creations in literature and art, if they carry through what they undertake. They also have a wonderful power of attacking anything that they plan to do, but they are apt to lose their enthusiasm and fail to carry a thing to completion. They underestimate their power and are very sensitive to any criticism of their work. It is their sensitivity towards beauty that ensouled evil will always attack. They are very wise in their day and generation, although not children of Mammon.

If a person feels he is a square peg in a round hole, and cannot adjust himself to his environment, let him pray to God through nature and, if he is worthy, the saints in nature may answer his call. A being who has gained God Realization (nature's will) can aid those of both natures (human and elemental) who call upon him. I have known a saint who died in the Roman faith to answer a prayer in ten minutes time, and I also know of a Mohammedan saint who answered a prayer that he should appear to a seeker, in five minutes.

We read of the miracles of the past, but we seldom perceive the miracles which are being performed every day in our midst by God-realizing men and women. In this connection we must not forget that the force works both ways, and that envy, hatred, and anger quickly contact our atmosphere with those powerful forces of nature and mind which exist in the lower densities beneath our feet.

What you evoke outwardly into your environment will evoke its reflection. The one thing most abhorrent to the higher elemental forces of nature is hypocrisy. There is a great secret to be found in nature which, when tapped by the student, produces a tremendous flow of energy. It is a consciousness in which he can rest and find peace, and it gives a greater urge to seek a knowledge of Truth. It is something which the student keeps secret in his heart. It is consciousness of truth and beauty, of power to discern loveliness in things which the world passes by. It is consciousness of the infinite and great Reality, which is so near, consciousness of its nearness, its love, and its beauty. But this secret remains hidden in the heart of man.

We look upon nature mostly with our normal vision, yet every part of nature has its overshadowing form. The trees, the rocks, and the flowers we see easily, but their overshadowing forms, their true beauty, only present themselves when we have gone deeper in our quest for the higher realization. The devas say that all things in nature have their higher counterpart. This higher counterpart is a radiation, or atmosphere beautiful to behold, and when seen for the first time by the student, he perceives in it the manifestation or vibration of the spirit.

When a person passes over at death, he perceives first the things which he saw upon earth, but, as he gradually evolves in perception, he sees the higher counterpart projection of these things. He sees the real tree, whereas before he saw only its objective vehicle. He also notices in the helpers who minister to him, a radiation which he had never perceived in mortal man, and in time by this radiation he measures their attainment into the light.

A Yogi, returning from a trip out of his body, shudders at the darkness of this world as he again enters his body. If man could only remember what he has witnessed when he leaves his body during deep sleep, he would strive for knowledge and truth, so that in the future he might no longer be chained by the law of cause and effect in this sphere of illusion called "the earth."

But the seeker must not forego the quest for adventure, for this will stimulate him to enter upon a voyage of discovery in the quest for Truth.

CHAPTER FORTY-ONE

NATURE'S CAUSEWAY

There is a division in nature which can be only symbolized. We will call it a causeway, or a sort of "no man's land." On one side of this division we find all the higher aspirations of man, all the best ideals that humanity has evolved, and like an army on the other side, stand the great beings of nature.

When the student arrives at a certain state of development, he represents the best in human conduct and experience, then devas from the opposite side, who can walk over this causeway easily, reach forth and lift up the student who is worthy, and place him in the center of the causeway. In this place, he becomes conscious of the light in the distance, and realizes that where he stands is a place of *nothingness,* and so he sets about seeking to be born into that light, and to unite himself with it.

The world from which he came is dark, but the world in which the devas move has an atmosphere like mother-of-pearl, and the landscape appears to have a rhythmic motion.

This causeway is, however, a place of nothingness, a void. No sound is heard as the student projects himself towards the light. As it comes nearer, more light floods his being. When it recedes, all is void, but he now sees only light, and to it he aspires for union, and he then becomes conscious of a great being beside him. He perceives a light is entering him, and as it enters, he grows stronger; he realizes that he is entering into his own world, into his own kingdom, and everything is changed.

There is one Truth and one Presence, and nothing else matters; all is silence, there is only the light. This is his entrance into his own "halls of learning," and he must remain in each of these halls, until he has received the wisdom of each life experience, and until he knows the real reason for his pilgrimage.

He is still an individual, but he is told that the time will come when his individuality will be broken up for union with its source. He discovers that, as he progresses, helpers from conscious nature arrive to aid him in his adventure, and that the "engineer" atom in his heart sends "instructor atoms" to guide him in his own "halls of learning."

Mantras, used rightly, lead to freedom, but if they are used improperly they cause the operator to be enslaved and bound by the powers he evokes. This is the so-called good and evil of magic. When the student meets his teacher, great stress is laid upon the care of the body and the use of imagination, but most students do not have enough patience and perseverance in the development of the physical body. It is the storehouse of all future strength, and although many a man considers himself physically fit, yet he little realizes what it means to make the physical body fit, alert, and ready for any call upon its structure.

The student who seriously takes up Yoga practice, no matter how old he may be, becomes youthful in his desire for adventure. He probes deeply into the world about him, and into the world within. It is a hazardous enterprise, and he realizes that life is worth living. With a strong urge to *know,* and to conquer himself, he seeks his sovereign goal of liberation, guiding his own chariot with quickened energies. He feels the Presence and the immortality of youth, and a quickening vibration surges through him, for he has discovered a rich abundance within, which he seeks to have and to hold. To be *free,* to *live,* and to gain *union* with the Truth which is within, is his quest.

Such is the journey of youth in the realm of his own spirit and, as he proves himself, he seeks to prove the world without, and to know the truth in history through space and time, and to probe deeply into the secrets of nature. He feels his own strength, governs his passions and desires with a strong hand, and chants a paean of praise glorifying the "Lord within, Youth the Adventurer!"

CHAPTER FORTY-TWO

STEPS IN DEVIC INSTRUCTION

We reach our first step in elemental devic instruction when we aspire for Truth, and the second step is that of observation.

We have to learn to observe upon two planes of consciousness, to observe and penetrate deeply with our mind the physical objects which we see about us; then, as our clairvoyance develops, we have to seek the manifestation of the spirit which is in all things.

It is our aspiration for Truth which places us en rapport with the information periods of the elementary intelligences. They impress us with their objects of thought, and to a certain extent we visualize these thought impressions. For instance, they will show us a tree, and with their power of radiation they will cause the tree to radiate its own atmosphere, until we discover that the objective tree which we see is only a shell form of a still greater tree. The real tree, or etheric double surrounding it, enlarges its form, so that it is often thirty per cent larger than the physical structure. Its wavering, quivering atmosphere of color has the power of expansion as well as of contraction, both outwardly and inwardly. The devas play upon a tree as an instrument is played upon by a musician and cause it, when challenged, to express itself in its tree character; thus, the oak and the pine tree stand far apart in their native character of expression.

The devas may cause the tree to give forth its own character of beauty, be it of masculine or feminine expression, and then they will say to you, "We have shown you the fruits of the tree, both in its higher and finer, and lower expression. When *you* can do this, do it likewise to the men and women that you meet. Bring the truthful character of their natures into expression, to be perceived by those about them for as *you* enter deeper into union with your own real man in nature you will find that the same laws that apply on our plane can be applied to those in your objective world of being."

This was known to the medicine men of the early American Indian tribes, for they took their pupils to nature, away from all physical contacts with men, and submitted them to the ordeal. In those days the medicine men whose prophesies did not prove true, met their death at the hands of their own tribe, for the Indians had their Golden Age, as well as other races, and they sought to obey the secret command of nature—honesty.

The early Druids also always impressed upon their hearers this great edict of nature—honesty. Those who are born underneath the sign of Taurus have a close relationship with the elemental worlds of nature, for, as the devas say, "Their feet are planted on the earth," and other signs of the zodiac also are important in dealing with nature's consciousness and the underworld of men.

Within the nature of men are untold depths of expression, for every man possesses an underworld of being and many submerged states of activity, and he possesses dynamic powers which, when tapped, will greatly surprise him. The average man today lives on the surface and is skating upon very thin ice, unless he seeks union with the consciousness of nature within the depths of his own being. Bubbles of greater realization, coming from the depths of his Neptunian nature, seek to impress him with a greater knowledge of his being and greater eagerness for self realization, but the bubble usually strikes the surface of the ice beneath his feet, and seldom registers its profound truth within his mental atmosphere. But if man does contact these deeper essences, he achieves the power to penetrate more deeply into the real nature of his being and environment, for he has an underworld submerged within him, and these planes of consciousness will relate him to the underworld of man about him, the underworld of crime.

We possess a microphone[38] at the base of the spine, which registers the vibrations of this world of evil and transmits the information to our human brain. The brain center at the navel, when fully developed in man, produces dictators like Alexander the Great, Mussolini, or Hitler, for it registers the *knower* con-

---

38   The Secret Enemy.

sciousness, and these men know intermittently what they can accomplish. For instance, when Alexander the Great placed his foot on the soil of Asia, he shouted, "Asia is mine," for he *knew* that which he could conquer.

To develop this center, the student in Yoga practice sits edgewise upon a chair with a belt tightly buckled round his abdomen, and rotates his body rapidly in the direction of the sun. This pressure placed upon the navel, this "churning of the butter," causes the atmosphere about him to ooze out and stand some two inches above the shoulders, thus producing a microphone which registers nature's will—intuition. Thus the student, aspiring through nature for Truth, receives from nature's will quick flashes of intuition, for this atmosphere is nature's sounding board in man, about which her will plays. It is similar to the vibration of the higher counterpart of fire, which is a cold vibration that enters the student's body between the shoulder blades, thus the experienced student can often answer questions correctly without thought.

This is called the *knower consciousness,* and many Yogis are most proficient in answering your questions without going through the process of *thinking.* As the devas constantly say, "Tell us what you know, not what you think."

When the student can realize this, he will try to answer a person's questions truthfully without thought, from his world of intuition.

The ordinary body today is like a beautiful musical instrument partly strung and out of tune, it hears, sees, feels, tastes, and smells a little of the real world about it. It lives in an environment of its own thought creation, and is a prisoner bound in a mire of illusion, like the frog in the moat is content with its own little world, paying no attention to the voice of the tree above which says, "Come up here, and I will show you a world you have never seen." Man does not realize that bliss and knowledge are within his reach, and therefore does not try to tap those planes of consciousness.

There is a main center in the throat called "the seat of Mercury," and it is most difficult for the student to develop this center, owing to its seemingly atrophied condition from disuse.

As this "seat of Mercury" (lord of the mind) is opened, it brings the student more closely into touch with the mind consciousness of the deva creation, and in his practice he chants a mantra which vibrates this center, calling upon the lords of the finer mind world to contact him, by an atomic link or chain, with these finer spheres in nature.

This is an exact science, known to the initiated in the East and West, and when the student is ready he receives personal instruction from those qualified in the development of these finer spheres of nature within him. In the West the teachers all aim for "God Realization," and there are specialists in each branch of Yoga. One master is perhaps adept in teaching the development of the physical vehicle, and another is a master in the art of observation, and a third is skilled in some other branch, each with the same objective.

It is quite difficult to explain how you are taught truth by the falsity of phenomena. The knowledge of that which is false, namely the use of phenomena which is really scientific, has nothing really to do with the phenomena of nature. This comes as a shock to the student, at least it did to me. We must learn to perceive the difference in magic, as professed by our conjurors, like Maskelyne or Houdini, magic created by man's inventiveness, and that which is built up from the phenomenal side of nature. A great teacher said, "You must have knowledge of how to place a man's mind, in order to take it off the intent of evil, and place it on something constructive and good."

Through clairvoyance one often finds that people have obsessions, of hatred, malice or anger towards a person, often with the intent to murder or commit a crime. Day and night, the man has a one-pointedness of mind for destruction. If you can remove or break that one-pointedness of thought, and attract the mind towards something else, you have a chance of preventing him from carrying out his formulated plan. If you can demonstrate to him by a simulative phenomenon, you take his mind off this preconceived idea, and bring the fear of God into his heart. Why waste your finer forces, when a simple simulative trick will bring about the required result?

It took me a long time before I realized that good can come out of evil, or what I had thought was evil. Often, among some of the colored races the fetish of an old stocking on a crooked stick before my tent caused the fear of God to enter the heart of the native, and my belongings were not molested.

No matter how humanity has evolved today, it still has its own fetishes. This was the greatest shock I received from my master in my occult teaching, but it often proved the means of protection for those in danger. The student is taught to use it in cases of great emergency to protect a great soul, while in the human body. He is also taught processes by which he can prevent the shock caused by an injury by the use of a counter shock.

Yoga is an extensive study of the philosophies of the world by which the student is able to acquire this information from within and check against historical evidence. The average man only realizes that there is crime going on around him, that the underworld of humanity preys upon the weakness and ignorance of others, but the Yoga student, as he purifies himself by aspiration and ascends into conscious contact with the finer spheres of being, discovers that crime has also ascended. He observes it often for the first time among the better class of humanity. He recognizes ignorance in the so-called leaders of the religious sects, and sees man-made religions at loggerheads with one another, witnesses the hypocrisy and ignorance of the self-styled holy men around him, and he perceives the selfishness and greed, the illusion and the falsehood—and with these he will have nothing to do.

His burning desire is to give help and aid to those whom he knows are seeking the cool nectar of realization and knowledge. The dying wish of a great saint who passed over some twenty-six years ago was that when she reached God Realization she might be allowed to bring that heaven to our earth, and today with various individuals we constantly have demonstrations of her power.

Just as we have specialized in the arts, so in the deva kingdom there are those specialists who analyze the real nature of our being. Instructors from the world of nature come to those who sincerely seek to be instruments of Truth. In the lower densities of matter we also find these same types of beings, seemingly instruments of Fate working in opposition to the universal good. It is these beings who teach the black magicians their secrets, so that the foolish and ignorant may suffer through experience and in time turn to good. The higher hierarchal beings say, "All men shall become good in time, and shall know God."

So we find in life that as the student gains extension of consciousness, and inwardly ascends his spiral path, he will always discover a world beneath his feet. Realize for a moment the crimes that have been committed, the torture that has been inflicted in the name of Christ, or in the name of Buddha, Mohammed, or Krishna! Why do people attempt to teach of the hereafter with authority, whilst they are ignorant of the world in which they live?

Life could well be symbolized by Nijinsky's dance to Debussy's music *Prelude a l'apres-midi d'un Faune*. Crouched on his rock, Nijinsky's faun watches some beautiful Greek girls dance. He gets up and shakes himself like an animal, seemingly drawing animal conditions out of the earth and joins the dance. The gods then clasp a silver sandal (symbolizing mind) round one ankle, and you perceive him gradually entering a mind world, and as he figures out the dance he catches up a gauze shawl which a Greek girl had dropped, and carries it to his rock, his whole nature changed, for love has dawned upon him, and he has become human. All this is brought out by the movements of the dance to Debussy's music in *Prelude a l'apres-midi d'un Faune*.

CHAPTER FORTY-THREE
VAMPIRE ENTITIES

We will now discuss another phase of the lower side of nature. As the devas stand in the presence of Truth and work constructively, so there are powerful forces, the lower counterpart of this devic creation, that have fallen deep into matter, who wage war, and bring destruction into the environments which they penetrate.

These lower aspects or devils are like men once good, who have fallen from their aspirations for truth and beauty and have been outlawed by humanity, and similarly there are elemental powers which have been evoked into the consciousness of humanity and which wage war upon all living beings. In nature we observe that there are constructive as well as destructive agents each following the law of his own being.

Within these planes there are entities which seek to draw out of the living and the dead those elements which provide them with food and vitality. When controlled by black magicians these agents are most dangerous to man, and in evoking them through ceremonial magic, the operator is often not able to control the power he seeks to enslave. I knew a man who intermittently had to defend himself against the onslaughts of such an entity; beads of perspiration would appear on his forehead at such moments and his entire physical organism was shaken by the struggle. This man was an authority upon theosophy and allied subjects yet was haunted by this secret fear which followed him to the grave.

When at so-called death a person's remains are placed in the grave, the disintegrating intelligences of nature begin to draw out of the body and liberate those elements similar to their own composition. The physical body must be returned to its natural elements, and this is the work of these atoms of destruction. Then there is another type of entity which seeks nourishment from the decomposing bodies of human and animal nature, and by them the properties of the body are disintegrated and returned to their natural elements, just as a leaf which falls may fertilize the earth, or serve as food for some other form of expression.

We find these types of elementals about our graveyards, where they sometimes find an astral shell similar to their own nature which they enter. Since these astral shells are often enslaved by the animal soul in nature, these beings, through domination of this astral shell, seek to draw nourishment from the human plane which, through the medium of the astral shell, they can more readily contact.

Sensitive people are most prone to attacks of these vampire entities, different classes of which exist in the intermediate world of being. They vary from the octopus class, with body like quivering jelly, to beings somewhat human in form, standing about four feet high. True to their animal soul these beings often run in packs and their movements are far more rapid than human movements.

During our sleep, especially, these vampire beings seek to draw vitality from the human body, and mostly resort to places where licentiousness, hatred, and envy abound. They are particularly attracted to brothels, and to people who harbor licentious thoughts. A magician, having power over elemental life, can cause these beings to clothe themselves in any form of costume that he may desire. Magicians in Nepal sometimes convey a message or frighten a person by sending one of these four-foot beings to you clad in a devil mask. These elemental apparitions often display a strong sense of humor, but the octopus type, rearing itself upon its tentacles, always presents a face of horror. These lower beings always convey an atmosphere like an impressionistic painting, horizontal, diagonal, and vertical lines, each paint stroke separated by a partition from the natural atmosphere.

As distinguished from these forces, beings which serve the "white" magician are beings of light, while forces of the "black" magician belong to the twilight world beneath our feet, and the shapes of some are beyond human comprehension. Sometimes they embody animal forms, such as black dogs or black pigs, and so forth. In the form of snakes the head is generally beautifully bejewelled with pendants similar to earrings.

Many people are born into the world who have contacts with, or are overshadowed by, these vampire classes of elemental life. As they grow up, they become conscious that they have the power of absorbing vitality from others. One very dear friend, when complimented upon her color and appearance of health, said, "I was feeling a rag when I started out to visit you, but when I got on the bus, I saw a very vital and healthy man, and I was fortunate enough to be able to sit beside him. Whenever I am with people, I always look out for the healthiest person that I can find to sit beside, and then I pick up in no time." Now this was a kind lady noted for her good works, but in this one aspect her personal selfishness predominated.

Another case was a so-called spiritual healer. She was a gentle lady known to many for her good works. When she left a room in which perhaps as many as eighteen people were sitting, everybody seemed to breathe a sigh of relief, because she had a habit of vampirizing the vitality of everybody in her presence.

On one occasion a lady came to me in great trouble; she was sorely in need of assistance. I went deeply inward, and I discovered her husband had recently passed over into a finer condition of life, and he asked me to give her this message, "When I was very ill from typhoid, you brought a healer into my room, and she ushered me out of my body, which was entered by the being who has treated you so shamefully for two years and a half—the beast who drank and gambled was not myself, but another being which the spiritual healer drew into my body. Remember that I have always loved you as I did before this thing happened, and I shall *always* love you." The poor woman burst into tears and said, "This is all that I want to know! You have answered my prayers. When my supposed husband recovered from the fever, his personality seemed strange, and I was living with a stranger in my house whose life was such that I cannot describe it. You have lifted a load from my heart." The spiritual healer who was called in at that time was the lady I have just mentioned who vampirized everyone.

As the atoms of destruction become stronger in old age, elderly people are often conscious of the vitality that they can absorb from the youth about them, but I have never yet discovered vampirism among people who do not lead selfish and self-centered lives.

Many black magicians have gained the power of giving life or death to individuals, and there comes a time in the student's life when he is tempted. Great powers are promised him by these fallen angels of the underworld if he will surrender his soul into the keeping of these Princes of Darkness. If you wish to advance along the path you can only dedicate your life to the service of God. This is a critical moment in the student's life, but if he earnestly aspires for Truth, he afterwards becomes aware that some of the greater beings of light stand ready to protect him. Out of the body the student learns to recognize the powers of evil. There is an understanding which passes between him and them, and if he goes deeply into the subject, he will discover that the deepest evil in nature will in time evolve to the higher good.

When the student has learned to use his own tools there is no animosity between himself and the craftsmen of the other path; they are like two fencers, each always balances his power and measures the power of his opponent. I have met great beings, brothers of the light, working in these depths to bring illumination to some occult student who lost his light through the ignorant use of experimental magic.

Just as we find black and white magicians working on the physical side of life, so we find them as denizens of the higher and also the lower states of being. The brilliance of intelligence in the fallen angels is fascinating, and they have great power over the minds which enslave humanity. Our great avatar has said, "The children of Mammon in their day and generation are wiser than the children of light."[39]

Nature scourges the children of light by periods of suffering and experience, but this causes them to evolve into the percep-

---

39   But their day is the astral day, and their generation the flesh.

tion of the truth of the Reality. The ranges of experience which we pass through bring us to self-thought, and the desire to know Truth. How dull life would be if one did not encounter opposition! Those who incarnate into a life of wealth often gain little real experience of life. It is from God that we came, so to God we shall return, and we ourselves can hasten or delay this pilgrimage of experience. The use of certain incense, a clean body and mind, a clean environment with natural surround- ings, if possible, and devotion to God, will protect one from the approach of these lower animal entities in nature.

All forms of sex imagination and distortions of thought con- tact these vampire conditions from the world beneath our feet, attract them into our atmosphere and, since the spiritual man gains his power from his organs of generation, he is most prone, if his thoughts are not controlled, to contact these conditions of the vampire class. Through proper control of our creative forces we liberate the higher counterpart of our seminal energy. This is a form of static electricity which liberates the soul of man from the prison house—the body. The Eastern Yogi says, "Kill your passions and desires." But the Western Yogis say you should control and govern them.

Often magicians, procuring the body of a person who has seemingly died, have held back the destructive elements from entering it, and have thus afforded an entrance for an animal soul. The body has retained its seeming health, but the mental- ity is of a lower order, able to do menial work only. Seabrook has described such beings in Haiti. It is a most pathetic thing to meet a person who has renounced his soul to the Prince of Darkness, for he hopes and longs for a chance to regain his lost estate.

Often such men are used to bring about the downfall of a country, that in the end a greater good or evil may result. They always have a look of martyrdom in their eyes which cannot easily be forgotten. Years ago a very holy man in a foreign country pointed out a man to me and said, "God sometimes brings about what is seemingly a great evil, but in time it brings about a common good." This man whom he pointed out had just returned from a pilgrimage to Jerusalem, and when I looked into his face, he registered the great sorrow that was there, and I knew that this man would be a martyr.

We cannot judge people until we know both the cause and the effect. This knowledge brings one in touch with the sorrows that evil can sometimes reflect into the mind. Great evil can be at times very beautiful. These beings of evil in the lower worlds are most beautifully proportioned (but not according to the Greek canons), yet in spite of their beauty they have an intensity of evil in their eyes. Some of them possess two pairs of arms and are magnificently clothed, yet their proportions are beautiful when analyzed.

Today many of our painters and modern sculptors are influenced by entities from the moon. They portray the human body differently from the canons of our age. If you study their work, seeking the truth of its expression, you can learn something, for our ideals of canons of beauty evolve forward or backward as we seek the light or the darkness, and the painter whose work was rejected yesterday often becomes a celebrity in a later time.

What can man, chained to the machine or desk for fifty weeks of the year, know of real beauty! He is the servant of the octopus of Mammon, with an ever-growing fear of losing his job, and of poverty! No longer an independent individual, he is the slave of a company, often overshadowed by Luciferian beings of our underworld. "What does it profit a man if he gains the whole world, and loses his own soul?" Man sometimes thinks he is buying cheaply when he is buying dearly. The worth of a thing determines its merit, and the cast iron hammer cannot take the place of wrought steel. An instrument or tool which is of good appearance but has no worth, betrays its owner at the critical moment. People will learn in time to save their money till they can get real worth and will apply this lesson to the art of right living.

CHAPTER FORTY-FOUR
TREE PEOPLE

There is much similarity between a man and a tree. The tree, like a human being, has its lungs, nerve channels, stomach, and intestines. It rids itself of its impurities through its roots like human beings. It is the action of this excretion which has much to do with bringing about poverty of the soil, for these excretions are either alkaline or acid.

When pine and beech trees are planted together, they render the soil alkaline, and this causes a cement-like layer to form about the roots, which prevents moisture from reaching them and retards the normal and healthy development of the tree.

Our flowers and trees all have their opposite complements which keep the soil fertile if they are allowed to commingle. The Druids and the monks of old were close observers of nature, and the oak tree was held by them to be the savior of the forest, for it is the health-giver, and when planted among pine and beech it counteracts all the mineral deposits formed by them.

Wherever it is planted it affords protection to the soil, and it is looked upon by the devas as the "great soul" of the forest, and it was consecrated to the element of fire. The vibration of fire, the highest of the elements, manifests through its vesture, and the Greeks held it in great reverence as the symbol of Jupiter, for it is truly the "lord of the forest," and wherever disease has ravished, it has been nature's instrument for bringing health to the soil.

The plant however becomes weak in its potential value, when man segregates it from the complementary plant or weed which accompanies it in its natural state. When the earth becomes worn out through extensive cultivation of wheat, it is because of the acidity which the roots of the wheat have infused into it, but such weeds as wild mustard (which thrives upon the acidity of the soil) return the earth to its natural health again.

In the deeper states of Yoga, the student becomes conscious of a vibration, as an alternating current, which can best
be analyzed as an alternating rhythm of strength and gentleness; and he observes that plants which in their natural state
give out acid excretions through their roots, are always blessed
by association with their alkaline opposites.

Science today has discovered that in raising sugar beets, the
ground quickly recovers its health if a little chicory is planted
at the same time to neutralize the soil. Likewise in art the
Chinese always balance strength and gentleness. When the
farmers closely examine the weeds that appear after a crop has
been harvested, they will read from nature's book the process
by which the devas seek to bring health and security to all
living things.

If the student will try to commune with an oak tree, he will
receive many illuminating impressions through his increasing
perceptions, and if he can merge his atmosphere with that of
the tree, he will find that it will give him a consciousness of
nobility, strength, and power, for the oak tree is truly the seer
and savior of the forest where, like a general, it watches over
the health and conduct of the others.

In the early days, the alchemists and Rosicrucians, by
noting the complementary flower or weed, recognized the
medical properties of each and used them medicinally in their
ministrations to their fellowmen. If sweets predominated in
the patient's food, they balanced these by adding vegetables
which were bitter to the taste and their rule of health was,
"Heal yourself, and keep your body fit by the things you eat."

The higher devas inform us that they have a process of
communication with beings, similar to their own nature,
which inhabit the earth. These beings work to develop the soil
into periods of activity, and periods of repression, when its
activity is seemingly dormant.

In time science will discover many things in the earth,
which have so far escaped observation. For instance, an
archaeological friend of mine near Stonehenge, dug a pit six
feet due East and West and six feet perpendicular, and on the
mound of thrown out earth there appeared most peculiar

flowers, but they would grow nowhere else except from the soil taken from a depth of six feet or more, thus showing that the different densities of earth hold different varieties of floral life. This soil when exposed to the sun and air, brought forth flowers entirely foreign to those which ordinarily grew in the locality.

The devas do not recognize the strata of earth in which the husbandman plants his seeds as a solid mass. To them it is an atmosphere interpenetrated by the activities of those atoms which exist in the subsoil; to them it has its movement and activity, but nothing solid, in the way that we would term a rock solid. To them it appears as a material which has fissures or lungs which breathe moisture in and out, and it is inhabited by myriads of elemental atoms which move in and out as nature breathes.

There is a lower class of sentient beings, which are not of the nature of minerals or of the gaseous vapor which the earth exudes. They have free movement through ordinary soil, and they pass through the interstices which separate the atoms. These intelligences are not looked upon with favor by the higher devic creation, for they are attracted to all kinds of refuse and decomposing matter of nature's excrement, such as manure or decaying vegetable matter, and when they find an outlet into the soil, for instance, in a manure heap, their vibration changes it so that it becomes a danger through infection to the human blood stream.

In thickly populated places, the soil often becomes so infected by the debris cast off from humanity, that this, may we say elemental bacteria, is extremely dangerous to man, for it is worked over by the parasites of elemental nature, and becomes dangerous to the human blood stream.

In places like China, even the vegetables carry this bacteria, through being grown on infected ground, and they are not safe for human food till they have been brought to a boiling point.

When we get away from human habitations and enter into the consciousness of nature, we find that she impresses us with her desire for moisture or water, and we also discover

that the subsoil itself has its own varying degrees of temperature, for the rise and fall of sap in a tree depends on the rise
and fall of the temperature in the subsoil.

Let us consider a grove of trees. They can occasionally
manifest the more active side of their elemental nature. Like
human beings, they possess an elemental structure which
enables them to leave their vehicles at night, just as man, in
his sleep, can leave his physical body.

People with etheric vision can often see "tree" people
(beings of the nature of trees) and they always present themselves in the form of trees, but with the power of locomotion.
In different parts of the world, gypsies are closely associated
with these tree people, for very often these tree elementals are
strongly attracted to human beings, yet they are usually of
a lower order of intelligence, and they often seek to frighten
and terrify the seer. Just as astral shells are found in and near
graveyards, so these forms will haunt the forests.

I know a man on whom I sometimes place my mind, in
order to know how he is getting on. Directly my thoughts are
centered on him, these tree people are immediately registered,
and they seem to give me historical evidence of the man's
former life, when he associated with Hungarian gypsies.

When people ask you for help, you often feel their elemental connection with nature's intelligence, high or low.

It may seem strange, but to the intelligences of nature, you
are like a foreigner entering a strange country, and you are
judged according to your conformity to their laws. They want
to know if you have acknowledged the jurisdiction of their
deva, and whether you will abide by their laws! When you
acknowledge their law and show the desire not to break it in
any way, then you sense a welcome from them. The acknowl-
edgment of their law is brought about by thought and physical action. Facing the East, you bow to the forest seven times,
then turning to the right you face the West, and your thought
and movement is projected there, as you again bow seven
times. Then, standing symbolically in the center, keep turning
to the right until you face the North. You project your mind
towards the North and bow seven times in that direction,

then turning to the right, face to the South, and carry out the same exercise. You have now formed two lines across, and at the junction of the two lines you stand facing the density of the wood.

You have now come under the protection of the wood and of the deva, and if you sit there often to meditate you will soon see a movement in nature and be lifted into the world of the fairy—the middle world of nature—and you will become conscious of peace and beauty. It will often bring you forgetfulness of earthly things, and then much wisdom can come to you from the forest.

A little waterfall and its surroundings are delightful to those who have the vision to look into nature's workshop, where the higher and the lesser evolved elements of nature work in peace and harmony, and the creations of the "tree" people, unperceived by normal eyes, absorb your interest. But behind all this phenomena is a great sermon of wisdom instruction which stimulates you to seek union with the Truth back of all phenomena.

The devas are constantly telling us that science has yet to discover the fixed principles in nature, and that when this is discovered then man will begin to realize his ignorance and lack of perception. He has made startling discoveries in his quest for Truth, but he has also been led into the byways of ignorance. In time he will realize that he has been dealing with protean elements in his study of chemistry, and that his search must be for the "fixed principles" in nature's manifestations.

Man has delved deeply into the science of chemistry, and is satisfied. Some day he will discover that there are elements in chemistry which are both fixed and fugitive. He will find that his fixed principles are subject to slow change, and that the compounds are also going through slow changes. The mineral forces in nature change their activities intermittently and work in an entirely new field of endeavor, and those minerals which are allowed access to their field of activity no longer attract but oppose them. This intermittent change is the stumbling block of all scientific research. A force may vibrate a thing up to its supreme moment, and then at the end of a cycle of time, say seven years, an entirely different rhythm begins to dominate it. It is an alternating rhythm of strength and gentleness.

In like manner, man has recorded his scientific experiments as absolute truth, and then discovered that the scientific truth of yesterday is not the scientific truth of today. For instance, yesterday it was said that the primary colors were red, yellow, and blue, but science today, according to Maxwell and Munsell, regards the primary colors to be orange, red, and blue-green, and these colors produce all the others in the spectrum. What a change in the science of color since the time of Newton!

It is the men of greater perception who teach others to see. Claude Monet, the impressionist painter, was ridiculed by science in his early days, but afterwards it was acknowledged that his method of painting light and sunshine was correct from a scientific standpoint.

When we enter into the consciousness of nature, and view her movements with the higher clairvoyance, we see distinctly movements, bewilderments, immensity, and a grandeur which, if spoken about to the scientific man today, would be disbelieved. Paul du Chaillu, the African explorer, was laughed at for writing about his "supposed" discovery of the manlike ape, the gorilla, but later science had to admit the truth of his discovery.

We are privileged to know a great soul, a native red Indian, who has a knowledge of nature's laws and remedies which science today would probably decry. He is a man who can do things which doctors are at present unable to accomplish. He once said to me, "If the white man had the graciousness of heart to approach the red Indian rightly, he might be given assistance which would prove of great benefit to his race. In the early days we were given missionaries and whiskey, and were driven out of our lands by the greed of the white man, but we are re-incarnating at this present time into the white race, and some day we shall regain that which we have lost—

but we hold our knowledge secret until the time nature shall call it forth."

The great souls among the red Indians today can produce the same type of phenomena which we hear of from Tibet and India, but their knowledge is adapted to their own climate and country. Some of the early Jesuit missionaries gained a good deal of information from them concerning the law of nature. The real priest is recognized by the real priest all the world over, regardless of his creed or costume. The initiated red Indians measure the spiritual man by valor, for it is spiritual valor which passes the initiate unharmed through any country or tribe.

The ideals of humanity vary according to fashion and circumstance. The "Gibson Girl" of yesterday, with her tightly laced waist, accented hips and breast line, shows the Victorian Age as it really was! Nowadays we never hear that famous Victorian expression "a fine figure of a woman." In the old days we were taught that fitness of purpose and position was the first rule in art.

Nowadays neither fitness nor art explains those ridiculous little pill-box hats the ladies wear for covering, which cannot possibly afford protection against wind, sun, or rain. This is an artificiality of fashion. As a great poet has said, "True beauty ends where intellectual expression begins."

When we recognize and acknowledge the laws of the devas, we are running true to the higher counterpart of elemental nature. People talk about the cruelties of nature, but if man looks about him, what has he to say for himself! There is a higher and a lower nature, as there is a higher and a lower man. The lower animal life of the woods destroys only that it may *live*, but man not only takes what he can gain from nature, but he also wages war upon his fellows in order to gratify his greed for wealth, power and possession.

An ancient Indian writer classified men and women after different types of animals. Science has not yet to our knowledge studied the similarity between animals and humanity, with the exception of the "bird man" type of aviator. The true type of airman is an exceptionally interesting study, for he typifies the elemental nature of air. One of them told me, "When I am up some thousands of feet, I think of the passengers behind me in the cabin, and I cannot help feeling that they are very inferior characters! I am in my element and I feel that I live in a world above them. Today I ran into a thick fog when I was returning with passengers over the Channel; my altitude gauge was useless for something was wrong with it, and as often happens, I had to reach port by intuition."

Many of these "bird men" are occult students, searching deep into nature's mysteries. I have also found that many of our best detectives have an extraordinary sense of perception and intuition, are strongly allied to elemental nature, and are very humane.

Unfortunately this trait is not shown in the conventional detective of the films which is responsible for an erroneous idea of American law and order! If the average American could meet the officials in our European cities he would be impressed by their courtesy, politeness, and sense of humor.

CHAPTER FORTY-FIVE

THE SEVEN-YEAR CYCLES

Much has been written lately about the seven-year cycles in men's lives, so we will go over into nature and consult the devas regarding this subject.

In nature there are periods of activity in the growth of trees and plants, and periods when the earth lies fallow. There are both progression and retrogression like the tides of the sea. As we observe men, we notice that there are moments of activity of mind, body, and soul.

The true character of a man's note is that vibration which builds up positive energy in his character. Man is the builder and should always progress in harmony with his true note of expression. Every man born is intended to ascend to a higher place and position.

To reach a higher or Golden Age of expression, from within and from without, is his natural inheritance, so that he can harmonize himself with the finer forces which go to make up nature's highest expression. Man was intended to become a commanding principle in nature. He has powers at his disposal of which he has never dreamed. The urge of his note or vibration has developed character which has assumed a monumental expression in nature, and has glorified the earth upon which he stands. Man is the master of his own destiny; yet he fails to realize that uncontrolled thoughts, passions and desires, speech without thought, envy, hatred, and malice cause movements which do not harmonize him with the keynote within. This disorganizes the harmony of the whole plan within and without, and thus brings about a retrograde movement. It does not mean that he is stopped in his evolution, but it withholds him from assuming positiveness, and it stops him from relating himself to the urge which nature's consciousness would give him. The pull from his "natural man" is withdrawn, for he has acted contrary to the wisdom of the Lord God of Truth within. Through lack of harmony with his central note he is not able to achieve the monumental objective for which he incarnated. Therefore, according to the cyclic law of being, he misses opportunities for this finer expression.

There is much of truth in the theory of the seven years interval, which the ancients had noticed in the development of man. There are also minor cycles, within the seven year cycles, which scientists will in time observe in nature. Nature reaches the crest of her development in fourteen years. This is the moment in nature when there is a greater abundance of rain, and when climatic change takes place over the earth. New elements are infused into the rain to take the place of those used up. Great electrical disturbances take place, for it is a time when the Titans of the earth manifest and grow strong in their power and energy, and infuse all nature with elements similar to an electric discharge, so that all nature undergoes a change at this time.

There is history preserved today in the akashic records written by an Egyptian priest many centuries before Jesus, which contains a description of these changes in nature. The title could best be translated as "The Divinity which lies beneath the Water, and under the Earth." The instruction is in the form of aphorisms, and can be tapped by any student of Yoga who searches for knowledge in this direction.

This ancient document tells of a past race of humanity which was destroyed, when the waters receded from the earth, and predicts that at some future period monuments and metal receptacles containing inscriptions which deal with the measurements of time and laws relating to climatic movements in nature, will appear out of the sea near the habitations of men. When these deposits are uncovered, historical evidence and curious instruments will be found which will stimulate the minds of many people. Humanity will discover they have acquired but little knowledge compared with that which will be found in these copper cylinders. They will realize that humanity has retrograded rather than progressed, and that the fist and hand of brass must crumble into dust. Man little realizes the marvels and wonders of science which have existed before his day and time.

When this historical evidence is found, the world will be longing for knowledge and truth. Much knowledge and strength for those who are poor and humble will be found on the ocean bed, and the great words of the prophet will be echoed into our world and time.

Man has been ignorant of the creative energy which these documents will disclose and will continue blind to this greater energy until he receives this knowledge. This ancient history has been preserved for the day when man shall become worthy to receive the greater knowledge.

In the beginning every man possessed his own light, but as he started to build himself castles and cities he pillaged the fields and burned and destroyed the habitations of others. He took upon himself to devise gods of his own, enriching them and covering them with jewels, until he slowly became ignorant of his own light and no longer followed the counsels of the elders. He cunningly devised engines and machinery and used them for ravishing nature, and enriching himself with spoils from the habitations of other men. He locked and barred his door to the elders who followed the direction of the light.

With his powers and cunning, he sought to subdue nature, and with his engines of warfare he has enslaved nature's elements to carry out his tortures and destruction. But the elders were not given to such devices. They taught their followers to bring the light of truth to the people. But, through the ignorance of the masses, the light diminished until the "beloved" lived alone in a secret place where they built temples and worshipped the light of Truth.

In time the common people were enfeebled by the destroyers, and the lawgivers of nature exterminated them with volcanic ash and eruption and flood. The door to the sea opened and these people sank into the slime of the ocean. But the "holy ones" who brooded in the silence and gave thanks to the light were left. They took up habitation in other lands where they taught the ignorant to become worthy of the light, teaching them agriculture and the fashioning of utensils, so that nature was pleased, and the land poured forth its abundance.

It was written of old that "the trees brought forth fruit, and the rocks poured forth rivers of oil."

The seers of today divide the world of nature into three divisions. Nature, as we see it with our human eyes—the middle world, the world of fairies, seen by those in whom the third eye is beginning to function, and the world seen by the seer and the Yogi—the higher world of the deva, whose costume is generally opalescent in color, becoming more dense at the foot of the garment.

The beings of the middle world, having power over mind stuff matter, show themselves as shining beings, in any costume which pleases their fancy. A friend of mine, a sylph, using our language, said that he had three suits of clothes. He taught me how to call him in a beautiful garden in the Highlands of Scotland, and if I sought to purify my mind and aspire for truth, he always appeared behind a copper beech in a shining robe of amber, which he would sometimes change to a costume of iridescent blue, sometimes in a headdress like some flower, such as a bluebell; ofttimes bringing a troupe of semi-human fairy children. He showed me the habitations which he could create with mind stuff matter for the pleasure of these multitudes of children fluttering in the air and on the ground. He called my attention to the work that the "little people of the fields" were doing, and showed me their nests of gossamer besprinkled with dew, sometimes hung behind a little waterfall.

This sylph was very learned in the ancient philosophies of the Renaissance Period, and sometimes he would show himself in his amber costume, which shone like the sun, and with a shepherd's crook. If he had appeared in this way to ordinary individuals, they would have thought themselves in the presence of Jesus.

The type of elemental being that appears to you is generally determined by your character of thought and aspiration, for it is said that you will always get your own reflection in nature. If you desire real knowledge, you must constantly aspire for Truth, for you can only attract the real nature of your own expression. If you have been depressed, or have been in the

company of those who are ill in mind and body, you pick up
their elemental conditions—the counterpart of your environment. Sometimes in one's travels, or through circumstances,
one finds oneself in a room or place where the inhabitants are
evil and licentious, and distrust in others abounds. To the sensitive, it seems as though he could cut the atmosphere with a
knife. You find this condition mostly in old Continental cities
and in old hotels, magnetized by mental and physical entities
of the worst kind.

A friend of mine had a little room which was his place of
retreat into the Presence. It was a place of aspiration and meditation, a cheerful clean room, with a chair, table and some
flowers, also the symbol of his order. Before entering this
room, he would stop a moment and seek to purify himself
when he was not able to take a bath. Then he would enter as if
going into the Presence. A doctor friend in a fit of anger and
temper wished to see him, and not finding him in his usual
room and knowing of his retreat, rushed in. He was thrown
back by invisible hands and received the shock of his life, and
he has never yet solved the problem of just what happened
to him. He was thoroughly unnerved, and when my friend
helped him to his feet and explained what his room was for,
the doctor said, "I am beginning to see that there *is* something
in occultism after all."

In out-of-the-way places, we often find little churches and
chapels of different creeds and religions which are places of
peace, magnetized by the aspiring thoughts of those who seek
help and light. Elemental Nature is herself a church or cathedral, where, if you enter properly with aspiration, you can in
time become conscious of the Presence. In the same way this
can be done in the deeper states of Yoga, but the key to this
church or cathedral is love, and when you have entered you
will be given the instruction best suited for your development.

The student is at first surprised at the reverence which
the gnomes, salamanders, sylphs and undines have for their
Creator, and what is so pathetic with the gnomes is their
childlike questioning to know more about God, for the Early
Church impressed upon them that they were denied immor-

tality until it came to deny and scout their very existence. They are conscious of the law of which they speak and of those guardians and sentinels in nature who watch over the development of the kingdoms of fire, earth, water and air.

Now nature, unknown to many, can have a startling influence upon the lives of old people. Her pressure lines upon man are to keep him from growing old, to keep him simple, enthusiastic, and childlike, for nature's consciousness[40] gives to humanity all that is beautiful and noble of the arts and sciences. The man who is touched by nature, pixilated is the modern phrase I think, will be always a child or genius, for he will be the instrument of the gods, who use him to bring inspiration to the human mind. The woman of any age who still loves to play with dolls and dollhouses, and who loves beautiful toys and china, will never grow old. There is always hope for the man or woman who never forgets to play; it is a mark of the genius. The wise man never grows up.

---

40   Intelligent forces working through nature.

CHAPTER FORTY-SIX
CHANGELINGS

Science today divides men and women into three groups, the male, the female, and the intermediate type. The third type comprises people with a woman's instincts ensouled in a man's body and those with a man's instincts ensouled in a woman's body. Science attributes this intermediate group, or so-called Changelings, to some defect in gland secretions. When educated and trained they are brilliant, and they make great artists, but they are unreliable according to the standards of the Western world. In their own sphere of consciousness they are moral, but are looked upon as immoral by the normal man or woman. They, like the denizens of the air, fire, earth, and water, look upon things from an entirely different plane.

Some of this type display dual characteristics, for a man may do a man's work, and yet at the same time he may have a strong urge to don the raiment of women. Also these changeling women are inclined to adopt things masculine. Science is beginning to realize that the glands and their secretions have great power in determining character in the human.

These changelings find themselves in a difficult position in society, for what is right in their world of nature may not be right in the world of man, and when they seek to obey their instinctive nature they may run counter to the moral laws of the Western world. When they are true to their instincts they live in constant fear that they will encounter the hatred of the human herd, and when they give way to their lower instincts they produce the skilled criminal who preys upon men and women through the passion and desire nature.

This type, when it resorts to black magic, attracts conditions which prey upon the minds and bodies of the healthy, and stimulate the hidden abnormalities which every human being possesses.

There are types who use their physical attraction in order to gain prominent positions and assured incomes without work, which is displeasing to them. They play upon the weak-

nesses of humanity, often stoop to blackmail, and are the
destroyers of high ideals in youth. But when they live according to their higher instincts, they have a power of introducing
beauty into this world of sordidness through music, rhythm,
and the arts. Feminine instincts in a man's body produces a
love of personal adornment, and he is attracted to his opposite balance in nature, but when a man's instincts exist in a
woman's body, she apes the garments of man.

Changeling people should not be condemned until they
are understood, and medical science is making great strides
in this direction. These types, though interesting, are obnoxious to the normal, balanced man or woman, and often a
pathological case is condemned and crucified by humanity,
when it should be given every assistance from modern medical
science and psychology. Confessions have been made to me
of experiences which the world would condemn, but under
proper mental guidance and mental treatment science was
able to effect a cure. In this changeling type the imagination
manifests in two worlds at the same time, and their sensitivity
is more highly developed than most people imagine.

Nature deals with people of this type who give way to their
lower natures. However, if they can live up to their high ideals,
they become vehicles for nature's higher expression. Their
ideals are easily crushed by the brutality of the world, nevertheless they have within them the qualities which make the
natural magician. Through ceremonial magic they can easily
evoke the lower conditions of nature into the atmosphere of
humanity. Frequently they are practitioners of black magic,
for the animal world beneath their feet attracts them, and in
their ignorance they evoke forces contrary to the law. They
have a great desire to possess things and always wish to be in
the limelight, hence they often become the medium of the evil
powers in the intermediate worlds.

One of their great arts is the power of ridicule, yet they are
most susceptible to it, thinking that any genius or brilliancy
of mind is tarred with their own brush. They live in great
fear of discovery. At the time of the arrest of a great poet in
England, the mob panic filled the channel boats with men

of this description leaving the United Kingdom, for fear had reached them.

Unless the student is positive, such minds often bring about conditions of thought (through suggestion) very distasteful to a seeker of light. A healthy and normal person may enter a room infected by such conditions, and in this way often inoculates himself with these same conditions. Disease of the body is very infectious, but disease of the mind is doubly so. The sadist who takes pleasure in paining people by talebearing and suggestion is a most destructive agent in society, and innocent minds often suffer untold injury through their spoken words.

A lady told me the other day that her whole vacation had been spoiled by what someone told her people were saying about her, for she said there was no truth at all in the suggestion which had been made.

Elderly people, especially women, are apt to suggest, through ignorance, to the young of their own sex that marriage may bring dire suffering and disappointment. These people are usually unloved females, and their condition can invariably be traced back to submerged sex inhibitions.

Maliciousness towards others places a man after death in the same thought atmosphere which he induced in other minds, owing to his jealousy at seeing other people happy. In all humanity there is a compelling instinct to become and to create. There is a compelling urge to express as individuals (or collectively in groups), and when this malicious type is thwarted they try to bring disaster to other minds, and it is only by being positive that these attempts can be prevented.

Where a man places his thoughts, there you will find him, for his will and imagination constantly create "thought forms," which the spirit in nature partly ensouls. He placards his mental atmosphere with these thought creations, be they of his lower or higher nature. This is why the Yogi finds the atmosphere of these criminal gigolos most offensive, for beauty of form and expression in both sexes is a target of the good or evil thought forms created in the minds they attract.

The actor and actress on the stage or screen are common subjects for the bombardment of people's minds. One screen actor, living according to the finer purposes of his nature, was the target of thousands of feminine minds. I could see the screen of protection, invisible to the ordinary eyes, which surrounded him, yet at the summit of his manhood, death ensued.

Few people realize how this bombardment of evil can enter any loophole in a man's character and dethrone him. One great soul, who was brought into prominence in the world, was under the tutelage of the great souls hidden from humanity. He had his audience, but for the sake of money, he changed the message which was given him for the world, because his editors thought it would offend the sensitivity of organized religion. From that moment he was never a happy man, for he had failed to give that light for which he had incarnated. But he left a pressure of love behind him which, in his next incarnation, should bring him into a consciousness of the light.

CHAPTER FORTY-SEVEN

OUR WHITE AND BLACK ATOMS

Within the pure blood of the aorta lies the *nous* atom,[41] and about it cluster the instructor atoms, similar to stars, which it uses to contact the mind of man. At the base of the spine lies our adversary,[42] a black atom, with its constellation of atoms. We observe therefore that we have two powers within us, the white and the black atoms, representing good and evil.

The chakra or nerve center at the base of the spine contains all the horrors and filth of our imagination, for it is the historian of all our evil experiences through all time, as we measure it. If we wish to know about the evil of the world, the spheres of darkness and the intelligence of evil, we have only to contact this center of our lower nature. By aspiring to the highest, by meditation and prayer for the attainment of light, the white atom in our hearts takes us over into the realms of intelligence and light. It rests with us whether we seek union with the God of light, or union with evil—darkness and ignorance.

Through Yoga practice, under the observation of a teacher, we are taught to balance the good and evil forces in our body, and it is only then we place our feet upon the Path. One student, when he was able to travel out of his body in full consciousness, found that it took him a year and seven months to observe the evil going on in this world, then his teacher told him, "Your aspirations are for the highest, you wish either to live the life of a recluse or monk or a life of service in order to minister to those who are suffering from privation and hunger. I have shown you the evil in the world, and now that your feet have been placed upon the Path, I shall not see you personally for some time, unless you stray too far to the left or to the right."

In the development of the body and the discipline of the mind, the student quickly realizes that it is far easier to contact his lower nature than his higher self which stands in the presence of Truth. The greatest trouble in the practice of Yoga

41 Sometimes called the engineer atom, or white atom.
42 Also called the Secret Enemy.

comes in controlling the adversary, which tries to absorb and direct the higher creative energy which he has brought into a state of fermentation. When this energy is controlled by the lower self it makes man a beast, when controlled by the higher self it gives him freedom.

The soul imprisoned in the human body is liberated by this process of calcination and fermentation and by this process finds freedom, and man's whole nature becomes changed, as he perceives the great activity in nature and his part therein.

After witnessing "out of the body" the evil in the world, the student's first realization on his return to the body is that he does not desire to live! An ordinary healthy moral man can little imagine the slime and horror, the filth, cruelty, and sadism which the innocent often suffer through the mental aggression of men controlled by the black atoms within their bodies! But the lesson to be learned by the student is the process by which he can put fear into the hearts of those evilly disposed minds which are about to commit such cruelty as cannot be written about. One great opportunity that Yoga gives us is the power to heal and help those minds which, through ignorance have come under the sway of black magic.

The heart of humanity in general is good, but there are men and women who have given way to their lower natures, and have become obsessed by their own evil thought creations, which elemental nature has partly ensouled. The "black" atom within us has a wonderful power of vision. It is a prophet of evil, and can show the student the evil that is to come upon this planet, for we must remember that we all possess atoms which are historians, and as such have registered all our evil deeds and tendencies both in this and previous lives. As we have already said, we must balance the evil nature with the good, so that both are neutralized. By this we mean that we balance the power of the "white" atom by that of the "black" atom within us, and by aspiration and prayer, and by seeking the guidance of Truth, we pass through the door of darkness, up the winding stairway and then through the door of Jesus or of Buddha at the top of our heads.

If we concentrate upon the symbol of our heart center, we bring it to the notice of our human brain, likewise with the spade, which is the symbol that represents the seat of the "black" atom within us at the base of the spine. The black magician, using symbols, and by the exercise of will and imagination contacts himself with this lower seat of power, and he thus contacts the lower worlds of evil which this center represents, and which he seeks to dominate.

The engineer atom of the heart can also easily contact our minds with this lower center, for as I said, it is the seat in the body of prophecies of evil, and the more it is contacted the more powerful it becomes, until it is able to enslave the man and link him with evil—with the sub-human, elemental, and still deeper worlds.

After an experience with these forces we thank God for the instruction and then seek knowledge and deliverance through the instructor atoms of our heart center. Many people have had dreams which can be more accurately described as "horrors," or nightmares. These are a small matter compared with the horrors of uncleanliness and filth with which the lower atoms contact us. But once our fingers have been burnt, one ceases to experiment or seek contact with these states of consciousness, and returns with greater eagerness to the light, the carrier of all life. Any person contacting these forces through the use of the will and imagination or through inquisitiveness, or the leaders of black magic, usually ends in both mental and physical degeneration.

In Yoga one is often confronted with one's higher self which is a being of great splendor and brightness, whose light may be too brilliant for one's eyes. One also meets the dark shade of his evil elemental nature, which strange to say generally takes the form of an old woman.

This book has been written to discourage people from participating in magical circles or spiritual seances which evoke forces from sources of which they are ignorant. We do however wish to encourage the seeker to aspire for the truth which is within, in order to illumine his intelligence and bring him into union with this consciousness. Thus he will discover his own "kingdom of heaven." The inner heart of humanity is good when men can understand each other.

All the great avatars give us the message that the kingdom of heaven is within. This was the early message of the great religions, which brought about union with God, but unfortunately many religions crucified the lightbringers and the message was lost to humanity. Differences of religious opinion have brought terrible suffering and unrest to the world, yet always it is the duty of every man to seek within, and where he places his thoughts, there will he also be, for light loves light, and darkness revels in its own shade.

Above all a man must be worthy and sincere in his efforts to gain the Great Realization, for it is his sincerity and right conduct towards others which helps him to build up contact with the higher planes of nature's consciousness. His longing and aspiration for Truth begins to change him physically and mentally, and he is easily recognized by the dark forces in nature and man, for they realize his attainments. The higher clairvoyance brings him en rapport with the higher forces in nature. A higher perception gives him the power to recognize people in whom the light exists. He is thus able to perceive the more advanced souls in humanity, and to recognize his teacher when he meets him.

The teacher's patience is often sorely tried by the student's lack of understanding, but if he is a real teacher he is able to unlock seats of consciousness within the pupil, and help him to the realization of Truth. Often when the pupil finds that he is gaining knowledge unobserved, he becomes conceited and wishes to become prominent among those with whom he is associated. The more ignorant the student, the more he is apt to radiate his own personality and desire to shine as a being with occult knowledge! An occult student once calmly informed me that his poems were on a par with anything that Shakespeare ever wrote. However, a little time afterwards he changed his mind.

I remember being present with a friend at a meeting of a small group devoted to research in the ancient wisdom. During the meeting my friend turned to me and said, "Is it

not too bad to have to sit still and say nothing!" The leader
was speaking with apparent authority of the personality of
a great teacher whom none of them ever met in the body.
Both my friend and myself had been privileged to meet him.
Finally, the leader, speaking of this distinguished man, said, "I
brushed sleeves with S— in Piccadilly yesterday evening." This
shows the amazing presumption of some so-called leaders,
and the credulity of occult students regarding the personality
of a great soul! Yet it reminds one of the blind leading the
blind, and both fall into the pit.

These great teachers, who are so wise in the greater wisdom, are very childlike in their everyday life, and the chief
recollections I have of one great soul are *his radiant health, the
clearness of his blue eyes, and his boyish demeanor. He was absolutely
natural in everything he did,* but you could never forget his
words, no matter on what subject. There was never any hurry
about him, he went about quietly conducting his own affairs,
but by observation you learned much from him. There is
far too much credulity in occultism, especially among the
younger students.

The interesting thing about this great soul was that when
I met him "out of the body" I met him in advance of his time!
A strange phenomenon you will say! Although he is clean-
shaven today, he wears a beard in the future, and I discovered
also when with him "out of the body" that I also had a beard,
but not cut square like his, and that my hair was becoming
gray on my temples. This was arranged to show me the things
which will happen at that time, when the Age arrives! So we
perceive that in reality there is no such thing as time or space,
for everything IS. Our difficulty arises from the fact that this
plane of consciousness is the common meeting place of what
we have come to call the past and what we call the future.

When we consider the white and black atoms within our
bodies, we discover that every man and woman partakes of
the nature of one or the other of these atoms. During sleep,
our bodies receive a foretaste of death, if the black atom rules
we delight in wrongdoing, for the black atoms desire to make
our bodies impure. The engineer or builder atom in our heart

seeks to raise our standards, and to build up the body, so that it may become a proper temple for the Lord God of Truth within.

Thus we carry about with us atoms of construction and of destruction. When the white atom leaves the heart at death, the forces of destruction take charge of the body to disintegrate it and return it to nature. Therefore when the white atom has left the body, it is dangerous for a sensitive to handle it without bathing or disinfecting his hands. This explains why post mortem dissection of the body is so dangerous, for through its corruption, it contains great danger to a healthy blood stream.

The masters in Israel were very severe with those who touched the body of a dead person. "Whosoever toucheth the dead body of any man that is dead, and purifieth not himself, defileth the tabernacle of the Lord; and that soul shall be cut off from Israel."[43]

The black magician often resorts to the graveyard to raise the astral spirit of some decomposing body. After death, when corruption has begun, the astral fluid becomes defiled and with the higher perception of clairvoyance one can perceive a faint spark or light within the dead body. The magician, if possible, causes this astral form to detach itself from the body, and he then seeks to control it, making it a messenger to do his bidding, just as the "black" hypnotist ushers the astral body out of the sensitive, often forcing it to go long journeys in order to find out things and listen to the conversations of people in distant places.

The normal sensitive naturally rebels at the strain put upon him, even though he may submit to these things. This has often been the method which certain police officials have used in tracking down crime, so likewise the "black" magician can control and dominate an astral entity from a recently buried body.

The higher self of the body gravitates to its own source, if it be good, but the lower self remains behind, a shadow in a land

---

43   Num. XIX:13.

of shadows, and it becomes the familiar spirit of the magician, for he can bend it to his will.

These spirits or astral forms, reeking with filth and corruption, often present themselves at seances held in the dark, and they are easily attracted to those people who delight in evil, for they bring to them similar conditions. They enjoy entering into the psychic screen of the sensitive, for then they can perceive the things of our world through our human senses. Sometimes an earthbound child entity will ask if he can step into your screen to register the things which you perceive through your five senses. It often affords these innocents great pleasure to step into your atmosphere, for with the earthbound entities what we call night is their day, and what we call day is their night, and that is why nearly all spiritualistic seances are held in the dark.

In Yoga practice, we perfect our bodies so that we can register the vibrations of the astral plane of our earth, and on that plane we can easily converse with those disembodied intelligences known as spirits. Many of them are partly ensouled by nature, and the Yogi will always attract those who have a likeness to his own nature. This is a plane of great pretense, and we seldom meet any intelligence approximate to our own.

The beings of intelligence and light come from those spheres which are on a par with our inner planes, and in Yoga practice we go inwardly into the finer vibrations of nature in order to register and contact these bringers of light and knowledge.

Although spiritualism, so-called, is a bridge over to something still higher, the Yogi is not interested in information from intelligences who are attracted to our own illusion world. The rule is that what you aspire to when you seek to purify your mind and thought you will attract from those spheres of a like kind in nature. Therefore it is possible to contact beings of intelligence who stand in the presence of God.

Communication with earthbound spirits, whose astral fluid has become corrupt, very often causes the communicant also to become corrupt, for as man is the victim of his environment, so close association through curiosity or otherwise, with these astral entities, nearly always brings about physical, mental and moral degeneration.

Where your thought is placed, there you stand, and often people with pure minds and clean hearts are enabled to be of true service to humanity, through meditation on the bringer of light and intelligence, thus procuring response from the finer spheres of nature's consciousness.

Sometimes a higher elemental being may overshadow a person. Take for instance the case of Joan of Arc. She claimed that St. Michael and St. George appeared to her, and told her that they were angelic beings, and undoubtedly their guidance enabled her to save the throne of France. But the angelic beings of nature's elements appear as sunlight, whilst earthbound spirits only emit faint radiance.

With the higher clairvoyants, the radiance of the light which emanates from these beings determines their nature and character, and the debased improperly called spiritualistic circles are but the playgrounds of depravity and corruption. There are many so-called mediums in the "racket," who easily gain information (from questioning their victims) which they pass on to others, who often blackmail the persons whose foibles are thus discovered. The professional racketeer in the spiritualistic game makes a point of gaining any outside information she can regarding any wealthy client, and unwise people who wish to know the outcome of an unfortunate love affair often give details regarding other people which makes blackmail easy. Most people are credulous and seek to know their future, and fortune-tellers reap lucrative harvests in consequence. This of course is dealing with that lower side of spiritualistic research, which has brought the study into disrepute. Every circle gets the reflection of its own composite character.

I have never known any real Yogi to accept money for the use of what the world would call his or her spiritual gifts. The only thing the Yogi may accept is food, clothing, and shelter for his head wherever he may be, and although I have heard of some who have received great sums of money, I have never known them to use it for their personal pleasure, but always for the good of humanity. Be it understood I have been speaking of the practice of the *Western* Yogis.

I have often thought what a waste of effort it is to find a Yogi spending most of his time earning his daily bread, when we feel that he should have income enough to supply his needs, so that he would have more time to devote to those who were seeking the knowledge which he possesses. We naturally question ourselves as to whether it is something missing in his character which causes him to lack freedom for his higher expression, and this is a question which has often puzzled me. Should you question a Yogi about this, it will be the only time you will see him stirred to the very depths of his being, and the answer to your question will be this. There is a type of knowledge which is denied to the Yogi, although it is sometimes disclosed to him before his death. Then he knows his destiny, and he may even learn the date of his own death which to him is birth into the larger life. The Yogi can see into the lives of others, and read the pressure lines of their destinies while on earth, but regarding himself he cannot see his end until he has passed through his Gethsemane. He makes many sacrifices for the good of others, and people with kindly natures are sympathetic with the Yogi and pity him or any real spiritual teacher, but they little know what the *real life* means to the Yogi who has become conscious of the Presence, from whence radiates bliss and intelligence, truth and beauty.

As the student journeys on his path towards union, and as he enters into each higher vibration or division of consciousness, the things of this world, which meant so much in his younger days, become less real. He sees people as children, gaining their experience through suffering, and he seeks to aid them in their attainment of self knowledge, for he learns not only to see the real pleasures in life, also he sees the suffering and the crimes of this world, and the longing in the hearts of his fellows.

The [black] magician seeks to evoke the denizens of the astral world and enslave them by the power of his will and imagination. Out of the body, we often watch the operations

of these magicians, and register with our higher senses of
perception the odor, filth, and degradation of the lower world.
We see the distortions which appear in the bodies and faces of
the magician and his associates, which register the abnormal-
ity of their make-up.

I once witnessed a friend whom I loved much, gaining his
first experience under the tutelage of a master black magician.
It would be impossible to describe the change in his appearance. He became like the deformed creation of an animal man,
and queer little pads appeared at the tips of his fingers. They
were working over the body of a person recently dead in which
was a faint gleam of light. This astral substance they were lifting out of the grave and slowly revolving as if on a spit. The
bestial odor was frightful, and the atmosphere was that of an
hallucination or dream of horror. But children have to learn
by experience, and although this friend of mine has done a
great deal of work for the good of humanity and is watched
by a great soul, I know it will be some years before he again
reaches the path which he originally followed.

Many youthful seekers for occult knowledge are instructed
by the magician that there is a short way of attaining fame
and recognition in the world through necromancy such as we
have just described, and thus often contact their lower world
whose sounding board is near the base of their spine.

Many of these black magicians themselves, educated and
powerful in their influence, seek help to regain the true light
which they formerly possessed, for there are many people who
have been looked upon as sinister forces in the world, who by
sacrifice and good behavior towards others, could regain the
Light which they formerly possessed, and great is the joy in
heaven when they accomplish this.

Sometimes also apparently sinister instruments which have
brought about the downfall of a country have turned out to
be instruments of the powers of good, working out the karmic
law. Sometimes we find that a man who has the reputation of
bringing about great evil, is most kind and humane to those
in his immediate environment. And men who have caused
suffering and misfortune to millions are often most delightful

socially. The political "boss" often says, "Give the majority what it wants, but feather your own nest at the same time."

The head of the "G-men" in the United States has said that one man in every twenty-five is a criminal. This presents a problem each must solve for himself, for Yoga is a process of reforming oneself. No one is in a position to assist another until he has accomplished the purification of his own life. When each man will think for *himself,* and bring peace and beauty into his *own* world of being, he will then be able to bring peace and harmony into the outer world about him.

Anyone who undertakes the practice of Yoga first detaches himself from the world about him; he does not allow himself to be caught up in his emotions or swayed by the mental pressure of dictators, and as he watches what is going on in his world within, he registers for the first time what is really taking place in the world without.

The country that seeks direction from God, receives that direction, and it is only by so seeking that a nation can gain the powers which exist in nature's consciousness, to bring abundance to the undernourished, and the light of the spirit into the life of man.

If we go deeply into historical evidence, we find that the great lawgivers and statesmen who earnestly aspired for right direction from God, received the benefit of that knowledge and that it brought peace and prosperity to their country.

A great Yogi covering a major political crisis once said, "The leaders of the country are blind; they do not know what to do for the country they represent; the light of direction being unsought is denied them; they work only for the pres-ervation of their party, and the real needs of the people are neglected through lack of devotion to God."

The real leaders of a country are prophets. They foresee the trend of things which are to be, and seek to forestall them if they are detrimental to the freedom of the individual. President Lincoln foresaw the conditions which were to come to pass in the United States, and sought to preserve the nation from such danger. Man, *know thyself,* that ye may sense this! As Solon has rightly said, "The best government is the government which does the most for its poorest individuals."

Today the strong must labor for the weak, and in order to assist the weak, a man must be strong in himself—strong to know and express God, the Lord God of Truth which is within. This is the great mystery teaching of the ages, the science of Yoga. Man must find God through the nature of his own being, and by so doing, he gains the law of nature's consciousness.

CHAPTER FORTY-EIGHT

SOURCES OF POWER AND YOGA PRACTICE

The source of all dynamic power lies in the secondary nervous system which operates on the nerve forces of the human organs similar to a spark coil in an automobile. All true power comes from the relationship which exists between the central nervous system and the secondary system which results in stepping up this universal dynamic power.

The Yogi derives his power by manipulating real solar energy, so as to raise the potential of his secondary output. But the "black" magician separates himself from the real source of his being, hence the activating solar energy is denied and in order to demonstrate he has to draw upon the lunar energy through the lower spinal centers, and this can only manifest on those planes represented by his lower nature. That is why he always seeks to drain the vital powers from his associates and victims. With him it is merely a case of survival, for he must draw force and vitality from the lower world either through the living or the dead; hence he wages constant war upon others, and when he fails, he dies. This mystery becomes more simple when the student realizes that man has a primary, secondary and tertiary nervous system. The tertiary system represents man's grossest nature or physical being. The Yogi consciously enters the mind world of his secondary system, with the aspiration that he may be able to unify himself with his true primary nature, his spiritual being, the Lord God of Truth within. In this is the difference between the white and the black magician. Thus where the black magician must fight in order to exist, the Yogi *must love in order to become the instrument of divine service.*

When we meet a "black" magician, either in or out of the body, we observe always a pathetic look of fear. He realizes that we have discovered his true character, and he is apt to draw from us love and compassion, for he is similar to a wounded animal seeking assistance. Meeting such people may stir one deeply, but the student must be careful that he is not

seduced by their personality and magnetism. They are merci-
less men who can *do* things, they have the power to kill, and
like the hunter they exist upon their prey.

It is only when we undertake our Yoga practice of entering
and studying the real nature of our being that we realize our
previous ignorance of ourselves and the world in which we
live. Life, real life, is something to be enjoyed, *and real enjoyment comes from love and sacrifice for the well being of others.* It is
only when we enter into the mind world of our secondary system that we begin to perceive and analyze the forces working
deep within our nature. We cannot perceive what is going on
within our own self-constituted world until we gain a vantage
point from which to observe it. In order to gain this position,
we must use the solar energy to step up the potential in our
secondary nervous system, and it is only when we come in
contact with a great soul that we begin to realize the greater
vistas and perception which they have obtained, and this
realization stimulates us towards the greater purpose of our
being.

There are forces and energies within and without which
must be tapped and controlled, if we would gain our vantage
point. Before very long man will contact the higher counterpart of electricity which lies within nature's keeping, and
will learn to control it as the Atlanteans did of old, and the
"white" magicians of later days.

Man has made this world uncomfortable, and the scourge
and flail of circumstances must fall upon his shoulders
until he regenerates himself in service for his race. Merlin, a
professed Christian and so-called magician, has said, "War
shall become so terrible that the nations shall call for peace."
But the individual must find peace within before he can
bring peace to others. It is only when we seek to serve our real
higher nature that we can find peace within.

The occult significance of suffering is generally demonstrated to the student by his teacher, for pain can be so
intense that it turns to pleasure. That is why many Zen priests
are crippled in some way, with their bodies badly scarred. This
experience of pain draws out impurities from the physical

vehicle, and many students have passed through it by a very simple process.

In Yoga, it is generally impressed on you that you should not discuss subjects which you are not able to demonstrate. This is a difficulty found in Yoga practice, for you must learn to demonstrate in others the things which you have discovered in yourself and the outer world. Yoga means union with the Lord God of Truth within, and it takes patience, hard work and discipline to gain any extension of consciousness.

After meeting your teacher, you must develop and discipline your body. Then you must learn the science of going inwardly to develop your finer forces. When you think you have attained to an extension of consciousness, you must demonstrate this in your teacher's presence, and there must be a sincere aspiration to know truth and gain knowledge. Eventually there will come a time in your training when you must learn to travel out of your body into finer (and also denser) spheres than your objective senses now register.

The writer spent nine months of hard work, living practically a hermit's life out of contact with humanity in general, and regarded it as a failure. After a year's interval he again attempted this union with nature, and after persevering for twelve months he came to the conclusion that it was beyond his power of achievement, so he renounced all desire to attain that union. Having renounced his desire, he suddenly felt himself being slowly born into the consciousness of nature without effort. Then he was given instruction and permitted to observe movements in nature known only to the adept.

Years before, while living among the red Indians, the writer had realized that some of them were in constant rapport with something in nature which he could not observe. The student will understand that there are realms of consciousness and activity not generally known, but which may be explored through effort in Yoga, but that this finer and higher knowledge can only be taken by forceful preparation and patient waiting.

Yoga practice teaches the pupil to discern what other people have seemingly overlooked. There are in Yoga "information periods" which are instruction courses from sources hidden from the ordinary mind. It is a process by which to unlock the door of our own house of experience where is recorded all the experience of our past as well as of our present life and activity.

As we progress inwardly, we enter into many different states of activity which exist within us, and from the standpoint of each of these states we view the activities of the objective world about us and take note of things which hitherto had escaped our observation.

If we aspire and are persistent in our practice, we discover a latent energy within us which, when evoked, brings us into a new world of consciousness and activity.

CHAPTER FORTY-NINE
THE LAW OF DISCRETION

The higher wisdom seeks perfection of character guided by the law of discretion. This higher wisdom can only be obtained through knowledge of the law of discretion, and the student must always be discreet and not give knowledge of the Truth to those who are not yet ready to receive it.

Now what is it that the law of discretion requires the student to conceal from the unprepared? It is a knowledge of the consciousness of nature as manifested in her different divisions. In order to gain this knowledge, we must enter into a conscious relationship with nature and her governing powers. To the great majority of people nature is a closed book; they perceive her objective semblance, but they do not realize or apprehend why she so expresses, what her relationship with humanity is, or her endeavor to bring into the world the law of her understanding.

Humanity knows little of the beings and intelligences in nature, or of the relationship which should exist between nature and man. Therefore, knowledge of the law of discretion comes from the instruction gained through Yoga practice, during which we enter into conscious rapport with the hidden intelligence and knowledge in nature. This instruction is similar to reading history.

We can study the rise and fall of a nation by studying the previous incarnations of its former inhabitants. We contemplate its end by observing gestation and birth of some new nation, composed in part of the reincarnated souls, from its school of experience. This is why history is said to repeat itself.

We appreciate the zeal of the pilgrims and the Crusaders, who for the sake of an ideal often walked barefooted to Jerusalem. Observe these reincarnated men of former days, doing with their hands today what formerly as crusaders they did with their feet. These men working with their hands today have the same ideal as in the former incarnations, but a more refined nature, and we find the higher ideals of socialism,

communism, and bolshevism entertained by these manual
workers, who are more intelligent than of old. Their ideal is to
deliver humanity from oppression. In these modern crusades
we have to remember the law of discretion which conceals,
until the proper time, the higher truths. Others more evolved
in knowledge and intelligence and living more in the mind
world have the same noble aspirations as these workers. To
them the governing power of this world will ultimately be
given. These minds, which are becoming spiritualized, have a
knowledge of the law of discretion, and although working for
the good of humanity, they still do not cast their pearls before
the ignorant swine.

There has always been a caste of intelligence on this earth,
composed of those who have acquired the greater wisdom
through a knowledge of the law of discretion, which nature's
consciousness gives. When the student is ready for it, he
becomes conscious of the conflict between nature and man,
and is taught how to remedy it, through the process of *knowing himself.*

Then we perceive that it is through a knowledge of the law
of discretion that man acquires the higher wisdom, which
nature's consciousness withholds from the ignorant mind.
Therefore we go to nature to gain knowledge and understanding, for man can only govern himself and his powers
intelligently when he has been passed by nature's guardians.
It is through knowledge of the laws of nature that man gains
knowledge of his Lord God of Truth within, for God is never
apart from his creation.

When the student makes the great discovery that his real
self is his "man in nature," the union between the higher and
lower self is quickly brought about. We often hear the phrase,
"If man could only live according to nature!" but man must
first remove from himself those conditions which nature
proclaims as unnatural, for her higher beings stand in the
presence of Truth. When we remove our unnatural conditions,
we also remove the ignorance within our mental atmosphere,
for nature's devas proclaim their teachings from the *knower
consciousness,* and this is what nature seeks to give humanity.

CHAPTER FIFTY

THE UNDERWORLD AND
ITS PRISON HOUSE

In the underworld of man there is a division of nature where climatic temperatures seldom vary. It is an abode of ignorance, despair, and hunger, and is inhabited by sluggards. There hunger causes acute physical suffering, for it is a hunger for the recognition and notice of beings above them, yet the density of their bodies prevents them from rising to these higher levels of intelligence.

Whenever there is dampness and moisture in our atmosphere, these discarnate beings can appear upon the level of humanity at night. Light is their enemy, and when the rays of the sun dissolve the globules of moisture, they sink back into their lower levels. You can gain very little knowledge from them. They can sometimes give their names, but if you want to aid them, they do not understand what help really means. They are surrounded by an atmosphere of despair and suffering, for they have not left a pressure of love behind them in their late earthly life. When a human being through misfortune is hungry or cold, these discarnate beings are attracted by his melancholy despair, for like attracts like.

The more intelligent of these nocturnal visitors gain some sort of recreation by tormenting human minds with an overflow of their own mental states and conditions. This may be likened to a sick man being surrounded by violent inmates of an asylum, subhuman beings whose earth lives have been steeped in ignorance or sin, and who very often inspire their victims to actions contrary to the law.

A suffering, despondent man has very little will power, and often acts upon the spur of the moment. These denizens of the lower world sometimes suggest to him when passing a shop that he should steal, and if he succumbs to the suggestion they are overjoyed because their victim has become subject to the fear and custody of the law.

Nearly all criminals are egotists and love to earn a reputation for cleverness, and this in the end invariably brings about their downfall. When the student is taken out of his body for the first time and accompanies his teacher upon a mental flight, he is not taken into these underworlds of being until he has become proficient in the art of levitation.

Later by passing into the deeper densities of the world beneath our feet he is shown the evil of the world, and when he returns, his first exclamation is, "I must take a bath," for he feels as if he had been into the Ghetto or the slum area of some foreign city.

As the student has now become deeply sensitive, his "light" is easily recognized by these dwellers of the underworld, and they are attracted to him as a moth is attracted to a candle. Many people on leaving their body in deep sleep, go to these underworld spheres in order to minister to these beings. What we here call mid-day has its correspondence there in what might be called the atmosphere of a London fog, and I have seen thousands of these beings collected together in an amphitheater listening to these helpers, for "out of the body" man has a double gift of oratory.

I at first heard with amazement the orations delivered by these helpers who on the earth plane are often incapable of making any speech. I even know of people who are looked upon as failures on this earth, but when out of the body they beam with intelligence and sincerity and are able to do a great work for God in these ignorant underworlds.

Just as this world of ours is divided into countries, so the ignorant of the underworld inhabit their own place. In one division are the indolent and stupid, in another those obsessed with anger and hatred, while, in other divisions men who are masters of eloquence and logic are grouped together; for also there are evil men of learning who have wrought destruction in previous lives.

The student will be astonished at the scintillating intellect of these scholars which is seldom to be witnessed on the earth plane. They excel in hypnotic pressure and often find channels of expression through contacting sensitive minds on our earth plane. The deeper the student descends into this underworld, the more brilliant and scintillating is the evil thereof, for the more we receive from the light of Truth, the more capable we become of descending deeper into the darkness of ignorance.

These brilliant intellects from the evil side portray to the student's mind what might be called the good of evil and the evil of good, and when he is "out of the body" there is that instrument within the student which measures the light of the spirit in any individual that he meets. This is his safeguard, and in the early days of his career he is taught to banish fear, but he finds that it takes real courage to work in these conditions.

Still there is an element in nature which removes fear from the human heart and gives the student courage to become the instrument of God's purpose.

There are still lower densities in nature, where the debris and filth of all time are collected. It is an area of slime and degraded intelligence, where the passions are quickly aroused against all who act contrary to the atmosphere of this under-world of being.

In this debris we find traces of the passions and desires of past civilizations as well as of the present, and the inhabitants which live in this slime have natures similar to those prehis-toric creatures that lived in the alluvial slime when the water receded from the earth.

The form patterns of these inhabitants do not conform to the human and animal life of today. They are monstrosities possessing an intelligence which is quick, ferocious, and alert, imprisoned in bodies ranging from forms like slugs, toads and spiders to malformed animals and human shapes.

By the use of seances, will, and imagination, these entities may be evoked into our world of being. Usually seances attract astral entities, seeking to draw upon mankind, but others are sometimes called up, who through misuse of the law have fallen into this prison-house from a higher position in nature. Like a brilliant financier, imprisoned for breaking the law, these entities retain brilliant intellect and the consciousness of evil wisdom. They also desire to escape from their prison-house and when, by magic, they are evoked into the world of

man they are able to attain their desire and to injure humanity.

There are many schools of the "left hand" side of magic
seeking to gain power and control over the youth of today,
particularly when they are rich. Youths, who are drawn into
these circles by curiosity, are invariably given opportunities
to gratify their passions and desires through sex worship.
It is difficult for one who has been enticed into ceremonial
magic of the darker side to become clean again, for there
is a law dealing with all "black" magic, which is that if the
hierophant fails he becomes the prey of the forces which he
has evoked. For instance, if he attempts to bring filth into
the places occupied by people whom he wishes to annoy (for
which he is often paid large sums of money) and fails because
his intended victims possess the knowledge of how to protect
themselves, he must persist more intensely and use every
means in his power to bring about the result which he desires,
for unless he succeeds, he goes under and often loses his life.

For this reason people have often been persecuted for years
by the malicious mind of a magician, realizing that unless he
succeeds, the evil power which he evokes rebounds upon himself, and the result is a quick degeneration of his physical and
moral nature. These black societies have their "rackets" and
are guided by master minds, who prey upon the curiosity of
those whom they wish to ensnare into their net. The student
of Yoga, after meeting his teacher, observes their objectives
while "out of the body" from a sphere of vibration which it is
impossible for these astral entities to reach. This is similar to
looking down upon them from a place just above the picture
molding of a room and observing what is taking place.

These entities have weight, and are of the consistency of
jelly. They also have great speed and quickness of movement,
and no man should experiment or seek the aid and activities
of these souls who have fallen so deep into matter. When you
meet a master of black magic "out of the body" and witness
his brilliancy of evil, you cannot help admiring his great powers, but you always hear ringing in your ears, "O Lucifer, Son
of the Morning, how deeply hast thou fallen!"

These scintillating intelligences often place men in prominent positions of wealth in order to influence them to become great destructive agents. There is an old Hermetic saying, "When your adversary cannot gain power over you when you are poor, he will make you rich, and his task may become easy."

A great magician, who had surrendered his soul to the adversary, once appealed to a great "white" teacher that he might be allowed to "come back," for he realized that devotion to good was the only way to freedom. Unfortunately these men always search for deficiencies in a teacher's character in order to undermine his work. They are past masters of ridicule, have a deep knowledge of the powers of suggestion, and they seek to break up the unity in any group which is dedicated to service or devotion to God.

They often train assistants to enter groups of instruction in order to work the downfall of the group leaders; they are clever in praising the work of so-called spiritual teachers, leaving a suggestion however which fires the imagination of the listeners.

Leaders in this warfare of good and evil often meet to measure their opponent's strength. Some of the greatest criminals in society seemingly live ideal lives, love their children, and bring beauty into the home. They are pleasant people to meet on the surface, for they are past masters in the art of dissimulation.

A friend of mine was of great service to a lady who was in distress in the last Great War. He told me that the lady's husband had always been his arch enemy, but the lady did not know this, and he wondered what the husband would say when he discovered who it was that had saved his wife's life! We have heard the old saying that there is honor among thieves, and we sometimes find examples of this among the racketeers of crime.

I was once invited to dinner to meet some very distinguished people, whose names are very well known all over the world. As the guests were passing into the dining room, a "personage" beckoned me to remain behind. He looked around to see if anyone had observed our delay, then he came up to me and shook his fist in my face, saying, "We hate you." This was a process of trying to cast fear into my mind; however, this great churchman afterwards asked me for aid, saying that his soul was in hell, and he wanted my friendship but he lived only three years longer. It interested me very much to find that among the guests were some of the great spiritual leaders of the land!

Now and then amongst the great religious leaders of all denominations you find the occultist and the Yogi. In the past these leaders have often been denounced and martyred by their followers because they failed to practice the law of discretion, but most of the great souls in our churches pass apparently unnoticed and unheeded by mankind.

Where there is light, souls will be drawn for encouragement and teaching. The world is athirst for instruction which will lead men to God Realization. The great initiate teachers say that every man whom the great Master Jesus looked at while on this earth has been unified with the Christ consciousness— God Realization.

It may be news to the student that the great devas in nature exalt the names of those who have gained God Realization, whether widely known as avatars, prophets, or known only to the few.

The sincere student sometimes contacts these great souls hidden from humanity, and he then realizes that it is chiefly through their efforts that great changes in the welfare of nations are brought about. It has been written that there was a man behind Washington, and those other great minds which brought the United States into being. Several good instances of great souls who remained behind to educate and enlighten the world are Savonarola, Dante, Botticelli, and Spinoza.

Ever behind humanity are these great souls working to bring light into darkness—working to bring the consciousness of Truth to humanity. In Yoga we often pray to the great light bringers who have been messengers to mankind, and we send them our love, but humanity in general does not think of these undying ones who are always watching over us and attracting us to nobler efforts to become fit instruments of God's purpose.

Man in general is like the frog, seemingly contented with the mud of his environment, and seldom knows or seeks to know what is above the mire.

CHAPTER FIFTY-ONE

THE LAW OF HUMAN SECURITY

One of the purposes of this book is to encourage you to open yourself to a new type of instruction, something which is not yet familiar to the Western world. Its source is a plan which was formed in the beginning of all time, but its expression has been withdrawn. It is again rising to the surface of the waters, and seeking to manifest in the consciousness of humanity.[44]

The older generation will greet with uncertainty or ridicule the proposition that nature has a right to exist according to her own evolution. But when we realize that there is behind everything a propelling force causing ideas to manifest in the relative terms of space and time, it is not difficult to approach the subject from this different angle.

When we push a large boulder over the face of a cliff, we can watch its descent until it finds a place of rest. Energy and force were needed to move it from its first bed, but we disturbed its equilibrium. We saw it descend and when, at last, it reached a position of security, it had wholly changed its original position. What had been the bottom may now be the top! Yet it had come to rest, and once more was secure.

But what security has *man* for his future? When his attitude towards life experiences a change, the security which he formerly thought he possessed may have passed away, and he will look about to discover some other promise of support and security. He is not aware that there is a law which gives security to all who will follow its precepts. Like a grain of sand on the hillside man is exposed to the weather and the sunshine, and a very slight avalanche will cause him to change his position. Perhaps he will be covered by the other grains of sand about him, and then his light is shut out. But the changing tide of circumstances or adversity is ever shifting mortal sand grains, and each individual experiences pleasure and pain and is well or ill nourished, depending upon his

---

44 Genesis 1-2.

own intelligence and the intelligence of those who share the atmosphere of his environment.

It is our present effort to return man to his proper place and position in nature, where consciousness has three divisions and we would have man become conscious of his own self and the self-created universe wherein he finds himself. This self-consciousness does not manifest, for instance, in stones or inanimate objects, for in them consciousness is imprisoned, but man is conscious of *himself,* which places him above the mineral, vegetable, and animal kingdoms. But he is not yet conscious of his self-created universe and its place in nature's plan. In his ignorance he does not realize that what he calls mind is the "watcher" which sees and records all things. But, seeing and recording things leads ever to the depths of illusion, and it is to discover some means of escape from this "watcher" mind that Yoga teaches us to look beyond objective knowledge to a state of consciousness, in which there is bliss and intelligence and in which the higher self in man resides. When in Yoga practice we pass through the mind world and no longer rely upon our physical senses, they are shut down and we pass into a knower consciousness or state of being known as nirvana, and we are then within the presence of truth and beauty.

All the great avatars have left instructions showing how to pass through the lower mind world into this consciousness where there is happiness and peace, and the basic principle of this instruction is *self education.* Every true student at sometime feels a strong desire to retreat inwardly, to remove from himself the conditions about him, and to seek union with the Lord God of Truth within.

The reader will realize that this process is diametrically opposed to the educational systems which man has evolved, which teach him to observe the things outside of himself and to contemplate and analyze the objects and changes which his senses can register. By such means man seeks to discover Truth through science and the activities of his human brain deal with material things. In the coming era of understanding man will adopt a new system of development, through which, by means of tenets of emancipation, he will discover the Lord God of Truth within.

The youth of today seek demonstrations of the things which people talk about; they seek to *know* things, and frequently say what they think, regardless of the sensitivity of those around them. They are reckless in their utterances and will not hesitate to say to the preacher, "You can fool others, but you cannot fool me." For this new vitality and vibration which is flowing into youthful humanity the old bottles will not serve, and youth demands to *know*. This demand will be answered increasingly by the knower consciousness within. Youth also demands opportunities to do and seeks for adventure and conquest. The vibration which carries him on disturbs the older generation about him, but as the youthful learn to think for themselves they will cease to be the tool or prey of older minds. Youth, the adventurer, questions everything. He quickly gains experience regarding his physical body and discovers that giving way to his passions and desires does not quench his thirst. He then begins to think about himself, his own place and position in society, and his own powers, and he realizes that under present day conditions he must conquer or go under. Unlike his ancestors he dares to question the meaning of it all, and then comes the urge to *know himself* and the others that are around him.

This struggle to know the Truth brings to him, for the first time, a slight knowledge of self, and as he meditates he realizes that a change is coming over him. Visions and vistas appear before his mind, and he begins to perceive things which others have not observed. If he earnestly seeks to know Truth, the intelligence in Nature will bring conditions to his attention, and inspiration to his mind, which will cause him to seek more deeply and earnestly for the consciousness of truth. If he persists long enough, he will discover that there are "engineer" atoms within him which connect his mind with information periods of instruction.

The secret of all Yoga practice is to learn from the "instructor" atoms within. These atoms can relate us to our own hidden books of knowledge which, through myriads of lives,

record our experiences. We must remember that our mind is
the "watcher," and that it has many volumes stored up for us
to reopen in some future period of development. These volumes will be made known through the aid of the "engineer"
atom within us, which will attune our human brain to the
frequency in which these records are preserved on the higher
plane.

Education begins with knowledge, and ends in God
Realization. The great beings in nature, those guardians from
whom the student of Yoga receives his instruction, constantly
admonish, "Tell us what you know, not what you think." For
they live in the *knower* consciousness, *i.e.* the plane on which
they know things without thought.

When we sum up our education by what we *know*, we
discover that we have attained little knowledge in our present
life. This is because our thoughts, minds and activities are
projected outwardly into this world of illusion which man has
created around him! It is by the process of going inwardly,
and by aspiration and devotion to Truth that we establish a
conscious approach to truth. The "Wise Ones" teach that we
must attain to the knowledge of the law of discretion before
the gates of true knowledge will be opened to our understanding. The education of the future which the cosmic hierarchal
ones disclose to the student is diametrically opposite to that
which the children of today are taught in ordinary education.
The child of the future will be the educator of the teacher, for
the teacher will ask him, "What do you know about this?"

In the curricula of today new revolutionary theories are
not welcomed. The discovery of a new law in chemistry disar-
ranges the other so-called laws of the past. The discovery of
a new law regarding religion is apt to change the expression
of the so-called other laws of benevolence and spiritual goodness. Thus the great avatars follow one another but seek to
adapt their teaching to their own time, place, and position.
Today, nevertheless, a new discovery is to be made by man. He
will learn that he is a changeling nourished by Mother Nature,
and that all understanding of Truth comes to him from an
inborn consciousness, inspired by the deathless solar fire.

Thus as man retreats inwardly he enters into a closer relationship with the Lord God of Truth within, his own "Kingdom of Heaven."

Because of ignorance of her purposes, and failure to interpret her manifestations, nature and her powers have not been fully realized by man, but if the student wishes to unite himself with her consciousness he must learn to serve her purpose. When man serves nature, nature will serve man, and unite him to the godhead within. This is the beginning and end of Yoga practice.

The mightiest of nature's Titans (the fourth class of sentient beings) are those who oppose the work of the devas. Among these are the thunder and the lightning, the wind and rain, which in their fury, oppose the devic inspiration and unite to destroy all that the devas build up.

The wind and the rain are divided against the lightning and the thunder, and both are often dominated by their atoms. These atoms, while imprisoned in the bowels of the earth, are energized by the earth power and are thus led to seek above the earth for freedom from their chains. Thus they escape out of the earth into the higher atmosphere where their energy is collected into composite powerful currents of activity, which being insufficiently refined are forced to return into the prison house of earth.

As it is with these elemental forces, so it is with man. He who is evil and delights in wrongdoing begets children like unto himself, and the end of them will be the same as his own. This is the meaning of the words, "Who knoweth the spirit of man which goeth upwards, and the spirit of a beast that goeth downwards!" The divine Creator alone knows whether they will ascend or descend.

Adam, having become impure in himself before conjugal union with Eve, begat impure offspring, but Abel, who was begotten in a state of purity after repentance, was consequently pure. Thus we learn why the two brothers Cain and Abel were so dissimilar in nature and character. Thus it was that Abel ascended early from the physical plane, while Cain begat his unnamed progeny in the land of Nod.

To a certain extent man has a foretaste of death during sleep, and it is then that the evil spirit is present to defile and corrupt. On rising we should wash our hands, lest we defile that which we touch. "And also I will cause the prophets and the unclean spirit to pass out of the land"[45] and He will swallow up death forever.

---

45   Zech. XIII: 2.

CHAPTER FIFTY-TWO
THE YOGA THEORY OF PEACE

In an atmosphere of depression, despair, or disaster, we find conditions that are easily absorbed. Then, when the newspapers dwell upon horrors or scenes of illusion and disaster, panic seizes upon people's minds and in such atmosphere, which is not healthy, or conducive to vitality, people are liable to collect all sorts of mental refuse and debris which press painfully against the silken fabric of their mind bodies, and react upon the physical.

The condition of our mental and physical bodies affects the aspiration atom within us, therefore happiness and laughter are good. Through our nervous system and by breathing, we induce the same conditions we aspire for into our bodies. Unhappiness or melancholia is as contagious as smallpox.

The person who worries reflects his distraught condition into the minds about him, and it matters not whether it is the worry of a moment, or a disease which can only be thrown off with the utmost difficulty. In the deeper states of Yoga, we learn the folly of worry and discover love and happiness, and a state of bliss and intelligence. Since these are the conditions of our heaven world, we aspire for their expression within us in our daily life.

When has worry ever done any good to a single individual? Ask yourself which you prefer, the sour cynic, or the genial philosopher? Shall we retreat into the darkness and ignorance of the past, or shall we press forward into the light of realization? These questions are for each to answer in the light of his experience.

By experience, we find it best to sail through life on an even keel, being neither too happy nor too sad, for when we can balance happiness and sadness, we find peace. By balancing the good and evil in things, we find a common starting point from which to go forward, and we observe that the fear of things to come can and does harass the ordinary mind more than the actual conditions of the present.

It is fear of a coming war that attracts the conditions of war, for the fear vibration draws into its vortex the conditions for its fulfillment. Through Yoga we can develop a condition of assurance, and discover a state of bliss and intelligence within us in which there is no fear. Once this consciousness is tapped, nothing else matters, but to attain permanent union.

Innocent minds suffer much through living within the environment of those who worry about things which *might* happen. Worry is the egotism of selfishness, and the worrier invariably concentrates upon his own position. Attachment to things and to persons is the cause of worry, and like a whirlpool, the worrying person draws others down into his condition of unrest. It is only by conserving our power that we can build up a reservoir of strength, and Yoga teaches us how to find peace, even in the midst of the conflict and agitation around us.

Yoga teaches us to use our powers inwardly, and not to expend them outwardly. We must accept our burdens gracefully, for when the student takes the Path, he is often plunged into ranges of experience which other men escape, in order to teach him to have command of himself in his environment, and thus learn the reason *why* he has been placed there. It is by this means that the student acquires a knowledge of the conditions about him, and the Law is that when one realizes why he has been placed in a certain distasteful position, and has solved the problem of adapting himself to it, he is freed from it.

The student of Yoga learns in time that he must give of his light to those about him, though this often means sacrifice of his own personal desires and wishes. A man in a workshop under a "boss" often kicks against the pricks, and wonders why he is so chained to circumstance. It is natural that he desires something better, but when he realizes that he has been placed in that position in order to gain a certain type of experience, so that he may be able to help those in his environment, then he achieves his freedom.

Whatever a man desires most in his heart, that he will ultimately achieve, but not before he has gained through experience, the knowledge of its proper use. A distinguished surgeon once said to me, "All my life I have desired to be a clog dancer, and I will some day, for I am only happy when I am practicing my steps. Do not give me away to my friends, but I must express myself in rhythm."

At the present time the world is going through a clarifying process, and a newer vibration is slowly and intermittently manifesting purpose in the human mind world. There are impulses of this glorious Dayspring of Youth which scientists call cosmic waves, that will bring humanity into closer union with the spirit of all nature which is about us.

There have been periods in history when the consciousness of this Dayspring in Nature was allied to the human understanding, and the Yogi finds moments of instruction given to him through this vibration. This instruction shows him the newer universe, when the human mind will be engendered with a new quality of perception, and will come to observe movements in nature and things close at hand which his forebears seldom noticed.

It is for humanity to return to the knowledge possessed in hyperborean days, which will bring about a close alliance between man and nature, and when men come to understand nature's laws and systems of government, they will begin to know themselves.

It is not until we become natural and childlike that we can remedy our faults, and gain the perception of God Realization. In other words, it is the return of the objective man towards union with his *natural man* in nature's consciousness—his higher self, that solves his problem of finding peace and happiness.

CHAPTER FIFTY-THREE
SELF-REALIZATION

The majority of humanity do not understand themselves any more than they understand the laws of nature. They have been given instruction, but they have gained little knowledge of the third division of consciousness, known as self-realization.

Man, conscious of himself, does not understand the process by which he can acquire knowledge of the *real self* that dwells in his "Kingdom of Heaven within."

The wish of every sincere student of Yoga is to extend his range of consciousness to an understanding of his real self, but his objective mind knows little of the real mind hidden behind the screen of his objective brain. He does not realize that he lives, moves, and has his real being[46] on other planes of consciousness, and in other worlds than those which his five objective senses register. He is sometimes conscious, by means of dreams and by the use of his imagination, that something is going on behind the screen which separates him from a knowledge of himself, but these flashes do not come through any one of the five human sense channels.

When we are deep in discussion, the only information we possess is that gained from worldly experience, and from books and newspapers, but the *real* knowledge of Truth can only be obtained through sincere aspiration and meditation. What the student earnestly seeks, he will find, if he will only persist in his seeking, and, in order to unlock the door through which he must pass in his search, he must first acquire knowledge of himself, and of his place and position in the universe.

Directly he seeks union with the Reality (Truth) within him, the process by which he can knock upon the doors of knowledge will be made known. By devotion to Truth he will slowly discover himself enlarging his powers of perception and that which formerly passed unnoticed becomes known to him. Bliss and intelligence is about him, but he has not

---

46   Acts 17:28: "For in him [God] we live, and move, and have our being..."

yet awakened into their consciousness. When seeking to obtain this through Yoga, we discover within ourselves all the instruction needed to regain our lost place and position in nature's environment.

Since man has ceased to conform to nature's will he has, during his evolution, fallen deep into matter and exalted his personal will. Therefore he does not rely for right action and government upon nature's guidance, although occasionally he has flashes of what he terms intuition.

At one period of his evolution man lived and moved and had his being in nature's consciousness, and in that Golden Age he obeyed the laws of nature, and was a man of nature. It is the aim and end of all the higher Yoga teachings to return man to the consciousness of nature, that he may follow again the dictates of nature's will—in other words, the aim of Yoga is unification of the soul with its source—God Realization.

A time comes in the student's training when he is taught to minister to those souls in darkness, whose whole atmosphere is one of torment and suffering. The average man little realizes that through his evil actions he burdens himself with the sufferings which he causes to others, and that he has to carry this burden until he has paid off his karmic debt.

Often after meeting his teacher, the student undertakes to clear himself in his present life of all his karmic debts. This brings him suffering and slavery under the dominion of his employer, but if he is sincere and will take the plunge, he can usually accomplish this in about twenty years of service.

On first seeing the student, the teacher measures the karmic debt that he has incurred in this life, through giving way to his passions and desires, and the student is often told that when he has worked off his karmic debts in this life, the teacher will take him on again for further instruction. This is the dark age for the student, but he must willingly accept his sentence. Often, in his ignorance the student does not realize that he has powers, both within him and without, which plead for his forgiveness and often shorten his sentence.

When at last he is free, and his shackles fall off, there is "joy in Heaven," for then he is able to take up his greater work and go forward in the process of becoming. During his term of bondage and service to others, he gains a great range of experience, and this gives him the power to aid others undergoing similar experiences. When the pupil is ready, the master will be at hand, and then there will be a joyous reunion, for the door is opened, and he perceives the light of realization and the plan and purpose of his incarnation.

As soon as the sincere student has paid his karmic debt, greater freedom of experience and greater knowledge than he has ever previously enjoyed come to him. It is not the rich who have the monopoly of the Light, it is more often found among the poor (those seekers of the light striving to end their karmic penalties). It is more often the tired and hungry heart whose soul becomes flooded with light.

Positiveness from the Yoga standpoint is an ever growing aspiration and desire for knowledge, in order to bring about our union with Truth. It is like a man who, after a long journey, sees his friend, and turns to meet him with enthusiasm and joy. This attitude of constantly seeking union with man's own God within, brings into his objective vehicle that sense of union which the objective man desires.

This gives him positiveness and power of subtle radiation, which will not allow the diseased atmospheres of men to penetrate his atmospheric screen of protection, and it is this pressure which evil minds recognize and hate. Men of a certain type cannot stand in the presence of a great soul, and we have recorded in another book an instance of such a man, who rushed from such presence saying, "I am unclean."

Sooner or later, we shall all stand in the Presence, and then for the first time we shall realize our uncleanliness. An adept will sometimes evoke the *knower* consciousness into a room. This vibration has its phenomena, for it is the higher counterpart of what we call *physical fire*. The adept beckons the candidate to come nearer to his presence and suddenly the student realizes all the good and evil of his nature. If the good predominates, he can enter into its vibration untouched, but if a great fear enters his heart he is unable to do this, and he will then seek to purify himself in mind and body in order to make the attempt again later on.[47]

In this vibration we can only speak the Truth, and when we develop our intuition (nature's will) and make our own personal will subservient to it, then we can attain to the *knower* consciousness, when we shall *know* things without thought, and feel the presence of the Reality within and around us.

It is this power which the masters use when putting the "fear of God" into the heart of the man who intends injuring an innocent in order to gratify his passions and desires. This is the real magician's wand, and it is by the use of this will of God that miracles are performed.

---

47   Fear is always a concomitant of evil and unclean lives.

CHAPTER FIFTY-FOUR

NATURE'S PROTECTION
AGAINST EVIL

Always there are two forces in nature, one which converges
and brings to a point, and one which has the opposite action
of expansion or dispersion. Studying the activities of the day
and night, we discover that in the day nature seeks to conserve
the energies of the plants, and at night seeks to draw out from
their leaves this vital energy.

In his eagerness and ambition, man has built up a mind
body out of all proportion to its original plan and purpose.
He has not learned to conserve the power within his mind
which will bring about determined action. He goes where his
sense takes him, and pours out a constant stream of mental
energy. A few things in the newspapers interest him for a
short time, but he forgets the things which do not interest
him, and when nightfall comes he is usually tired in mind and
body.

We must not forget that the mind is the instrument of
the body, and the body is the instrument of the mind. Each
day man goes through the process of muckraking the debris
which his mind cast off the day before. The result is that
everything about his mental screen is his own mental offal,
the manure and debris of his passions and desires. He finds
that he has little control of his mind, and witnesses the recurrence of the thoughts which aroused his former passions and
desires.

By what is commonly known as wrong thinking, he
slowly builds up an accumulation of thought forms which
constantly recur to him and arouse pride, envy, lust, hatred,
and malice. These form a screen about him, and, if persisted
in, they will shut out the light which formerly illuminated his
mind. They make up his self-created universe.

If man will aspire for truth and knowledge, seeking to be
kind and benevolent to all beings, he will in time erect a wall
about his mental atmosphere which will reflect the things
of his higher nature, and allow the light which is within

him to shine forth. A certain type of man, carrying with him the debris of unclean thoughts and abnormal desires, is apt to bring long-dormant similar thought forms into the atmosphere of other minds. On the other hand I know a man who can change the whole atmosphere of the room when he enters; the original conversation changes also, and constructive thought is stimulated, causing the mind atmosphere in the room to take on a newer and finer type of expression.

When we seek to remove this foulness of the mind by aspiration and the desire for knowledge we make a discovery. We find that a movement from nature is coming into our atmosphere, and is placing a screen of protection about us which shields us from the atmosphere of an ignorant or diseased mind. We also discover that devotion to God and the desire to know Truth is immediately recognized by the consciousness in nature, and she affords us a wall of protection.

Many city dwellers, ignorant of the reason, often have a strong desire to put their hands and bare feet on Mother Earth. This brings about a change of polarity in our systems, for unknown to us nature gives us of her secret nourishment.

Out from the earth in the beginning came our physical structure, and unconsciously, when we love nature, she restores to our vehicle the energy of which it has been long deficient. This approach to Mother Nature should be practiced in the sunlight before ten o'clock in the morning. It will be found most helpful to neurotic people whose mental screens have been endangered through the filth of desire and the larvae of vice collected by ignorance.

The reader must realize that the second power in this world is money, but the first power is the attainment of wisdom (Truth). The evil man possessed of money is a colossal force, whereas a starving man stealing a loaf of bread has been known to suffer twelve months of hard labor. Few people today can resist the power of money and, in this way, justice is defeated.

The ignorant will always wage war upon those possessing intelligence, for both recognize the "caste mark" of destiny which separates them. Always, when mob ignorance rules, destruction has its harvest. That is why the wise men of this earth live in seclusion, and seek neither wealth nor fame. The Master Jesus left his seclusion to teach the multitude. He had studied and travelled extensively in the East. When Jesus said that John was great in the kingdom of heaven, he had in mind a real place on earth.[48] The records of Jesus' travels and studies still exist in the ancient temples of the East.

Although today we possess certain chapters of the New Testament, the Yogis inform us that there are other chapters in existence, one especially, relating to the physical travels of Jesus. These will be returned to the world when the law of nature calls for their appearance. Spring comes and calls for the budding of the leaves, which autumn returns to the ground. Even so, the teachings of the great avatars are given to humanity. Like another spring, another avatar makes his appearance, and new teachings fitted for the present needs of humanity are given forth.

But the essential truth is always the same. Some accept and some reject the message which the great avatars have given to humanity, but the Truth remains always the same. The great Infinite Reality is very near, yet in order to become at one with its creation and express its truth, we must seek its consciousness.

Truth and Beauty! What wonders these words symbolize to the Yogi as, going inwardly, he stands in the Presence, always seeking at-one-ment with his Creator. Could man but realize how foolish it is to injure anyone, how in so doing, he retards his own progress into the consciousness of Truth and steps down to the level of the beast, he would guard well his words and deeds.

In Africa there is a tribe known as the "Clan of the Lions," each member of which has killed a lion with a spear, and eaten his heart. They believe that when they have eaten the lion's heart, they then possess its qualities of strength and courage.

---

48   It is suggested that the occult concept of John the Baptist—the voice crying in the wilderness—is the rational mind preparing for the coming of the Christ, or knower consciousness to the individual Ego, the awakening of the rational intellect. See Matt. xi:7; Luke vii:25.

Strong and fearless as the lion is, if we do not interfere with him, he kills only to provide food. Mr. Martin Johnson said that the lion had so many amiable qualities, he had sworn never to shoot another. Mr. Rudolph Steiner told his extremist vegetarian disciples that they would not get to heaven by what they put into their mouths. Yet, what we believe, we become, and an initiated member of the Lion Clan, through his belief, probably acquired somewhat of the courage and power of the king of beasts. Therefore, he who constantly aspires and believes he can attain to the consciousness of the Truth, will attain it sooner or later. When he learns how to knock at the door, it will be opened. This is a law which the seeker must remember. If a man earnestly seeks for light for seven years, and is considered worthy, he will come in contact with a more advanced soul who will give him his first instruction in the process of unlocking the door, for the wise men are conscious of a man's light and aspiration and will minister to him, for those who have attained to higher realization can bestow it upon the less evolved.

Unlocking the door is a process of bringing to birth a possession within one, by the aid of a teacher; it is a process of introducing a man to himself; a process of teaching him to observe that which he has never before seen in this life; a process of going "within himself" and opening his own gate of knowledge.

CHAPTER FIFTY-FIVE

THE BLIND SPOT

Modern civilization has encouraged the growth of the luxury liner and the pleasure cruise. Studying the activity of the myriads of men who have brought the work on the vessel to completion, we are first impressed with the endeavors of the designers, engineers, decorators, and artists whose brain and energy have provided the luxury boat.

The captain and the men down to the most menial servant have gone through a long course of instruction and toil in order that those in the possession of wealth may exhibit their vanity and egotism. Many of these men, earning salaries barely covering the necessities of their mode of life, do not appear to hear or notice the things going on around them.

There are always passengers on these boats who, afraid of being alone, are followed by the "Hound of Heaven." The makers of the family fortune seek rest and a change of scene, but the ambition of the younger members is to gain recognition from a higher strata of society than they were born to.

The women folk of the "idle rich" are very similar to the bowerbird of Australia, which Darwin wrote about. The females of this species of bird build a promenade with an arch, and line it with the colorful things they can collect from nature, and then they parade back and forth in order to attract the male species. As this type of woman grows old, she still seeks to carry on the illusion, and often resorts to cosmetics in an effort to conceal the ravages of Time, that hound of fear ever yapping at her heels.

When a person finds that he cannot spend an evening alone with some good and stimulating book which will make him think, he should begin a survey of himself and try to penetrate into the future for which he is heading. Men and women are glorious creations and it is a glorious thing to have strong passions and desires. When we learn to aspire for the finer things of life and control the passions they can lift us into a higher stratum of consciousness where we discover intelligence and bliss.

Man must seek the Presence of the Lord God of Truth within, and try to find and heed his own soul, and not lose it. Youth demands the finest creations for the gratification of vanity. Art has an ennobling quality and brings to youth a type of refinement which expresses itself. Then they compare the things surrounding them with the things others possess, and frequently the possession of something of real artistic merit, such as a picture or painting, will transform the bedrock character of man, and bring out the hidden and finer expression from within.

Contrast an English railway station in London, with an American depot in any of our large cities. The one represents old conditions and the past, and the other the fertility of a newer mind and a more useful expression. When the Boston Library was opened, its marble stairways and mural decoration by Puvis de Chavannes so impressed the hoboes, who always seek warmth in our public institutions, with their beauty and symmetry, that for over a month they did not desecrate the building by spitting on the floor. This hobo type peruses *Burke's Peerage* more often than any other book, and I imagine must be seeking for some trace of eminence in their family name. People of this class often say to me, "When the spring comes, I must get away and lie under the trees."

This type of soul (often lower than the beast of the field) continually speaks of the attraction of open air life, and of their hatred towards humanity. They are a parasitic class of unfortunates who often glory in wrongdoing, and prey upon the labors of honest men. They are pathological cases, and difficult to heal. Like the beast of the field they are often good and humane to their own kind, though destructive to those outside their world. Strange to say they have not the ordinary man's sensitivity to pain, and in minor surgical operations they often take no anaesthetic, but merely ask for a "fag" or a drink.

As above, so below. The hobo class of humanity is only the reflection of another class higher up in society. Both are parasites, and inimical to the welfare of the community. By the cinema, the youths of this type are stimulated to become heroes, as well as to emulate the gangster and the hobo of the screen. Much petty pilfering is done by youths ranging from fourteen to seventeen years of age. A Scotland Yard officer once caught three youths fourteen, fifteen, and seventeen years of age. For sometime they had been raiding "shut up" shops in a certain residential neighborhood. The fathers and mothers of these boys held honorable positions in society, but the boys had provided themselves with complete kits, comprising masks, burglar tools, etc. When they determined to raid a shop they made a plan of the place, beforehand, then they broke in, ransacked the shop, and did a tremendous amount of damage. They were caught lifting a radio set out of the window. When the parents were summoned to the police station, each protested the innocence of his boy, until shown the individual equipment and loot which had been taken from him.

Moving pictures do not usually show the end which overtakes their gangster heroes. In some Continental cities, the criminal is given a drug in coffee, known as the "talking drug." When questioned under this influence, he will talk freely, thus doing away with the brutality of "third degree" methods practiced in America. This drug is now used with great success in Russia, and under its influence the soul in man only allows him to speak the truth. Its use was suggested in America, but the legal fraternity said that they gained money by protecting the criminal, and that they would be "out of a job" if this drug were allowed to be used on him. The drug has been introduced into England by a foreign syndicate, and has been used by women gangsters in order to get money from the victims whom they induce to drink with them. Under the effect of the drug, a man will honestly tell these women how much money he has in the bank, and will unhesitatingly write a check for any sum which they may demand. Of course he is kept a prisoner in the apartment till the check is cashed.

The ordinary man does not take much interest in things which do not affect him personally.

Often the foreign element in a country work harder and are more thrifty than the original inhabitants, but their canons of honor differ, and these conditions bring about hatred and sometimes persecution of the minority. The Chinese live and thrive on fare that would starve any other national. This is the chief thing Japan is afraid of. But as a rule we usually find the disturbing criminal element comes from the foreign infiltration.

The student of reincarnation today will find that many Americans have lived in Oriental bodies. There is a strong similarity to the Koran in Mr. Wilson's Fourteen Points which were the basis for the Peace Treaty at Versailles, and his pronouncements were certainly those of a Mohammedan soul. Abdul Baha, the leader of the Bahai movement, when asked why he was going to America, answered, "I go to collect and bring together in a unity the Bahai souls living in American bodies." This is why Oriental teachers of different sects find such response to their teaching on American soil.

Once when I was talking to a great red Indian initiate, he said, "Our Indian souls are incarnating into American bodies today and if you will study the faces of the white people in the Middle West, you will find the characteristic features of the Red Man, the feminine mother eye, and the male jaw and cheek bones. I recognize a Red Man in a white body as easily as the scientist does the geological formation of a country. In the future these Indian "white men" will respond to the Indian call for Truth."

CHAPTER FIFTY-SIX

NATURE THE LAWGIVER

Man, in his greed, will heedlessly sacrifice anything in order to attain his end. Each day a forest disappears to provide logs for the mills, with the result that destructive nature is becoming more active and summers and winters are becoming more severe. Cyclones and tornadoes do not recur where virgin forests still exist, for the tall trees temper the effect of the destructive agencies. Nature, however, steps in and penalizes man for his destruction and wastage of her bounty.

In England, during the Great War, much oak and other timber was cut down to provide necessary pit props. It will take at least ninety-nine years of reforestation before this damage can be remedied. When the trees covering the sides of our mountains are destroyed, torrents of water carry away the fertile earth, and eroded stony deserts are formed. Today even the small trees are ruthlessly cut or broken down in the process of logging, and reforestation by artificial means is necessary. The more man destroys the handiwork of nature, the greater the calamity to future generations. But there is another angle to this law, for we are told that in proportion to man's destruction, nature shuts down on the activities of his memory.

If the citizen who destroys one tree will with love and reverence plant three others in its place he will form an alliance with the consciousness of nature which will afford him a shelter of protection. Devotion to God through kindness to nature will redeem man from such ignorance. As man destroys the trees and vegetation, nature's supply of oxygen is reduced, and oxygen is man's elixir of life. There are many places on the earth today which afford man an earthly paradise, because the climatic conditions are tempered by the bounty of nature's vegetation and man receives his full supply of oxygen. When a man who has lived close to nature enters the great industrial sections of a city, he will experience difficulty in breathing and a sense of oppression. Smoke from the factories, especially where soft coal is burned, causes havoc and destruction among humanity because the soot with which it is laden clogs the lungs, and the gases rob the blood stream of its oxygen. Nature's purifying oxygen is diluted with carbon oxides, and men and women are "born tired," live in exhaustion, and die in despair. The impurities man liberates in the air are brought into his own system, and he should realize that he is suffering the penalty of his own acts.

Nature looks to man to help repair the calamities which he creates, and whoever works to alleviate the misfortunes of nature unconsciously redeems himself. There are many real lovers of nature who beautify their houses and gardens, and on them nature bestows her love and affection. I have heard many sensitive people say, "Love comes to me from my garden for the care I bestow upon it." However, people seldom exert themselves outside their own environment or seek to remedy the destruction which others have caused. While nature seeks to bring happiness to her children, she often weeps over the desecration of her bounty which Christmas brings, when the small fir, pine and hemlock trees are uprooted and sold over the counter for a few cents each.

A dear friend of mine, whose nature is of the "sylphid" type, once purchased a small Christmas tree for her drawing-room, which she painted a silver bronze. It is most beautiful when decorated, but she said last Christmas and has said for several years, "I shall save it and use it again next year, for I never wish to kill another fir tree." She had been to one of the big shops, and had seen hundreds of these small trees piled up to provide a passing thrill for the children and grown-ups at Christmas.

The devas have prophetic knowledge and they often inform the student what catastrophes are to take place when the Titans within the earth will be released to work destruction and havoc among mankind. Our modern Sodoms and Gomorrahs will in the fullness of time all suffer the due penalty which their destructiveness has brought to nature. When a place becomes so saturated with evil that it becomes destructive to the pure in heart, it remains only a matter of time when it will be razed to the ground.

I have witnessed the manipulation of natural forces by an initiate during one of the great commercial crises in America, in order to prevent nature's penalties being too severe. And if it were not for the great immortals now living, the aftermath of the last great war would have been terrible beyond the conception of man.

Man comes naked into this world, and naked goes he hence. The perfection, the experience, which he gains to bring him into the consciousness of Truth can be summed up in one question, "What did he learn about himself?"

I have been privileged to read messages which certain Yogis wrote before they passed out, and the knowledge they had gained was of true spiritual worth, even though the whole life experience could be summed up in a single phrase. They also wrote minutely about knowledge they had gained in far distant countries, in order to enable the reader at some later date to open the book of the daily life and customs of a people who are today known only through archaeological research. Some of the writings of these seers gives an insight into the daily life and religious observances of past civilizations, and when the will of nature allows, humanity will be given information about Lemuria, Atlantis, Cush, Egypt, and Asiatic and African cities of which today we know little.

This information will become available to those who are seeking to abide by the laws and edicts of nature's consciousness (natural law). But until a man passes the border which separates him from nature's consciousness, and lives according to her law, he cannot enjoy her bounty and protection. The devas often say, "How few we find in humanity who can become our spokesmen to redeem man into an understanding of our purpose in humanity's endeavor."

The great light-bringers to our earth have said, "Thou shalt not kill," yet today mankind is recklessly killing other human beings by pestilence, wars, gas, greed, and the adulteration of nature's products. Could the total be known, the entire loss of life through the Great War would be negligible in comparison to the killing going quietly behind the scenes through man's violation of natural law.

Disease is becoming so subtle that science is baffled to ascertain its cause or cure, and there is a new disease developing which will attack the membranes of man's astral and mental bodies, for man in his ignorance releases powers and forces into the atmosphere, the effect of which on the human brain and man's causal body sheath he little knows.

After many years the manipulators of the X-ray are beginning to learn how to protect themselves from injury. This discovery, which has been of the greatest service to mankind, produced martyrs before the operator learned to safeguard himself against its subtle effects.

The average person seldom realizes that there are many pathways to God, and that there is one through science, wherein nature instructs humanity, and although many martyrs are sacrificed, yet when man lives the natural life according to nature's law, he will live to a greater age, gain a greater knowledge, and enjoy a greater freedom from disease and annoyance. From the acquirement of knowledge comes wisdom, and wisdom points the path that leads to the "place of understanding."

There are many today, generally unheeded by the populace, over whom nature has cast her Shekinah, and these are our "wise men." We have many politicians, but few statesmen. The devas often speak of the wise men in nature, meaning those men who have attained to her wisdom. These men are given great powers to ennoble the mind of humanity, and protect the innocent, and in proportion as they increase, the level of human accomplishment is advanced.

CHAPTER FIFTY-SEVEN
PERIODIC ILLUMINATION

Our first periods of instruction give us a general outline of the knowledge best suited for our present day development. Later, intermittent vibrations come to us from the "sounding board" of nature. These vibrations of intelligence only tap the consciousness of man periodically, just as in astrology the planets, through the shifting of their positions, vary in their influence over us. At certain times, for instance, the planet Jupiter strongly influences the mind of humanity, then his power wanes and seemingly disappears for a time while Saturn, Venus, or Mercury take the stage. So it is with nature's vibrations, which call to us intermittently, and give beneficent instruction, and it is during these information periods that the arts and sciences are able to bring into existence things previously dreamed of.

These intermittent periods of instruction make possible the materialization of newer ideals of a constructive nature to nullify former periods of destruction, and to the student these periods bring discoveries which had been lying dormant in the recesses of his being.

The enlightened minds which work for the good of others, and have a strong desire to attain perfection through the arts and sciences, will shortly make a great discovery which will bring about a new world concept of man's relationship to his brother man and to his Mother Nature.

That new type of intelligence that is springing up in the heart of man is a desire to *know himself*, his brother man and nature. This is leading to the great discovery of this New Age, when mankind will work with enthusiasm for the common good, regardless of inherited principles handed down through the dark ages of his forebears.

Man has been slowly exterminating himself through ignorance of the laws of nature. Individually and by slow degrees he is becoming poisoned, because he lacks the knowledge of how to help himself. In this New Age of discovery, he will be taught how by following natural laws he may eliminate from

his system those poisons which bring about premature death.
He will be taught right living (which is a process of right
thinking) and his natural place and position in society, and
in time he will insist on having food in which the natural elements are not adulterated.

Man suffering from bodily disorders can no more enjoy
happiness than a wireless set can attune itself to a broadcasting station when its component parts are broken or worn out!

Until the advent of white settlers the native people were
a noble race living natural lives. At the present day this once
noble race is nearly exterminated through disease and customs brought to them by civilization. As an example of this,
we have only to look at the natives of Tahiti, and at the Zulu
tribes in Africa, the Indians of America, and the Kanakas of
Hawaii.

Man's greed and inhumanity has placed the nations of the
world in the position in which we find them today. Because of
his unnatural life, nature has shut down on man's power of
memory, and he is gradually exterminating himself through
the efforts of the so-called Christian nations to conquer
each other. Men are denied their natural rights by taxation
and extending state control over the individual in order to
prepare for some still greater war. Weapons of war quickly
become obsolete through more modern inventions, and each
country seeks to produce powerful destructive agents, for all
of which the individual has to pay. Fleets of planes are being
constructed so fast that those of yesterday are out of date,
and tomorrow will see the present product condemned to
obsolescence.

Eventually no place on earth will be free from the destructive hand of man. Russia can bomb England within seven
hours, and before long even America's stretches of ocean
will not be protective barriers against the aerial warlords of
destruction.

Neither the actors nor humanity realize that the destructive agents who cause so much suffering by the sword, quickly
meet their *own* doom. Most of the leaders who brought about
the great Russian revolution have been shot by their compa-

triots. And the law of karma will exterminate in shame the totalitarian war makers of today. The great initiates speak of this karmic law in nature, which hastens the punishment of those who initiate strife and destroy life with lethal weapons. While they reign, no country is secure, for such leaders are true to their birthright and have no heritage of position or leadership and no integrity of purpose. Yet they can cause old traditions to change and the security of a peace loving nation to disappear in a watch in the night.

In order to find any true security, man must return again to the laws of nature and endeavor to obey them; then a Golden Age will again manifest; man's instinctive nature will be reborn; and he, possessing nature's will once more, will thus gain her bounty.

It is for man to choose whether he will be governed by his personal will, or his Lord God of Truth within. Our great avatars have all said, "Do unto others, as you would they should do unto you," and in this New Age they add, "Give unto nature that which you desire her to give unto you."

CHAPTER FIFTY-EIGHT

CORRECTING MIND MALFORMATION

Man's self-esteem often brings him into conflict with his own real nature, and this gradually results in a malformation of his mind. This malformation is caused by the spoken word which in his haste to acquire that which he selfishly desires, he recklessly utters contrary to his real character of being. Desiring to have his own way, man begins by saying things which are untruthful and injurious to others, and upbraids anyone who stands in his way. He may do this by seeming praise which is subtly belittling, or by an open diatribe. But the "watcher" within, elemental lord of his mind, sits in judgment upon his speech, hence the spoken word has ever been a cause of man's suffering. Envy, malice, and hatred manifested through the spoken word dominate the character of the mind, and the watcher passes judgment upon a culprit for thoughtless speaking. The dynamic forces which he has energized from the underworld beneath his feet by vocalization turn and prey upon his mind, disorganizing it, until his own thoughts become an obsession tracking him night and day. It is to escape this torment that men seek pleasure.

The wise man will say little, and think before he speaks, striving to ennoble everyone who hears him. He realizes that the mental forms a man builds during life, he takes away with him at his death. The good type of thought which the pressure lines of vibration show at death lead him into the presence of Truth, and such men arrive at their true height of attainment, and are never earth-bound. On the contrary, the man who is untruthful and envious, and who disowns any allegiance towards the common good of the community, finds his own level in those spheres of which he has made himself a representative while on earth.

It is very interesting to talk to an earth-bound spirit, and sometimes it is difficult to make him realize that he has passed over. He comes to you as he did while in the earth life and demands that you should do certain things for him. One earth-bound spirit who had been a "boss" in business, wanted

me to go and see the executors of his will because he said they
had not carried out his orders as he desired. When I said, "Do
you not realize that you are dead?" he answered, "Yes, I know
that, but I want you to do this." I said to him "My friend, I
cannot see that you have left much love behind you." And he
replied, "I see my family who seem to hate me." I asked him
if he could see a far distant star with its minute light, and
he said, "Yes, when I close my eyes I see it." I answered, "My
friend, that is your salvation. Whatever good you have left
behind you will help to bring you to that star; try to go there."

Emotional people, especially at one phase of their lives, will
feel a glow in their hearts after attending a religious revival,
and will think that they have found God. This emotion may
last all their lives, and cause a transformation in the entire
character, but with most it lasts only a short time. Still the
light is brought into the human *heart*. Many unemotional
people live most of their time in the *mind* world, and if they
aspire for truth, the light of the spirit will enter their mind
world also.

Illumination of the mind brings about a complete change
in one's self-created universe, for as the Yogis say, the light
of intelligence has entered it. When this happens, man com-
mences to receive instruction in the laws of conscious nature,
and a desire dawns within him to attain nature's will, and
to renounce the physical will, which he has built up, thus he
becomes conscious of Truth. This knowledge and power and
the use of nature's will he possessed in the Golden Age, but
in his journey down through the Age of Silver into the Age
of Copper, he began to build up a personal will, and it is this
which now dominates him in this Iron and Steel Age. Thus
he has lost all memory of natural law, and the use of nature's
will.

After illumination the student experiences the complete
change of mind which accompanies it. Nature takes him
under her jurisdiction, and he returns to his long lost mother.
It is the return of the "voice crying out in the wilderness" for
union between the physical and mental man.[49]

---

49   Consider the scripture story of the prodigal son; also the story of Jesus
     and John the Baptist.

It is the beginning of a composite unity, when man and his elemental twin are locked in the embrace of love, the "man of nature" with the conscious man as we see him become one. This is symbolized in the Baptism of Jesus by John, who represents his elemental soul, *the worker of miracles, with a knowledge of natural law,* and with the power to bestow that consciousness. Man's creative world, which he has built up about him with mind and physical activity is detrimental to nature, for it is opposite to anything that we can perceive in nature's operations.

Man asserts himself as he desires, he does not seek to ascertain what nature would have him do. He is deaf to the appeals of the "natural man" within, and to the approach of nature's intelligence from without. If man will only seek union with his own true nature of being, the Lord God of Truth within will align him with nature's understanding.

Humanity does not know the part that nature plays in human affairs for we seldom realize that our physical, mental, and spiritual bodies are made up of nature's component elements. Science has explained to man that he is of a mineral, fluidic, and airy nature, and has told him that when he inhales, he brings the oxygen atoms of nature within his system. Seen with the eye of the Yogi, man is a semi-transparent and gaseous being, and the ultra violet rays reveal how translucent his body really is.

When man realizes that he is composed of the elements of earth, air, fire, and water, he will have some knowledge of his composite body. Science recognizes that man is like an iceberg in the sea, which shows only one-ninth of its real size above the surface, the rest being unseen and submerged.

Nature's will takes charge of our bodies while we are asleep, and causes the broken tissues of our bodies to be built up.[50] This makes it interesting to speculate on how long the most learned doctor or scientist would live today if the upkeep of his body depended entirely on himself. The student of Yoga seeks to unify his objective self with his own Lord God of Truth within, and when he seeks this union (the merging of

---

50   As Shakespeare says, "Sleep, that knits up the ravel'd sleave of care."

his "natural man" with his lower counterpart) nature instructs
him in the building up of a physical body, which is developed
and brought into harmony with nature's vibrations.

The development of the "third eye" (which is a purely
scientific process) gives man an extended range of vision. By
its development, he slowly begins to perceive a new world
of being about him, for it gives him power to discern the
activities going on in several divisions in the world of man
and nature. In Yoga practice, as the student goes inwardly, he
discovers that the organs of perception (hearing, seeing, feeling, smelling, and tasting) each has a higher counterpart, and
he seeks through these to attune himself with and register the
vibrations of the different divisions of nature.

The mother usually gives her child its spiritual knowledge
and training, but it is Mother Nature who restores to him his
lost heritage. Man must seek Truth, to enable Mother Nature
to harmonize herself with him, and reveal the "forbidden
knowledge," for nature is the custodian of the wisdom knowledge by which she has guided the great seers and prophets of
the past, and her books are ever open to all who seek union
with her.

CHAPTER FIFTY-NINE

THE AWAKENER

It is realized that these teachings are contrary to the accepted ideals of our time which consummate the failure of some six thousand years of human history, therefore the time has arrived for man to take an inventory of his failures and revise his view of life in order to conform it to the Reality.

Our practice has been to analyze the mind of an individual by regarding its determined expression, but the Creator has placed within the mind of every inhabitant of the earth the divine expression which he will sooner or later assume, and this can only be accomplished by bringing to birth and experimenting with the opposition of his real character of expression.

A man threatened with abuse will invariably reveal some expression of the true character of his mind. If you present to a man's mind your attainment to the consciousness of truth, he will naturally either accept or deny it. In the future, therefore, accept a man's understanding and character as he expresses it, and then try to evoke his true manifestation of expression. This is an overhead process of bringing the good and evil within him to manifest; first accept him as you find him and then by the more subtle use of Yoga evoke the truth and by analyzing his power to accept or reject Truth, bring to the surface his real character of expression.

By spraying a man with the vibration of the consciousness of nature, he will come to its directing impulse. By this means he can be slowly brought into a consciousness of his own ignorance of Truth.

When a man for the first time comes under the vibration of nature's consciousness he will realize his falsity to Truth, as well as the calmness of the vibration and the peace which is flowing through him from nature.

Nature's subtle vibration, transmitted to others through you, will determine their true character of expression regardless of their desire to protect themselves; therefore, when you meet a person throw this divine attribute of nature into his consciousness. By doing so you will give him a precious antidote to the evil working in him. Thus through personal contact in your future work, you must bring to birth in the pupil the knowledge of his own finer expression, in order to give him the power to achieve, and make manifest the possession which you have cast into his atmosphere.

In the ether of nature there lies the awakener—that sovereignty of spirit which brings into activity the hidden powers within man. These powers remain dormant in humanity and are seldom disturbed, though it is possible for man to become the instrument of the "Awakener," and attain to a consciousness of the bounty which Mother Nature bestows on those who seek union with her and work in her service.

A manifestation of nature's awakener is the great need of humanity today. Then man will realize his true character and experience within nature. To prepare for the awakening is the part which the forerunners always perform when they have attuned themselves to nature's fixed principle, and the underlying streams of energy which, though seldom experienced, lie hidden within all men.

The student will recognize that the divine energy in man cannot be separated from the divine energy in nature. The awakener in nature is your brother "man of nature" and he awakens you by sounding his vibration into your objective being, so that you consciously re-establish yourself in nature's being. Union between objective man and his "higher self" is in nature's keeping.

The great devas in nature give the student his first and finer perception of the reality which exists within. They seek to bring peace between the objective man and his Innermost which, during incarnation, lives and moves within the keeping of nature. They teach that the sovereignty of the spirit exists in every living thing in nature.

Man does not comprehend what is going on within him. He knows little of the workshop within his body and is ignorant of the laws which govern it. The devas say that a man should scribe his own circumference, placing his mind upon the point at the foot of his compass. Man not only scribes his own circumference, but the circle which he has scribed represents the conscious limit of his mental expansion. Though man looks out beyond his circumference into the objective world, he seldom turns around and looks inwardly to the true center of his being. Yet through all flows the real spirit of his Being with which he must attain to union by expansion of his consciousness. He must seek inwardly, not outwardly and must aspire for more light, and yet more light, in order to become conscious of the "pure light" at the center of his circle.

If you would gain knowledge of light, begin by discussing darkness. If you would consider Truth, begin by discussing falsehood, the opposite. Plan a lecture on these lines, and if you wish to speak on good, commence by discussing its opposite, evil. The modern preacher talks about the beautiful sunrise or sunset, or of the gifts of nature. If you would instruct your hearers, place their minds upon opposite conditions, which will stimulate them to seek the cause.

Man becomes sick because of a breakdown of law and order in his system, caused by mental, emotional, or physical defilement of his body, either by his ancestors or himself. The so-called "bad" man is usually a pathological case, some organ or center of his body being malformed through ignorance of the Law.

Seek always for what a certain character in history did not achieve, and by so doing you acquire a clearer understanding of what he did not possess, and why. By a similar process you can arrive at the motivating influences in the circle of your acquaintances.

CHAPTER SIXTY
WORKING WITH NATURE

Just as the tiny twig, the strong branch, and the rugged trunk of the tree are bent by the prevailing winds, so the great Truth which lies so near to us will direct man to the sanctuary of his God.

It is the pressure of nature's consciousness upon humanity which slowly folds men into her embrace. The manifestation of good in man is bound to be shown forth eventually, for the good ultimately must prevail. In order to reform criminal tendencies we must find the hidden good in mankind.

God will eventually overbalance evil, and the psychologists of the future will seek to bring into activity the good hidden deep in the nature of the subject. It is by bringing the good side of the man into ascendency that the criminal comes to lead an honest life. This cannot be done if the offender is constantly reminded of his previous crime. He should be forgiven and no reference made to his past which the good in him is seeking to efface.

If man has committed a criminal offense, suffered the penalty, and is trying to lead a normal life, his fellow men should not raise his past against him. They should encourage the good in him so that he may heal himself. People who are trying to live clean and good lives, and have become discouraged, often confide in occult students. Sometimes they are hounded by their fellows for acts of which they were quite innocent.

Remember that the second edict of nature is honesty. The student should approach every man with the idea in his heart that "this is an honest man." If his fellow man has been dishonest in the past, this approach will give him courage and strength and greater power to eradicate the former tendency.

I remember being with a great Yogi when we met a lady in the street who had tried to ruin him, and had been an agent to destroy his work. To my surprise he spoke to her as if she were one of his greatest friends. When we parted from her I called his attention to the destruction which she had done to his work, and he looked at me in a surprised manner and said,

"I had forgotten all about it." He met the world as he expected the world to meet him.

The great leader of the Bahai was hated by a Mohammedan who used to curse him in the street. This hatred had existed for many years, yet when this beloved teacher heard that the man was in great distress and poverty, he went to his house and seeing that he was suffering from cold, covered him with his own cloak. The Mohammedan could not understand this action, but later on his animosity and hatred vanished.

The hatred which a man entertains in his heart causes him more damage and suffering than the person to whom he projects it.

Nature's consciousness supports right action in all things. There are great beings with whom the student is sometimes able to converse, and the work of one of these teachers is to bring back to the student's mind his acquired information of the laws of natural phenomena gained in previous lives. Next to this teacher stands the Lord of Compassion, who returns to this student his memory of past experiences, when he possessed the power to remove bad conditions from his pupils.

The Master Jesus cast out seven devils from Mary the Magdalene and the Lord of Compassion stimulates these powers within the student, so that he is able to lift conditions of suffering and sorrow from people, in order that their minds can be re-established in nature's purpose.

There is also a great lord of the "money mind," a great master who is able to manipulate the gold specie of this world. Certain sections of humanity have a greater consciousness of the "money mind" than the average person would give them credit for. Because they were persecuted in all countries, the Jews have always had to carry their worldly possessions on their persons, and have gradually developed a "money mind" which can easily tap the consciousness of the world of "finance," as well as the world of "precious stones."

If the occult student can tap the atmosphere of a great financier, he will find out much about the powers attending the concentration and the development of "money sense." A friend of noble birth once confided to me his financial difficulties and I afterwards discussed his affairs with a very well known American financier. Inside of five minutes this man had formulated a plan which would place my friend upon his feet, and I was able to bring a meeting between them.

As the worthy Yoga student progresses in his practice, the initiate will ask one of these great lords (specialists in their own lines) to assist him in recovering from within, the knowledge of his past achievements gained through many lives on this earth.

In every good deed, or intention of doing good to others, we have the backing of nature's consciousness, but those people who wage war against nature lose their powers of memory. It is a curious fact that in primitive countries where all natural life is respected and loved, the natives have phenomenal memories, which is a cause of great surprise to visitors from the Western world.

In order to obtain nature's "push" for good fortune and success, man must have an honest intention to do good without any pressure of individuality and personality behind it—in other words he must be impersonal in his honesty and good intent. But in any such action he should ask the Lord God of Truth within him for wisdom; mere personality plus goodness and honesty often turns out a "white haired boy" in the family!

Personality should enter as little as possible into any good action. A man may say to his child, "I am giving you this because you have been a good boy," but this father is pushing his personality into the boy's atmosphere, which nine times out of ten brings fear to birth in the child's mind. Love only comes from the giving of freedom to others, for it cannot be chained to the personality of a man or woman. Love should make no demands, for fear approaches when freedom is restricted. It is unselfish love given with no demands which links people together, as married people would find out if they gave each other their freedom, and were honest with each other.

CHAPTER SIXTY-ONE

NATURE'S RESERVOIR
OF KNOWLEDGE

In Nature there exists a great dome shaped elemental temple which has been built up through aeons of time by the composite thought of the leaders of our race. From this a composite thought energy comes forth which heralds a new age. These heralds give forth their knowledge and instruction to the wise men of the tribes—a secret knowledge which they hold intact—and when they have perfected this knowledge, they pass it down to the long line of leaders, so that they can stand in the presence and the glory of this shining orb.

Thus, they have slowly instilled into the mind of humanity a knowledge of the divine concerns of nature and God, and their instruction was given to those brethren of the Rose-Cross who stood in the Presence. They divided and assembled themselves into different groups of humanity, so that the Ancient Wisdom Teaching should be held intact in groups separated from other groups, in order to allow the toilers of humanity, when worthy, to group themselves about the sacred edifice and be given secret instruction regarding the laws by which the edifice of nature is built up.

In all the different settlements of humanity, there were to be found groups who were guardians and custodians of nature's laws regarding her association with man. But the lawgivers of humanity (religion and jurisprudence) appointed themselves as dictators in their own self-constituted universe. Thus the Church and the State still seek to fortify their own interests, heeding not the prophetic voice crying in the wilderness. Hence the custodians of the natural law gave forth their knowledge secretly in their disguised literature.

Through the craftsmanship of their own hands they wrought into the edifices which they constructed, symbols of nature's teaching, so that in some future time man might, through craftsmanship, come at the understanding which nature can give to him when he is worthy of her appreciation.

The Egyptians, placing the symbol of the winged globe over the entrance to their temples, and the builders in the Middle Ages in their craftsmanship, have left to humanity the symbol of all that is needed to be known regarding the alliance of nature and man. Those who have eyes to see can read both their symbols and the book of nature, through understanding of the fixed principles which nature unfolds to the sincere craftsman.

Man has only to knock and the door of Truth will be opened to him. He has only to seek, and he will find the key to the lost instruction. But he must first, through discipline, perseverance, and aspiration for Truth, be taught how to knock and how to seek. When he has asked for and learned this, then instruction will be given by those truly enlightened ones who hold the secret of the divine laws of nature's self-government. Then, and only then can man stand in the presence of the Lord God of Truth within and partake of the peace which passeth all understanding.

GLOSSARY

THE BROTHERS.—A Fraternity that has existed before man descended into matter, and who have worked and still work out in the world upon the Path of activity. They only appear as an active Brotherhood when the cosmic energy of a Dayspring of Youth brings them into manifestation to shield and bring its vibration and intelligence into the minds of those who seek their Innermost. When this cosmic energy is withdrawn they seemingly disappear from the world. The real name of the Order is only revealed at the initiation of a disciple. One of the tenets of Order is mental levitation or the process of travelling out of the body.

.   .   .   .   .

THE DAYSPRING OF YOUTH.—A cosmic hierarchal energy that appears at the beginning of a new age in man's development. It is now entering this world, and, through Yoga practice, the student attempts to tune himself into this directing consciousness and intelligence that is to revert man to an understanding of Nature's laws.

ATOMS.—Minute bodies of intelligence possessing the dual attributes of Nature and man.

ASPIRING ATOMS.—Those higher forms of energy and intelligence that, through Yoga practice, the student attracts to his physical and mental body.

NOUS ATOM.—The minute image of perfected man within the left ventricle of the heart.

SECONDARY SYSTEM.—These are centres or ganglia of the sympathetic system that extend each side of the spinal column and are contacted by the student when he aspires in his Yoga practice to enter his inner planes of consciousness and relate himself to the finer forces in Nature. They also review and re-experience him in his past lives and in those periods of inner development ahead of our objective time.

THE THIRD EYE OR PINEAL GLAND.—Through Yoga practice this seemingly atrophied organ within the head vibrates and attunes itself to man's nervous energy, and becomes the organ of the seer who visualises the activities of the finer states of consciousness in Nature and man.

DESTRUCTIVE ATOMS.—The opposing forces of Nature in man that seek to retard his development towards the Reality.

ATMOSPHERIC SCREEN.—A silken-webbed lining that holds the mental body in alignment to the physical body and is covered with a multitude of node points through which are received as well as transmitted thought-vibrations to and from the human brain.

NODE POINTS.—Small, truncated, cone-shaped projections.

THE SECRET ENEMY.—The principal atom of evil in man that directs the Destructive atoms.

INFORMER ATOMS.—Atoms that had worked for the Secret Enemy, but who have been liberated by the Aspiring atoms from bondage. They are a link between the Aspiring atoms and the atoms of the Secret Enemy and inform us about the nature of the evil plans that threaten us from the Secret Enemy and from outside influences.

THE ASTRAL BODY.—A sheath of radiant, fluidic atmosphere that envelops the physical form and is seen by the third eye. It registers our passions and desires and is a remnant of the past.

CAUSAL BODY SHEATH.—This is a lower atomic substance that registers racial consciousness and tendencies, and possesses the qualities of our individual parental stem.

DEATH ATOMS.—When the Solar and Lunar forces cease to operate in the body, and the Nous atom has left the arterial bloodstream, these Death atoms watch over the disintegration of man's lower vehicles and return the imprisoned atoms back to their natural elements.

THE ADVOCATE.—A powerful, collective atomic entity, otherwise known as the Higher Self, created from the best of man's aspirations during his descent and evolution through matter. It is the intermediary between man and his Innermost, and pleads for the remission of our past evil after we have reviewed this through Yoga practice.

THE ELEMENTAL ADVOCATE.—Similar to the Advocate, but created in our elemental past. It possesses the same attributes and works in union with the other Advocate. These two are known in zodiacal terminology as Castor and Pollux.

WHITE MAGICIAN.—They who seek to serve humanity impersonally and obey the directions of their Innermosts according to the degree of their occult development.

MANTRAS.—Sound invocations that the student uses to harmonise his body and its centres with the finer forces in Nature and man.

DETERMINATIVE ENERGY.—An energy that determines Nature's expression and that the student seeks to attain and obey.

THE SILVER SHIELD.—Through Yoga practice atoms called Transformation atoms of a higher voltage are attracted and formed into a mental shield that protects the student from opposing forces in Nature and man. It is the temple in which the Master atom of the mind will reside and is the condenser and transmitter of the powerful voltage of the Innermost.

MASTER ATOM.—An atomic energy within the seminal system that represents the student's individual record of intelligence gained through past experiences. When the Silver Shield is developed the Master atom ascends from the seminal system into the Silver Shield and becomes the intelligence that instructs the student about his mind-world and mental inheritance.

TRANSFORMATION ATOMS.—(See Silver Shield.)

INNERMOST.—That part of the Reality (GOD) within man that the Yogi seeks to attune himself to before attaining cosmic consciousness.

CENTRAL SYSTEM.—Represents the brain and spinal cord with its seven principal ganglia or atomic centres, and is the instrument that aids man to release—through Yoga practice—his Innermost from Its prison house of the body. (See Solar Force.)

SELF-DEVELOPED UNIVERSE.—That universe that man has built up through eternity under the guidance of the Innermost.

SOLAR FORCE.—It is of the nature of static electricity and remains latent in man till evoked and used through Yoga practice. This force can be governed by man and is the instrument the Innermost uses to build up Its solar or spiritual body.

SEMINAL SYSTEM.—The organs that create life as understood by man and by the student as the depository of the powerful forces attained to and made known to him in the elemental and objective states of his past. This brings about the birth of the Solar force.

INITIATE ATOMS.—Those atoms within the higher counterpart of the seminal system that relate the student to periods in advance of his time, and possess the attributes of a great Initiate's atmosphere.

SCHOLAR ATOMS.—Those atoms an atomic centre that relate themselves to the objective mind of the student and in his deeper
states of Yoga inform him of his inner and objective attainments gained through countless lives.

PARENTAL STEM.—The individual expression of the Reality from which
the Innermost sprang, and the directing force and individual
expression of the student and his race.

Index

Architecture, 71
Art, 9, 34, 41, 46-47, 71, 93-94, 98, 119, 130, 135, 173, 194, 197, 211, 219, 228, 236, 238, 243, 274, 277, 300
Arthur, 194
Artist, 31, 56, 103, 121, 128, 173, 191, 196
Artistic, 173, 300
Artists, 40-41, 47, 94, 104, 128, 135, 151, 251, 299
Arts, 13, 121, 229, 250, 252, 307
Ascetic, 31, 150
Asia, 61, 120, 156, 227, 305
Asleep, 313
Asp, 158
Aspirations, 40, 42, 74, 119, 155, 204, 223, 231, 255, 272, 326
Aspire, 183, 265
Aspires, 1, 6, 12, 29, 45, 91, 102, 136-137, 147, 163, 167, 186, 199, 207, 223, 234, 298, 325
Aspiring, 2, 29, 65, 78, 98, 150, 209, 227, 249, 255, 325-326
Aspiring Atoms, 325-326
Assimilate, 181-182, 200
Assist, 10, 12, 19, 61, 75, 81, 89, 115, 132, 139, 155, 158, 161-162, 196, 214, 265-266, 321
Assistance, 62, 133, 145, 195, 233, 242, 252, 267
Assistant, 85, 87, 277
Assyria, 83
Astral Body, xii, 186, 260, 326
Astrology, 83, 307
Astronomers, 152
Astronomy, 83
At-one-ment, 120, 132, 145, 297
Atlantean, 9-11, 74, 188, 268
Atlantis, ix, 9-10, 159, 305
Atmospheres, 148, 160-161, 163, 185, 219, 287, 293
Atmospheric, 12, 147, 149, 293, 326
Atmospheric Screen, 293, 326
Atomic, 2, 12, 22, 67, 97, 110, 142, 197, 209, 228, 326-328
Atoms, x, 7, 19-20, 41, 67, 75, 79-80, 95, 127, 135-137, 143, 152, 169, 182-183, 208, 224, 231, 234, 239, 255-257, 259-260, 283, 285, 313, 325-328
Atrophied, 5, 227, 325
Attention, 3, 30, 77, 139, 203, 217, 227, 248, 283, 319
Attitude, 49, 63, 73, 89, 98, 161, 195, 207, 281, 293
Attract, 30, 40, 55, 67, 77-78, 95, 126, 135, 139, 169, 175, 228, 235, 241, 248, 253, 261, 275, 299
Attracted, 232, 239-240, 252, 261, 273-274, 327
Attracting, 279
Attraction, 34, 61, 78, 88, 102, 131, 169, 214, 251, 300
Attractive, 116, 206
Attracts, 33, 36, 41, 46, 60, 77, 147, 208-209, 251-252, 273, 288, 325
Attribute, 2, 315
Attributes, 91, 114, 251, 325-327
Attune, 18, 30-31, 67, 95, 103, 107, 135, 141, 160, 284, 308, 314, 327
Attuned, 15-17, 156, 316
Attunes, 2, 29, 70, 325
Augustus, 130
Aurora, 31
Austerity, 83-84, 126
Australia, 299
Automobile, 214, 267
Avarice, 197
Avatar, 20, 48, 133, 203, 212, 234, 297
Avatars, 37, 57, 69, 81, 134, 138, 144, 178, 199, 217, 258, 278, 282, 284, 297, 309
Awake, 77, 137-138, 142
Awakened, 55, 205, 208, 292
Awakener, x, 315-316
Awakening, xi, 181, 185-186, 316
Awakens, 1, 25, 316

Your book reviews matter.

Glorian Publishing is a very small non-profit organization, thus we have no money to spend on marketing and advertising. Fortunately, there is a proven way to gain the attention of readers: book reviews. Mainstream book reviewers won't review these books, but you can.

The path of liberation requires the daily balance of three active factors:

- birth of virtue
- death of vice
- sacrifice for others

Writing book reviews is a powerful way to sacrifice for others. By writing book reviews on popular websites, you help to make the books more visible to humanity, and you might help save a soul from suffering. Will you do your part to help us show these wonderful teachings to others? Take a moment today to write a review.

Donate

Glorian Publishing is a non-profit publisher dedicated to spreading the sacred universal doctrine to suffering humanity. All of our works are made possible by the kindness and generosity of sponsors. If you would like to make a tax-deductible donation, you may send it to the address below, or visit our website for other alternatives. If you would like to sponsor the publication of a book, please contact us at (844) 945-6742 or help@gnosticteachings.org.

Glorian Publishing
PO Box 209
Clinton, CT 06413 US
Phone: (844) 945-6742
VISIT US ONLINE AT gnosticteachings.org